FROM SCARS TO STARS

REVOLUTIONIZING RECOVERY THROUGH
TRAUMA-INFORMED CARE & LIVED EXPERIENCE

FROM SCARS TO STARS

#1 BESTSELLING AUTHOR AND NOMINEE OF *THE PULITZER PRIZE*

JOEY PAGANO, MSW, LSW, CRS
& JODIE PAGANO, BSW, CRS

Proofreader: Blair Parke
Book Editors: Blair Parke
Book Publicists: Joey Pagano, Samantha Showman & Jodie Pagano

From Scars to Stars
Revolutionizing Recovery Through Trauma-Informed Care & Lived Experience

First Edition

ISBN   Hardcover
        Paperback
        Ebook

Book Cover Design and Interior Formatting by 100Covers.

This book is dedicated to our mothers, Cindy and Diane; fathers, Timothy and Joe; son, Zavier; daughter, Gianna; sisters, Samantha and Cynthia; brother, Xavier, and nephew, Tyler. A special shout-out to Dr. Scott A. Cook, Kellie, Cheryld, Dawn, Mark, Lee, Mindi, April, Dani, Carl, Abigail, Sam, Flip, Raymond, Bob, Robbie, and George.

Most importantly, prayers for our lost loved ones, the people who only stayed for parts of our journey. For those who never stuck around or were taken from this world way too early, there will always be a moment of silence for them.

CONTENTS

PROLOGUE

Pittsburgh, Pennsylvania, 2024: Nestled between avenues of dreams and alleyways of despair stands Whispers and Words, an enchanting coffee shop intertwined with a bookstore. In this place, the lustrous sheen of hope glimmers amidst the worn-out pages and old wood, standing defiant against the looming shadows of the town's darker corners.

Husband and wife Joey and Jodie Pagano find their haven within this unique blend of aroma and literature. Their roles aren't limited to mere observers, scribbling notes in the coffee-stained margins of life. They're warriors, drenched in the trenches of the ongoing war against substance use disorder (SUD). Their eyes have captured the raw agony of souls ensnared and the triumphant flutter of spirits reborn from the ruins. They've borne witness as the indelible marks of addiction transform, over time, into galaxies of redemption.

As you prepare to turn these pages, understand that they aren't just ink marks on paper. Every chapter unfolds amidst the cozy corners and bustling counters of Whispers and Words, as cinematic and vivid as any scene from a golden-era film. They're intricately choreographed sequences resonating with the passions, perils, and promises of those entrenched in the fight against addiction.

On your next visit to this beloved establishment, imagine that while sipping on a freshly brewed coffee or perusing an old novel, you overhear a whispered conversation, a tale mirroring the very essence of these writings. In that moment, realize that you're not merely stepping into a story but plunging into the heart of a revolution. A whirlwind of sentiment, resilience, and revelation awaits. So, settle into that familiar chair, breathe in the fusion of caffeine and paper, and let the Pagano duo navigate you through this intricate labyrinth, from the muted anguish of scars to the radiant embrace of the stars.

INTRODUCTION

The Convergence of Two Worlds: A Clinical and Personal Journey

The Rising Crisis of Substance Use Disorders

Upon entering Whispers and Words, an unexpected nook beckons you—one where books seem to converse with cups. Amid the shadowy alcoves, the aroma of coffee mingles with the narratives of *The Scribe's Sanctuary*. The gentle hum of whispered conversations dances with the mellow notes of an old gramophone.

As you draw nearer, an enigmatic figure framed by a sun-drenched bay window becomes apparent. A man, spectacles reflecting the wisdom of years past, holds your gaze. This is Professor Robert Albus Brinker, your guide and narrator throughout this unique journey. Next to him rests a substantial book, its title clearly visible, enquiring into the complexities of substance use disorders. It's as if the professor is close enough to perceive the multitude of lives entwined within its pages. It's only a short time before you discern that this man isn't merely a passive reader. He serves as a bridge, gracefully uniting the world of clinical insight with humanity's raw, heartfelt stories. Among these tales, those of Joey and his wife, Jodie stand out. They are termed "care navigators" within these pages, mirroring their roles at the Center of Excellence (COE)—an opiate use disorder program (OUD). While their role title suggests case-working, it's evident that they are much more. Their very essence, shaped by their education and passion, resonates with the spirit of social workers. They shepherd souls through daunting odysseys.

The professor's voice, rich with emotion, beckons you closer. He shares stories of Joey's encounters with temptation and Jodie's unwavering determination, painting a vivid, emotional landscape. His words capture the heartbeats of many—some fragmented, others healed, all intertwined in a poignant dance of despair, hope, and restoration.

When the final word is read, you realize this isn't a mere introduction but a portal—a gateway into a realm where clinical sagacity braids with the human spirit's fierce tenacity, reshaping beliefs with each revelation. Now, with the comforting blend of aged paper and coffee grounding you, you're ready to delve deeper into a journey that promises enlightenment, challenges, and profound insights.

In the shadowed, often overlooked corners of our globe, a silent yet devastating storm brews, threatening to engulf everything in its wake. Though some are tragically familiar with its power, for many, it remains hidden, cloaked in stigma, and mired in a fog of misconceptions and societal ignorance. The escalating substance use disorder (SUD) crisis cannot be distilled to mere digits on a page or sterile data in an annual report. It is a haunting ballad of pain, longing, and despair, searingly etched onto the souls of countless loved ones—our kin, our friends, those we work with, and those we casually pass on the streets.

Imagine, if you will, standing precariously at the very edge of an immeasurable and foreboding chasm. Beneath you, the engulfing darkness epitomizes the cruel grip of addiction—a grip that promises solace but delivers ruin. From this abyss emanates the heart-wrenching screams of countless souls, their voices laden with the weight of vanquished dreams, sundered relationships, and once unshakeable self-worth now torn asunder. This descent into the jaws of addiction represents more than just a physiological dependency. It symbolizes a heart-wrenching emotional and spiritual nosedive, a vortex of anguish, hopelessness, and paralyzing loneliness.

One does not need to look deep into scholarly books to fathom this crisis's sheer scale and depth. Over the past few years, recent statistics paint a stark and alarming picture: millions from every continent are trapped by SUD. They are most frequently victimized by opioids, alcohol, and methamphetamines, among other substances. However, these figures, cold and impersonal as they are, only tell a fraction of the story. Beneath each number is a living, breathing individual, a wealth of experiences, dreams, and potentials. Every individual battling SUD embodies a unique tale, a narrative rich with hopes deferred, ambitions unfulfilled, and familial and social ties strained to near-breaking points. Joey and Jodie knew this all too well, while also battling SUD. Their personal battles often echo the more significant societal conflicts we face against misinformation, deep-seated prejudice, and the distressing scarcity of meaningful, effective treatments.

Nevertheless, it is imperative to understand that this issue extends beyond mere data, no matter how startling. At its core, the substance use crisis is intensely emotional, deeply personal, and profoundly spiritual. Those ensnared by SUD struggle against guilt, shame, and self-loathing. This is not merely a stumble on life's complex journey; it is akin to being trapped in a maze, an intricate web of paths where each twist and turn only plunges them deeper into the clutches of despair, pushing them further from redemption and hope. Families and friends, too, bear the brunt of this crisis. Their faces, lined with pain, bear witness to the transformation of someone they cherished, their once vibrant essence now dulled, almost extinguished, by addiction's relentless assault.

However, in the heart of this darkness, there are glimmers of hope. Just as the first rays of dawn pierce the most profound night, this overwhelming sea of sorrow is punctuated by beacons of hope and resilience. Increasingly, voices are rising from the gloom, demanding reform, advocating for empathy, and clamoring for a shift toward trauma-informed care. For, you see, SUD is not solely about chemical allure. Often, lurking beneath is an array of trauma—deep-seated wounds that have been left to fester, untreated and unacknowledged. Recognizing and addressing these wounds is essential—it could be revolutionary, reshaping the recovery landscape.

Stories of resilience emerge from this morass of despair like phoenixes rising from the ashes. Consider Joey, whose journey took him to the very brink of oblivion and back. His saga of recovery, redemption, and rediscovery is a testament to the incredible fortitude and adaptability of the human spirit, capable of overcoming even the most harrowing of adversities. In parallel fashion, there is Jodie, whose tale offers invaluable insights into the myriad of challenges faced by those who stand by, seemingly powerless, witnessing the relentless ravages of addiction in those they hold dear.

These stories and countless others resonate with a potent message: even in the bleakest moments, even when all seems lost, hope persists. The darkest hour is, indeed, just before the dawn. Moreover, dawn, with its promise of renewal, is inevitable. As we journey further, delving into the intimate intricacies of Joey's recovery and Jodie's poignant experiences, let us commit ourselves to understanding, to truly feeling and empathizing, and to joining hands as one unified force, ready to combat the tidal wave of the substance use disorder crisis that threatens to overwhelm our global society.

Joey's Personal Recovery Journey and Jodie's Experiences

Amidst the complex tapestry of human experiences, the stories of Joey and Jodie unfurl like soulful ballads, echoing pain, courage, deep affection, and rebirth. Beyond addiction, their tales capture a remarkable metamorphosis, emphasizing the unyielding spirit that exists within each of us, waiting to be awakened.

Joey's narrative unfolds like a heart-wrenching sonnet that gradually evolves into a triumphant anthem. A decade free from the paralyzing grip of substances is not just a number; it signifies a rebirth, an emergence from the very depths of despair. Enveloped by the consuming shadows of addiction, he teetered on the precipice of oblivion, contemplating an escape from the relentless torment. Nevertheless, even in that seemingly endless chasm of hopelessness, a tenacious spark refused to be extinguished—a beacon of potential and defiance against his internal adversaries.

This unwavering determination led Joey to Club Serenity non-profit recovery group, a sanctuary for wounded souls. Not only did he seek solace, but he metamorphosed into a guiding light for countless others. As he navigated his path of self-discovery, Joey pursued academic enlightenment, amassing a wealth of knowledge through four degrees, and molding himself into a licensed social worker. With each achievement and life he touched, Joey was not merely enhancing his credentials but rebuilding, redefining, and redeeming himself.

Parallel to Joey's tale, Jodie's narrative brims with an intricate blend of vulnerability and unyielding spirit. For seven agonizing years, Jodie confronted her innermost demons, displaying a steadfastness that both challenged and inspired. Embroiled in the fierce clutches of substance use disorder, her bond with Joey was incessantly tested, teetering on the precipice of dissolution.

The sanctuary they sought in love threatened to submerge under addiction's overpowering torrents. Yet, the sheer purity and fervor of genuine love possess the remarkable fortitude to navigate even the stormiest of seas. Their union, resilient in its essence, encapsulated far more than a mere romantic connection: it symbolized a united front, a testament to their joint odyssey toward healing, self-discovery, and an evocative metamorphosis.

The foundations of Jodie's emotional tempests trace back to her formative years. Adopted into a loving home, Jodie often grappled with a gnawing sense of alienation during family gatherings. The echoing sentiment, "I felt lost in a room where people cared for me," underscores a poignant paradox that trapped her. The revelation of her adoption, precipitated by a school parent's indiscretion and a forced confession by her mother, Diane, left a young and impressionable Jodie reeling. "I felt so different," she would often lament. This seismic shift in her self-perception was punctuated with moments of deep-seated trauma, casting long, lingering shadows over her psyche. Yet, in a transformative moment, the birth of her daughter, Gianna, breathed a rejuvenating essence into her life. In Gianna, Jodie discovered a tangible extension of herself, a balm to the wounds that had festered for years.

Amidst Jodie's struggles with trauma and addiction, her cousin Andrew emerged as her beacon of hope. Providing more than shelter, he offered unwavering belief in her potential. His support showcased the transformative power of human connection, highlighting how one person's kindness can profoundly alter another's trajectory.

Further complicating her emotions were the rigid, dogmatic principles that governed her upbringing. Ensnared in a paradigm where her intrinsic nature perpetually clashed with established norms, Jodie often felt adrift, always seeking an elusive affirmation from her family. She emerged from a familial cocoon where hushed whispers substituted candid conversations, amplifying her feelings of isolation.

Jodie's narrative is a stark reminder that behind every struggle with addiction lies an intricate maze of experiences, traumas, and unvoiced yearnings—a poignant tale of resilience and rediscovery against overwhelming odds.

However, their expedition was not without its battle scars. The corrosive effects of addiction did not solely confine themselves to Joey and Jodie. The ripples extended, distorting the very fabric of their familial bonds. Their children, the silent spectators to the disarray, faced the agonizing ordeal of yearning for their parents from the periphery. Despite the challenges, the resilient threads of love, although tested, remained intact.

Fast forward to today, Joey and Jodie are monumental beacons of inspiration, representing hope and resilience to countless souls ensnared in addiction's labyrinth. Their odysseys emphasize the profound depths of human emotions, the nadirs of despair, and the zeniths of redemption. They serve as poignant reminders that beyond every grim statistic, every label, and every judgment lies a deeply personal, profoundly human tale—a narrative replete with adversities but also teeming with immeasurable potential.

Diving deep into Joey's experiences, we uncover an individual with multifaceted academic and personal expertise. With years of dedication in mental health, Joey's impressive roles as a licensed social worker, a recovery, family, and forensic specialist, and his extensive association with a large behavioral health agency exemplify his commitment to the cause. His vast training in diverse areas, such as motivational interviewing (MI) and trauma-informed practice, highlights his proficiency. Nevertheless, his personal touch, unyielding empathy, and compassion—qualities honed through his recovery journey—truly distinguish him.

A poignant moment from 2011 underscores Joey's tumultuous past. Outside the Pittsburgh, Pennsylvania suburb, Charleroi police station, he made a despairing call to his mother, conveying a depth of desolation that left her heartbroken. This moment marked a turning point; his decision to walk into the police station and seek help epitomized his undying will to transform his life. His subsequent experiences, the incarceration, rehabilitation, and chronicle of his recovery journey, *No Addict Left Behind*, co-authored with Dr. Scott A. Cook, MD, MPH, stand as a testament to his unyielding determination and resilience.

His mother, Cindy, still vividly recalls the anguish of witnessing her son's battle, her desperate attempts to save him, and her overwhelming relief upon knowing he was safe. Jodie, resonates with the perpetual challenges of addiction, underscoring the importance of mutual support, understanding, and the unwavering belief in the power of recovery. Their shared journey, interspersed with moments of profound despair and invigorating hope, encapsulates the essence of overcoming life's adversities.

Amongst these evocative tales lies a singular message—the overarching significance of narratives in understanding the complex journey of recovery. Joey's harrowing experience in an emergency room and his poignant recollections of being labeled, mistreated, and judged highlight the deep-rooted societal prejudices surrounding addiction. His plea for a compassionate, empathetic, and understanding approach underscores the importance of personal narratives in redefining societal perceptions.

Through these powerful personal journeys, we transition seamlessly into a broader, encompassing discourse—understanding the intricate dynamics of trauma and its profound implications. With Joey and Jodie's narratives serving as the foundational bedrock, we are poised to search deeper into trauma expertise and its relevance, creating an amalgamation of personal experiences, academic insights, and clinical expertise, painting a comprehensive portrait of addiction, recovery, and the transformative power of resilience and support.

Trauma Expertise and its Relevance

Amongst the silent chambers of our hearts, memories linger. Some of these memories bring us warmth and tenderness, returning us to happier times. However, others whisper sinister tales of pain and despair. These latter memories, residues of traumatic episodes, often act like phantom shackles, silently directing our actions, shaping our beliefs, and sometimes ushering us into the treacherous maze of addiction. Peering into the abyss of trauma is not just an academic endeavor. It is a brave endeavor to illuminate the shadowy corners of our souls, seeking to comprehend the anguish that bubbles underneath our everyday personas.

When trauma is evoked, it is not limited to mere physical harm. Emotional, psychological, and even intergenerational traumas hold paramount significance. Visualize the child, isolated and yearning for parental love, the battle-hardened soldier battling the demons of war even in peace, or the individual suffocated by societal judgments due to their identity. Their scars may not always be visible, but they cast a long, haunting shadow, shaping perceptions, molding behaviors, and sometimes pushing the soul to seek solace in substances. The profundity of trauma expertise goes beyond superficial understanding.

It seeks to unravel the intricate dance between traumatic incidents and the subsequent emotional aftermath. Why does a heartbreak in adolescence lead to destructive patterns in adulthood? How does a brutal memory erode one's sense of self-worth? Embarking on such quests allows us to see beyond the trauma, delving into the very essence of the individual.

So, why does this matter? The relevance is monumental. Behind every substance abuse, behind every numbed emotion, there often lies a trauma recounting its devastating story. To overlook this elemental core is akin to watering the leaves of a wilting plant, ignoring its parched roots. Truly addressing trauma means creating sanctuaries for these stories, ensuring the individual is recognized, empathized with, and, above all, deeply understood.

The emergence of trauma-informed care heralds a pivotal shift in perspective. It signifies our collective awakening to trauma's profound intricacies and, more importantly, underscores the indispensable nature of empathy. The domain of trauma defies mere clinical detachment; it beckons for profound emotional engagement. It compels us to momentarily bear the chains that enslave another, forging pathways of genuine healing.

As you examine these words, grasp this truth: trauma expertise transcends cold data. It is a unique prism, refracting the myriad hues of human fragility. This prism shows that addiction is not a standalone disorder but a heart-wrenching scream emanating from deep traumatic chasms.

Having emphasized trauma expertise's intrinsic value, it is essential to situate it in a broader framework. It is a cornerstone in the edifice of understanding and healing. This foundation sets the stage for the subsequent chapters, merging the profound insights of trauma expertise with intimate personal odyssey through addiction's labyrinth.

Historically, trauma was confined to the visible and immediate. However, as physician and trauma expert, Bessel Van der Kolk astutely illustrates in *The Body Keeps the Score*, trauma surpasses superficial injuries. It etches itself deep within our neural fabric, influencing the holistic process of recovery (Van der Kolk, 2014). Such traumas, dormant for years, may suddenly awaken, perplexing even seasoned observers. Behaviors dismissed as mere rebellion or addiction might, in essence, be poignant cries echoing from traumatic pasts (Felitti et al., 1998).

Physician and addiction expert, Dr. Gabor Maté's writings elucidate the intricate nexus between trauma and addiction. In *In the Realm of Hungry Ghosts*, he portrays addiction as more than a mere chemical dependency. It emerges as an emotional refuge from the oppressive weight of past traumas (Maté, 2008). Similarly, *Seeking Safety* by Najavits underscores the intersection of post-traumatic stress disorder (PTSD) and substance abuse, emphasizing the allure of substances as temporary havens from anguish (Najavits, 2002).

Addressing trauma demands a multifaceted approach. Maxine Harris and Roger Fallot assert that trauma-informed care transcends mere acknowledgment. It requires environments tailor-made for trauma survivors, facilitating trust-based exploration of their stories (Harris & Fallot, 2001). As White suggests, peer support serves as a sanctuary of shared stories where understanding transcends words (White, 2009).

Recognizing trauma, however, is just the prologue. As highlighted by Miller and Rollnick's *Motivational Interviewing*, understanding the motivations stemming from trauma can pave the way for enduring transformations (Miller & Rollnick, 2012). This aligns with Marlatt & Witkiewitz's emphasis on trauma-informed harm reduction strategies (Marlatt & Witkiewitz, 2010).

SAMHSA underscores trauma's multifaceted nature and pervasive impacts (SAMHSA, 2014). Research like that of Dube et al. (2003) illustrates the nexus between early-life adversities and substance abuse, underlining the need for trauma-centric therapeutic interventions. Furthermore, blending cognitive behavioral therapy (CBT) with trauma-informed practices can craft a holistic healing path, as Kar (2010) posited.

As elucidated by Krystal, Neumeister, and Charney (2004), the neurobiological aspects of trauma shed light on trauma's ability to reshape neural circuits, culminating in behavioral alterations. The intricacies of self-regulation failure, outlined by Heatherton & Wagner (2011), further spotlight trauma's neural aftermath.

To fully grasp addiction and its myriad manifestations, one must navigate the turbulent undercurrents of trauma. As Goleman (1995) posited, emotional intelligence is instrumental in this endeavor. By melding trauma expertise with lived narratives, we sow the seeds for a more empathetic and effective healing journey.

Ultimately, the dance between trauma and its myriad expressions—addiction, behavioral shifts, or emotional storms—is a testament to human resilience. By bridging the chasm between trauma expertise and personal narratives, we embarked on a journey of profound understanding, empathy, and hope. As we venture forward, we will further explore this symbiosis, delving into the primary objective of this book: weaving the profound insights of trauma expertise with personal odysseys, offering a beacon of hope for those trapped in addiction's clutches.

The Goal of the Book

Each thread tells a story of joy, despair, hope, and resilience in the human existence. However, some threads bear the weight of profound traumas, weaving patterns of pain that culminate in the complex picture of addiction. Within these intricacies lies a profound revelation—the undeniable link between trauma and addiction. This book, *From Scars to Stars*, embarks on a journey to illuminate this connection, unraveling the intricate dance of pain, vulnerability, and healing at its core.

Picture a world where every person who stumbles into the grasp of addiction is seen not as a mere statistic or a lost cause but as an individual bearing scars from deep-seated traumas. Such scars may lurk beneath the surface, masked by the numbing effect of substances, yet they are the silent scream that drives many toward the path of addiction. Recognizing this profound connection is not merely an exercise in empathy; it is a clarion call for change in how we approach addiction treatment and recovery.

At the heart of this book lies an unwavering belief: that in understanding trauma, we hold the key to revolutionizing addiction recovery. By placing trauma at the forefront of our discussions, we do not just acknowledge the pain: we seek to understand its origins, its manifestations, and, most crucially, its healing. Trauma-informed care is not just a buzzword: it is a compassionate, holistic approach that recognizes the whole person, the sum of their experiences, and the depth of their pain.

However, understanding is but one piece of the puzzle. True healing requires insights gleaned from those who have navigated the stormy seas of addiction, faced their traumas, and emerged stronger and wiser. These are not mere anecdotes; they are the compass that points toward genuine recovery. By merging the insights from lived experiences with trauma-informed care, this book seeks to present an approach that is not just clinical but deeply human.

You, dear reader, are invited to witness and feel the weight of these narratives. To understand the tears behind every relapse, the silent strength in every recovery story, and the profound need for an approach that intertwines understanding with experience. With every page, you will delve deeper into the souls of those battling addiction, feeling their pain, hope, and indomitable spirit.

This is not just a book; it is a movement. A call to action for therapists, caregivers, physicians, loved ones, and society at large to redefine how we perceive and treat addiction. Beyond the clinical terminologies and methodologies lies the realm of human emotion. Moreover, within this realm, the battle against addiction can be won. We owe it to ourselves and those we care about to recognize the profound interconnectedness of trauma and addiction, and to champion a treatment approach as multifaceted and holistic as the humans it seeks to heal.

Now, as we stand at the threshold of understanding, let us take the first step into a world where trauma and addiction are not seen as separate entities, but as interwoven threads in the fabric of human experience. Join us in Chapter 1: The Fabric of Trauma and Addiction, as we begin our deep dive into the intertwined narratives of pain and hope, scars and stars, despair and redemption.

CHAPTER 1

The Fabric of Trauma and Addiction

Trauma as a Precursor to Addiction

In the cozy nook of our favorite coffee shop, Whispers and Words, a golden light washes over the readers, creating an atmosphere where the past meets the present. Here, the distant echoes of stories merge seamlessly with the soft rustling of pages and murmured conversations.

Engrossed in his novel, Joey occasionally sips his dark expresso while Jodie, at a nearby table, remains captivated by the swirling patterns in her latte. For her, the whirls in her cup are symbolic, much like the chapter's essence. They are reminiscent of the intricate dance between trauma and addiction, where individuals often plunge into the depths, seeking solace in a fleeting high. It's a dance mirroring the complex workings of the mind, where scars of the past drive one toward substances for respite.

As Jodie lost herself in her thoughts, Joey's words from a past conversation echo in her mind: "It isn't just the biochemical reactions, but the cascade of emotions they bring forth." It's a poignant reminder of the fragile line between painful memories and the allure of intoxication. Their glances meet, conveying a shared knowledge.

They both understand the intricate details they're about to unravel, a narrative where pain and dependence are intertwined. It explores the scientific and emotional intricate fabric where every tear and mend has its story.

With resolve, Jodie flips open the page, ready to dive deeper into the complex relationship of trauma and addiction. Their shared quest for understanding beckons; the exploration is about to commence.

Both recognize the depth of the journey they are about to embark on—a tapestry rich in texture, where individual threads of trauma and addiction weave a story that's all too familiar yet deeply personal. It is a journey into understanding, not just of the science but the soul, where every experience and every emotion is a piece of a puzzle waiting to be deciphered.

Taking a deep breath, Jodie turns the page, ready to uncover the intimate relationship between trauma and addiction, a voyage that promises to be both enlightening and harrowing. The stage is set; the journey begins.

Joey leaned against the worn brick wall of his childhood home in Charleroi, Pennsylvania, of the Mon-valley, allowing the memories to flood back: the laughter, the family holidays, and the warmth of loving parents. However, connected with these joyful memories were flashes of trauma—moments of inexplicable emotional pain, which, over the years, provided a fertile ground for his descent into addiction.

Similarly, despite coming from a seemingly idyllic family background, Jodie found herself spiraling down a similar path. In the quiet spaces between family gatherings and celebrations, traumatic shadows lingered—shadows that no one talked about, yet whose effects were visible.

As Van der Kolk aptly posits in his seminal work, The Body Keeps the Score, trauma, whether a one-time event or the result of persistent emotional neglect, finds a way to embed itself deeply within our psyche (Van der Kolk, 2014). It becomes an insidious force, steering many toward substance abuse as a means of escape or self-medication (Khantzian, 1997).

In Joey's case, every shot of heroin temporarily dulled the pain of those buried traumas. For Jodie, each encounter with illicit drugs provided a fleeting moment of relief, a brief escape from the internal storm. Despite their similar backgrounds, they both exemplified the alarming findings of Felitti et al.'s Adverse Childhood Experiences (ACE) study. This ground-breaking research unveiled the undeniable link between childhood trauma and the propensity for addiction later in life (Felitti et al., 1998; Dube et al., 2003).

Trauma can be likened to an emotional scar—a lasting testament to past injuries. Moreover, as scars can be sensitive, so can these emotional wounds be easily inflamed by life's stressors. For Joey and Jodie, addiction emerged as a misguided salve, albeit with its devastating consequences. Substance abuse, though momentarily alleviating, merely compounds the emotional pain, leading to a vicious cycle of trauma and addiction (Maté, 2008).

However, amid the narrative of pain and struggle, silver linings emerged. Joey often recounted the invaluable support he received from his peer group during his recovery—a testament to White's assertion about the transformative power of peer-based addiction recovery (White, 2009). Their shared experiences became a beacon of hope, a tangible reminder that recovery, while challenging, was attainable.

Joey, too, had his moments of enlightenment. One summer at an inpatient facility, amid his struggle, he attended a harm reduction workshop (Marlatt & Witkiewitz, 2010). There, he met others who, like him, sought to understand their triggers and patterns. This knowledge, though seemingly basic, was a revelation. Recognizing his patterns and triggers became the first step in Joey's arduous journey toward healing.

It is essential to acknowledge that trauma, though a significant precursor, is not the sole cause of addiction. Genetics, environmental factors, and other complex interplays contribute to this intricate mosaic (Kreek et al., 2005). However, by addressing trauma's role, we open avenues for trauma-informed care, a paradigm shift that places the individual's lived experiences at the center of recovery (Harris & Fallot, 2001).

Draped within the shadows of Joey and Jodie's experiences lies a universal truth—that the human psyche is a web woven of not just experiences but also the myriad interpretations of those experiences. The worn bricks that Joey leaned against were not just the foundations of his home but were repositories of deeply etched memories, each brick seeming to whisper tales of joy, love, hurt, and abandonment. His fingers might trace the rough surface, feeling the bumps and grooves just as his mind navigated the highs and lows of his past.

Although paralleling Joey's journey in many ways, Jodie's journey had unique intricacies.

Behind the luminous façade of family celebrations, the invisible weight of unspoken words bore down on her. Silences often speak louder than words. The whispered confidences never shared, the stifled tears, and the forced smiles at gatherings all contributed to the ever-growing chasm between her present reality and buried traumas.

The nuanced dance between memory, trauma, and substance use is as intricate as it is profound. Just as a piece of music can evoke many emotions, triggering cascades of associated memories, the environment we immerse ourselves in plays an instrumental role in dictating our mental responses. Joey's childhood home was not merely a backdrop; it was an active participant, a silent witness to his life's symphony of emotions. Jodie's familial environment, with its blend of joyous occasions and overshadowing traumas, played a symphony of its own, harmonizing and clashing in equal measure.

The external world often mirrors our internal chaos. The streets we walk, the homes we return to, and the spaces we inhabit are not just physical entities. They interact with our psyche, sometimes as gentle caresses and sometimes as harsh reminders. The profound insights of researchers like Van der Kolk and Felitti do not merely investigate the individual's psyche but reflect a broader societal pattern, urging us to recognize and address the intricate dynamics between environment, trauma, and addiction.

In these intertwining narratives, what stands out is the incredible resilience of the human spirit. The paths to recovery, laden with obstacles, also shimmer with hope, often illuminated by supportive peers, enlightening workshops, or the sheer will to heal. Joey and Jodie's stories serve as poignant reminders that in our quest to understand addiction, we must transcend beyond the individual and encompass the collective, embracing the environment, society, and culture in our narrative.

Joey and Jodie's stories underscore the undeniable link between trauma and addiction. Nevertheless, more importantly, they highlight the human capacity for resilience and recovery. Our understanding of trauma's neurological implications is ever-evolving, a testament to the complexity of the human brain.

As we look deeper into the intricate world of recovery and healing, it becomes imperative to understand the neurological underpinnings of trauma and addiction. We owe it to Joey, Jodie, and countless others to explore this nexus further in hopes of finding sustainable paths to healing. Let us now explore into the "Neurological Aspects of Trauma and Addiction" to understand the science behind the pain and, most importantly, the recovery.

Neurological Aspects of Trauma and Addiction

The human brain, a marvel of evolution, is sculpted by joyous and jarring experiences. At the crossroads of our personal histories, traumas, and addictions can powerfully rewire this intricate organ. To understand this interplay, one must research into the underlying neural pathways and see how experiences, especially those rooted in trauma, leave imprints that often lead to addiction.

Joey, with his carefree swagger, and Jodie, with her fragile poise, have danced with these twin demons. While their journeys differ, their brains share tales of relentless pain and unyielding hope.

When trauma strikes, the brain's alarm system, the amygdala, becomes hyperactive. It keeps sounding the alarm at the faintest trace of threat, leaving an individual perpetually on edge. Van der Kolk describes this process as the body "keeping the score." Traumatic experiences alert the brain, waiting for the next threat (Van der Kolk, 2014). Such persistent stress reshapes the brain, eroding regions essential for judgment, self-regulation, and discernment.

These changes are not merely academic constructs. They manifest tangibly in Joey's impulsivity and Jodie's heightened sensitivity. When Joey impulsively reaches for a drink after a traumatic flashback, it is a testimony to how his prefrontal cortex—the seat of judgment and impulse control—has been compromised (Heatherton & Wagner, 2011). Meanwhile, Jodie's addiction of choice was opiates. This began as an attempt to numb the relentless cacophony of her amygdala, her substances of choice providing a temporary reprieve from her traumas.

Moreover, here is where addiction enters the fray. The surge of dopamine, the neurotransmitter of pleasure and reward, becomes a siren song for a brain reeling under trauma. Dr. Gabor Maté suggests that many who grapple with addictions are, in reality, attempting to address old wounds, stating that "addictions always originate in pain, whether felt openly or hidden in the unconscious" (Maté, 2008). They are self-medicating, albeit destructively.

However, amidst these tales of neurological reconfiguration and substance-fueled escapades, there are also stories of resilience. Jodie recalls moments of fleeting clarity amid her addiction haze when the warmth of genuine connection or the simplest acts of kindness became her dopamine source. Joey reminisces about a guitar riff, a forgotten melody from childhood that stirred something within, hinting at neural plasticity and the brain's inherent capacity to heal and rewire (Krystal et al., 2004).

Research consistently indicates that meaningful human connections can foster recovery by activating the brain's reward pathways in healthy ways (White, 2009). In their recovery journeys, Joey and Jodie found solace in peer groups where shared traumas and triumphs became catalysts for healing (Davidson et al., 2012).

One poignant memory stands out. After a group therapy session, Joey played that same guitar riff in his head, the melody now acting as an anthem of his healing journey. Jodie moved and danced with abandon, symbolizing her liberation from the shackles of her past. This dance, observed by others, became a symbolic testament to the power of neural resilience and the possibility of rebirth.

However, the duality of trauma and addiction is not solely a neurochemical narrative. The emotions, experiences, and environments interlace with these chemical cascades, perpetuating a cycle that's hard to break. Najavits termed this the "cycle of trauma and substance use," illustrating how one feeds into the other, creating a relentless loop that can seem inescapable (Najavits, 2002).

As we turn the page, we will explore this intricate dance between trauma and substance use, understanding how they feed off each other and exploring ways to break the cycle. Like the riveting tales of Joey and Jodie, it is a chapter of both despair and hope, chaos and clarity. It beckons to explore the cyclical nature of trauma and addiction and the paths to breaking free from their grip.

The Cycle of Trauma and Substance Use

The intimate dance between trauma and addiction, painted against the vast canvas of human emotion, is heart-wrenching and profoundly enlightening. One might ponder how trauma, an experience of deeply distressing or disturbing events, entwines itself with addiction, a relentless grasp of a substance or behavior. The answer lies in the very fabric of our existence, sewn together by threads of emotions, experiences, and the human psyche's innate desire to find relief.

Joey once described his childhood as "a collage of chaos." After each tumultuous night, the echoes of hurtful words and the suffocating silence etched deep scars in his psyche. Joey found peace temporarily, in the syringe. Heroin numbed the searing pain of those memories, a balm for his festering wounds. Van der Kolk (2014) aptly notes in The Body Keeps the Score that trauma leaves an indelible mark on our physiology, making victims more susceptible to addiction as a means to escape their relentless torment.

Similarly, Jodie's initiation into the world of drugs was not an act of rebellion, as many perceived. It was a desperate cry for help, a means to mute the rigid, unbending doctrine she had to suit up and march to like the beat of a drum. Addiction became her fortress, shielding her from the outside world yet imprisoning her in a cell of her own making. Maté (2008), in In the Realm of Hungry Ghosts, poignantly highlights that addiction often stems from a place of pain and anguish, making it more of a coping mechanism than a mere choice.

The emotional labyrinth that trauma survivors navigate is intricate. Feelings of shame, guilt, and a relentless internal cacophony of self-blame drown out reason and logic. Harris Fallot (2001) emphasizes that the system often fails to recognize these intricate emotional nuances, pushing survivors further into the clutches of substance use as a form of self-medication (Khantzian, 1997).

However, amid this grim dance between trauma and addiction, a glimmer of hope emerges. Joey's story did not end in despair. In the pit of his addiction, he found a beacon in the form of a peer support group (White, 2009). Among fellow survivors, Joey unearthed the power of shared experiences, empathy, and the indomitable human spirit. This communal bond became his lifeline, pulling him from the abyss of his past traumas and addictive tendencies.

Jodie, too, discovered solace and strength in unexpected places. Encounters with compassionate therapists who employed trauma-informed approaches were pivotal in her recovery journey. Najavits (2002) underscores the significance of such approaches in her work, Seeking Safety. Integrating understanding of trauma with substance abuse treatment empowers survivors, enabling them to confront their past and carve out a future free from the shackles of addiction.

The narratives of Joey and Jodie illuminate an essential truth. In contrast, trauma may sow the seeds of addiction, but the inherent resilience, the capacity for connection, and the power of informed, compassionate intervention can break this cycle. Understanding trauma's role in addiction is paramount for professionals in the field and society. We hope to sever the deeply entrenched links between past traumas and present addictions through empathy, education, and effective intervention.

Addiction does not define Joey or Jodie. Instead, it refined them by giving them stories of endurance, resilience, and eventual recovery that shined as testaments to the indomitable human spirit. Their tales are but two threads in the intricate fabric of trauma and addiction, weaving together despair, hope, agony, and redemption.

As we further explore, let us remember Joey and Jodie and countless souls like them. In their lived experiences, trials, and triumphs, we find profound insights into the human psyche, addiction, and the boundless capacity for healing.

Furthermore, as we turn the page, we explore deeper into the lived realities, laying bare the raw, poignant real-life narratives of trauma survivors.

Real-Life Narratives of Trauma Survivors

Abby's eyes flitted across the room, glancing at the empty pill bottles and the faint trace of white powder on the coffee table. They were remnants of a battle she fought every day, a battle against memories of a trauma that refused to fade. Just as scars tell tales of past wounds, Abby's addiction spoke volumes about her deep-seated pain.

As Van der Kolk stated, "The body keeps the score" (2014). For trauma survivors, their bodies often bear the weight of unspeakable experiences, and substance abuse becomes an avenue to numb that pain, albeit momentarily. Abby had endured years of emotional and physical abuse in her childhood. Her body became a canvas, illustrating her pain through various means, including substance use. Nevertheless, understanding trauma and addiction requires peeling back the layers and diving deep into the intersections of physical pain, emotional scars, and the unyielding grip of addiction.

Maté (2008) explored the profound connections between trauma and addiction in his work, *In the Realm of Hungry Ghosts*. He observed that the root of addiction often stems from emptiness, a void created by past traumatic experiences. For Abby, every drug was as an attempt to fill that void and escape from her past's haunting flashbacks.

The same narrative unfolded in the life of Shane, who was once a promising college athlete. A car accident stole his dreams and left him with chronic back pain. Shane's story is familiar: a prescription for pain relief that became a lifeline. Pain pills provided a brief respite, not just from physical pain but also from the overwhelming grief of lost potential. He soon spiraled into addiction, with opioids being his only refuge from his new reality.

However, it is crucial to highlight the more profound complexity of trauma and addiction. Harris and Fallot (2001) argued that service systems must be designed with a trauma-informed approach, understanding the myriad ways trauma manifests. For Abby and Shane, their substance use was more than a mere desire for pleasure; it was a desperate attempt at seeking safety (Najavits, 2002).

Amidst the turbulence of their lives, Abby and Shane found solace in peer-based addiction recovery support. White (2009) championed the transformative power of such groups, emphasizing that individuals with lived experiences bring a unique, empathetic perspective that can catalyze recovery. Through sharing their stories, Abby and Shane found they were not alone in their struggles. Others, too, had faced the sinister dance between trauma and addiction.

Moreover, there were silver linings. Abby began using art as a form of therapy, creating masterpieces that narrated her journey. Her artwork not only became a cathartic release but also offered a beacon of hope for others, illustrating the possibility of finding beauty amidst chaos. On the other hand, Shane began mentoring young athletes, teaching them resilience and the importance of mental health.

However, despite these glimmers of hope, it is paramount to understand the nuanced and multifaceted relationship between trauma and addiction. For many, like Abby and Shane, substance use might start as self-medication (Khantzian, 1997), an attempt to regulate overwhelming emotions. However, this seemingly short-term relief can lead to a lifelong battle with addiction.

Indeed, research has shown that adverse childhood experiences significantly increase the risk of illicit drug use (Dube et al., 2003). Abby's tumultuous childhood and Shane's tragic accident created a fertile ground for addiction to take root. And while interventions can help

(Livingston et al., 2012), true healing requires addressing the underlying trauma.

Yet, it is essential not to view individuals like Abby and Shane solely through the lens of their trauma and addiction. They are more than their scars. They are testaments to the human spirit's resilience and the innate desire to heal, connect, and find purpose. As Lieberman and Van Horn (2009) highlighted, giving voice to the unspeakable, acknowledging the trauma, and finding avenues of self-expression can pave the path to recovery.

This intricate fabric of trauma and addiction, woven with threads of pain, resilience, and hope, sets the stage for our exploration. These narratives serve as a poignant reminder that while trauma might leave indelible marks, the human spirit's resilience can shine through the darkest nights.

As we transition from understanding the complex jumble of trauma and addiction, exploring the multifaceted pathways to recovery is imperative. Every journey is unique, but they all share a common destination: healing with hope.

Pathways to Recovery

In the vast embroidery of human experience, trauma and addiction weave an intricate pattern, often interlacing in ways that are difficult to disentangle. The resonant words of Van der Kolk assert that *The Body Keeps the Score* highlighting the profound manner in which trauma inscribes itself upon both the psyche and the body, making its presence felt long after the triggering event has passed (Van der Kolk, 2014).

Joey and Jodie know this all too well. Their struggles with addiction, at times so overwhelming that it seemed life would snuff them out, were often exacerbated by underlying traumatic experiences. Nevertheless, their stories are not mere chronicles of pain and struggle; they serve as living testaments to the transformative power of recovery and the resilience of the human spirit.

As Maté describes, addiction can be visualized as souls roaming the "Realm of Hungry Ghosts," an allegorical domain where unquenchable desires torment individuals (Maté, 2008). The ghosts are not only those addicted to substances but are haunted by past traumas, seeking refuge and solace. Joey's battles, for instance, were not solely against the substances; they were, in essence, battles against his traumatic past, against the shadows that constantly whispered from the dark corners of his mind.

Jodie's journey was no less tumultuous. The whirlwinds of emotion, the agony of dogmatic actions, the beckoning shadows—every challenge she faced was external and internal. In her darker moments, trauma seemed like an ever-tightening noose. However, with every step toward recovery, she rewrote the fabric of her life, transforming scars into constellations of hope and resilience.

However, it is crucial to understand that addiction does not manifest in a vacuum. The Adverse Childhood Experiences study by Dube et al. (2003) underscores the alarming connection between childhood trauma—abuse, neglect, and household dysfunction—and heightened risk for substance use in adulthood. Joey and Jodie's harrowing experiences were not unique, but representative of countless souls trapped in similar vicious cycles.

To add depth to this understanding, consider the perspective of Khantzian (1997), who posits that individuals often resort to substances to "self-medicate"—an attempt to numb or regulate emotions stemming from traumatic events. This hypothesis illuminates why individuals like Joey and Jodie, scarred by past traumas, might find solace in the transient escape provided by substances.

But hope is not lost in this intricate weave of trauma and addiction. The lived experiences of Joey and Jodie radiate like silver threads in this textile, providing tangible inspiration. Their recovery, rooted in trauma-informed care, twelve-step support, and sheer determination, stands as a beacon for countless others lost in the abyss of addiction. Leveraging trauma-informed approaches, as highlighted by Harris & Fallot (2001), can revolutionize recovery processes, ensuring that underlying traumas are not overlooked but are addressed as pivotal aspects of holistic healing.

Joey and Jodie's tales also emphasize the significance of peer support in the recovery journey. The camaraderie, understanding, and mutual support provided by peers have been found to offer substantial benefits in addiction treatment (Tracy & Wallace, 2016). Joey's connection with fellow survivors, for instance, was not just about shared stories; it was about collective strength, about drawing upon shared experiences to forge a path forward.

As the chapter unfolds, the interplay between trauma and addiction becomes evident, stitched together by Joey and Jodie's raw, authentic silver linings. Their stories emphasize the power of human resilience, the importance of understanding and addressing trauma in recovery, and the undeniable value of shared experiences and peer support.

However, understanding this intricate relationship is just the beginning. As we transition to Chapter 2: The Role of Empathy in Recovery, the focus shifts from broad conceptual frameworks to the mighty emotional connections vital for healing. We will explore how empathy, when sincerely expressed and deeply felt, becomes a transformative tool in recovery. By immersing ourselves in our clients' experiences, understanding their unique struggles, and genuinely being there for them in their most vulnerable moments, we pave the way for true healing. Through this profound, empathetic connection, the seeds of recovery find their most fertile ground.

CHAPTER 2

The Role of Empathy in Recovery

The Role of Empathy in Recovery

As the cafe within Whispers and Words hums with its quiet life, patrons slowly gravitate toward a corner of the bookstore where the warmth of empathy blankets everyone. This sanctuary, adorned with overflowing bookshelves and the ever-constant tick-tock of an antique clock, carries the silent stories of countless souls. The atmosphere, imbued with the resonances of countless confessions, is a testament to the healing journey of many.

Joey and Jodie Pagano, settled in plush chairs beside a burnished table, symbolize the beautiful intersection of professional acumen and the visceral pulse of firsthand experiences. Their world is a haven where trauma and addiction are viewed not as adversaries but as layers of the human story, begging for acceptance and comprehension.

Between them rests an oft-referenced book, its margins filled with scribbles and underlying passages, evidence of their unwavering commitment. Each notation reminds us that authentic recovery is anchored in presence, genuinely seeing another's soul without filters or preconceptions.

Emotionally tinting, Jodie murmurs, "Every session here feels like we're walking alongside them in their shoes, doesn't it?"

Joey, eyes deep with understanding, replies, "Each story is a reflection, echoing moments of our journey. To be present isn't just about being here; it's delving deep into that realm between wounds and wonders."

Outside, the world continues, oblivious to the sacred dance inside the room, but the feeling is unmistakable for those who step foot in this haven. Here, one is indeed seen, truly understood. As the clock continues its relentless ticking, the Paganos remain anchored in their mission, guided by a blend of education and emotion, ready to traverse the intricate pathways of the human psyche. The journey is not just about healing but a celebration of resilience, a testament to the transformative power of true presence. The tale continues ever deeper into the heart of what it means to recover, rise, and truly live.

Empathy, an innate human capacity often misunderstood or overlooked, becomes the golden thread stitching the mosaic of recovery. It is the bridge between the healer and the wounded, the guide that fosters an understanding beyond words (Goleman, 1995). Joey and Jodie Pagano, having navigated the tumultuous waves of addiction themselves, knew the incredible potency of empathy firsthand.

In a world where addiction was often misunderstood, misconstrued, or dismissed, genuine empathy was like the comforting touch of a loved one. They remembered the glimmers of compassion they had occasionally encountered on their own rocky journeys—those rare moments when someone genuinely sought to understand their experience without judgment. Moments when the chilling grasp of addiction momentarily loosened, replaced by the warm embrace of genuine human connection.

According to Van der Kolk (2014), trauma leaves an indelible mark on the psyche, transforming how one perceives the world and oneself. This profound alteration in perception often becomes a chasm, separating the trauma victim from those who have not experienced such devastation. Empathy becomes the bridge spanning this abyss; it is not merely about understanding someone's pain but about validating it.

Dr. Maté (2008), in his seminal work, In the Realm of Hungry Ghosts, delves deep into the intricacies of addiction, highlighting how society's lack of empathy aggravates the already overwhelming burden of addicts. The external judgments, prejudices, and stigma encountered daily by those battling addiction often reflect their internal torment (Livingston et al., 2012). Joey and Jodie had experienced this duality: society's disdain mirrored their self-loathing. However, they also remembered those who showed them empathy, lighting their way through their darkest hours.

Empathy in the therapeutic realm goes beyond mere words of solace. White (2009) notes that peer-based addiction recovery leverages shared experiences to foster a deep understanding; Joey and Jodie were living embodiments of this approach. Their past battles with addiction and the scars they bore became beacons of hope for others. Their lived experiences were not just stories: they were lessons, guides, and, most importantly, proof of the possibility of redemption.

This tangible, empathetic connection can be the difference between recovery and relapse. Miller and Rollnick (2012) affirm the potency of MI, a technique rooted in empathy. By validating a person's experiences and emotions, one can help steer them toward positive behavioral change.

Drawing from their personal encounters with addiction, Joey and Jodie recognized that empathy was not a static, one-time gesture. It was an evolving, dynamic practice. As they listened to countless narratives of pain and despair, they realized that every individual's experience with addiction was unique, shaped by a myriad of factors ranging from genetic predispositions (Kreek et al., 2005) to traumatic childhood experiences (Dube et al., 2003).

However, empathy is not without its challenges. Kar (2011) highlights the risk of vicarious trauma among therapists, where one can become excessively affected by a client's traumatic experiences. But Joey and Jodie's histories with addiction, rather than being a weakness, fortified their resilience. Their pasts taught them the art of balance—being deeply empathetic without becoming submerged in another's pain.

Empathy, as they discovered, was also a two-way street. As they reached out to others, their interactions with those on similar journeys enriched their understanding of addiction's intricate labyrinth. Each story, each tear, each smile was a testament to the transformative power of genuine human connection.

Empathy is the anchor in addiction recovery, keeping individuals rooted when tempestuous emotions threaten to sweep them away. Joey and Jodie knew this all too well. As they journeyed forward, hand in hand, guiding countless souls toward healing, they did so with an unwavering belief in the power of empathy.

As we explore deeper into the world of recovery, one essential lesson emerges: while knowledge and techniques are vital, it is the genuine human connections, built on understanding and devoid of judgment, that genuinely heal. As we explore the significance of non-judgmental approaches, we will discover how these connections, rooted in empathy, blossom into a powerful force for transformation.

The Importance of Non-Judgmental Approaches

On a bitterly cold morning, Joey and Jodie, survivors of an addiction that nearly snuffed the lights from their souls, found themselves in a dim, unwelcoming clinic. They were no strangers to judgmental eyes and whispered conversations. "Isn't that Joey? The one found on the street last month?" or "Jodie? She once had such promise."

However, amidst these covert exchanges, there were silver linings. Joey recalled when a nurse gently took his arm, looked into his eyes, and said, "You matter, Joey." It was a simple act devoid of judgment that made all the difference. For Jodie, the therapist never faltered in her belief that Jodie could recover. She always said, "Your past does not define you." These professionals practiced non-judgmental care, and their impact was real to the couple.

The weight of stigma related to substance use disorders is suffocating (Livingston et al., 2012). It weaves into the fibers of societal norms and prejudices, perpetuating the false belief that addiction is a sign of weakness or moral failing. This stigmatization, rooted in misunderstanding and fear, becomes a significant barrier to seeking and obtaining proper care (Maté, 2008).

However, an approach grounded in empathy and non-judgment can bring revolutionary changes in recovery trajectories. It can transform a dim clinic into a beacon of hope.

The theory behind a non-judgmental approach is embedded in the broader framework of trauma-informed care (Harris & Fallot, 2001). Recognizing the intricate dance between trauma and addiction is vital. According to Van der Kolk (2014), trauma can profoundly impact the brain, mind, and body. These lingering effects can, in many individuals, manifest as substance use disorders, a desperate attempt to self-medicate or cope (Khantzian, 1997).

Joey's addiction, for instance, was rooted in a history of being bullied by persons, agencies, and the military (Dube et al., 2003). The weight of his trauma remained unaddressed until a trauma-informed therapist, practicing non-judgment, helped him connect the dots after addiction had already sunk its claws into him. For Jodie, her substance use began after a rigid, unbending doctrine controlled her decisions. Though buried deep, the painful memories affected her choices, leading her down the dark path of addiction. The simple act of being heard and understood, without judgment, was her first step toward healing (Najavits, 2002).

Nevertheless, why is a non-judgmental approach so transformative?

As Goleman (1995) described, emotional intelligence emphasizes the ability to understand and manage our own emotions and those of others. When professionals harness this ability, they can form therapeutic relationships without bias. They can truly "see" the individual before them beyond the addiction. This rapport, built on trust and understanding, can significantly enhance the effectiveness of interventions, making recovery a tangible reality.

Miller and Rollnick (2012) emphasize this in their work on MI. By taking a collaborative, person-centered form of counseling, they argue that individuals are more likely to find their motivations for change, free from external pressures or judgments.

Remembering Joey and Jodie, it is clear that amidst their tumultuous journeys, there were moments when non-judgmental approaches made a profound difference. Joey's connection with the empathetic nurse and Jodie's bond with her healthy support were not mere chance encounters; they were transformative intersections that redirected the course of their recovery.

However, there is still much work to be done. For every Joey and Jodie, countless others are still trapped in the shadows of judgment. Our collective responsibility is to dispel the myths surrounding addiction, challenge our biases, and foster environments of understanding and empathy.

To do so, we must lean into the lived experiences of those who have walked the treacherous path of addiction. Their stories, filled with pain, resilience, and hope, hold invaluable insights. They remind us of the profound impact of non-judgmental care and the indomitable spirit of the human soul.

As we transition into the next segment, let us dig deeper into these lived experiences. Understanding their intricacies and complexities will illuminate the myriad of ways they can guide, inform, and revolutionize our approach to recovery.

Leveraging Lived Experience in Understanding Clients

In the mosaic of recovery, each individual story is a singular tile, an experience unto itself, glistening with a myriad of colors representing pain, hope, trauma, and triumph. Among these myriad tales, Joey Pagano's poignant narrative, as documented in his book, *No Addict Left Behind*, stands out as a beacon of hope and resilience.

When the word "addiction" is uttered, the societal lens often stigmatizes and isolates individuals, ignoring the immense strength it takes to break the chains of addiction and chart a path to recovery. Joey's stories epitomize this resilience. As a veteran, he battled not only the external adversaries but the internal ones, with the weight of stigma doubling down on him. Rejected by the system that was supposed to support him, Joey's life became a battlefield ridden with addiction, shame, and rejection. Yet, in the face of adversity, he survived and thrived, securing a governor's pardon and overturning his army discharge (White, 2009).

However, his journey was not an isolated climb. The year 1994 marked a rock-bottom moment in Joey's life. A high school graduate with memories stained by bullying, every day was a struggle. With an aching heart, he yearned to escape the torment, even if that meant oblivion (Harris & Fallot, 2001). However, a flicker of hope within him led Joey to higher education, and as we speak today, he stands just six months away from attaining his Doctor of Social Work (DSW). This transition was not simply a change in circumstance; it was a metamorphosis of a broken spirit into a phoenix, rising from the ashes of his past.

Jodie's journey parallels Joey's story, equally drenched in pain, hope, and redemption. Joey and Jodie trudged through the tumultuous terrains of failed marriages, with addiction often looming like a dark cloud overhead. Instead of resigning to despair, they found hope in one another, weaving a new narrative emphasizing the power of human connection, understanding, and empathy in recovery (Tracy & Wallace, 2016). Their union is not just a testament to love but a salient example of how lived experiences, shared and understood, can pave the path to healing.

The lived experiences of Joey and Jodie underscore the essence of what Van der Kolk (2014) described in The Body Keeps the Score. Their bodies, minds, and souls bore the brunt of trauma, yet they also held the key to their healing. These narratives exemplify the concept that recovery is not merely the absence of addiction but the presence of purpose, connection, and love.

Their stories' emotional landscapes encapsulate the essence of empathy in the recovery process. Empathy is not just about understanding another's pain: it is about feeling it, living it, and then using that profound understanding to foster healing (Goleman, 1995). It is about diving deep into the abyss of another's trauma and emerging with insights and actionable solutions for recovery. For professionals in the field of addiction recovery, leveraging these lived experiences can be a game-changer. Such narratives provide an authentic understanding of the nuanced challenges faced by those grappling with addiction, enabling professionals to design interventions that are not just clinically sound but emotionally resonant (Harris & Fallot, 2001).

The potency of empathy in the recovery journey is further accentuated when viewed through the lens of trauma-informed care. This approach is not about what is wrong with an individual but what has happened to them (Abuse, 2014). It recognizes that trauma, whether stemming from bullying, childhood adversities, or societal stigmatization, plays a pivotal role in addiction (Dube et al., 2003). Acknowledging and addressing these underlying traumas can significantly revolutionize the recovery process.

In many ways, the stories of Joey and Jodie are tangible manifestations of the power of lived experience in understanding addiction and charting pathways to recovery. Their stories are more than just tales of survival; they are symbolic of the role of empathy in understanding the intricate interplay of trauma and addiction.

However, understanding is just the first step. As we investigate deeper into this journey, it becomes paramount to translate this understanding into actionable strategies that resonate with those battling addiction and empower them toward lasting recovery. In the next segment, we will inquire into the intricacies of "Practical Techniques for Client Engagement," harnessing the power of empathy to foster a transformative recovery experience.

Practical Techniques for Client Engagement

Though brightly lit, the room was filled with shadows of the past. Joey and Jodie sat opposite their counselors, faces etched with tales of addiction and recovery. Their eyes spoke of pain but also of hope, resilience, and the will to rise above their past.

Emotions play a crucial role in the journey of recovery. It has often been said that addiction numbs feelings, pushing one into a cocoon of oblivion. Breaking free requires facing the whirlwind of suppressed emotions head-on, and that is where empathy makes a world of difference.

Maté (2008) profoundly captured this sentiment when he wrote of the profound loneliness and pain felt by those battling addiction. A poignant reminder that understanding, patience, and compassion can work wonders in the recovery process. In this context, empathy does more than "feel"; it builds bridges, allowing professionals to truly engage with their clients on an emotional level (Maté, 2008).

The Power of Empathy in Recovery

Let us examine Joey's story more. He often spoke of the chasm he felt between his past and present self. The darkness of addiction seemed like a never-ending abyss until he experienced a compassionate approach to treatment. Joey shared, "When I walked into therapy, I felt seen for the first time, not as an addict, but as a human being with dreams, fears, and emotions."

Recalling the words of Van der Kolk (2014), our bodies and minds are deeply interconnected, bearing the brunt of trauma. Acknowledging his trauma and its link to his addiction was transformative for Joey. With his counselor's empathetic approach, he gradually released the heavy chains of shame and guilt, replacing them with self-awareness and acceptance (Van der Kolk, 2014).

Jodie's journey echoed a similar sentiment. "My addiction," she said, quivering, "was my safety blanket against the world that seemed too overwhelming. Every time I tried to quit, the fear of failing rushed into my mind." The trauma-informed approach, as emphasized by Harris & Fallot (2001), underscores the importance of recognizing the interplay between trauma and substance abuse. For Jodie, an empathetic counselor became the beacon of light, illuminating her path toward healing and self-discovery.

Empathy is the golden thread in the rainbow of recovery, weaving a connection between the healer and the healing. As we examine deeper into "The Role of Empathy," it becomes abundantly clear that fostering genuine empathy is both an art and a science. While empathy may seem innate to some, enhancing its depth and effectiveness often requires intentionality and method. To aid in this journey, a meticulously curated list of techniques follows. Each technique, backed by research and seasoned with lived experiences, holds the potential to revolutionize our empathetic engagements. By harnessing these techniques, we elevate our understanding and elevate the very essence of therapeutic connection. Dive in and discover these transformative tools for fostering empathy.

Techniques for Fostering Empathy

1. Active Listening: More than just hearing words, it involves absorbing the emotions beneath the words. This fosters a deeper connection, letting clients know their experiences and feelings are valid (Miller & Rollnick, 2012).

2. Validating Emotions: By acknowledging and validating clients› emotions, we lay the foundation for trust, which is vital in the recovery process (Goleman, 1995).

3. Sharing Stories: As illustrated by Joey and Jodie›s experiences, stories can be powerful tools in the therapeutic setting. Not only do they provide insights into clients› lives, but they also build a sense of camaraderie, demonstrating that recovery is indeed possible (White, 2009).

4. Building on Strengths: Instead of focusing solely on the negatives of addiction, it is vital to recognize and celebrate the strengths and resilience that clients bring to the table. This positive reinforcement can act as a catalyst for change (Marlatt & Witkiewitz, 2002).

5. Incorporating Trauma-Informed Care: Recognizing the link between trauma and addiction is vital. By adopting a trauma-informed approach, we can address the root causes of addiction, thereby facilitating holistic healing (Najavits, 2002).

Amidst their addiction's stormy clouds, Joey and Jodie discovered silver linings. Joey, with the support of his counselor, channeled his passion for music into a therapeutic outlet. Those chords and melodies became his anchor, pulling him back every time the tides of addiction threatened to engulf him.

Jodie, on the other hand, found solace in being of service. Each non-profit outreach service commitment became a testament to her journey, becoming a tangible example of her struggles and triumphs. Their stories are powerful reminders that amidst the darkness, there is always a glimmer of hope, a silver lining waiting to be discovered.

As we journey alongside our clients, weaving through the intricate maze of their emotions, we must recognize the transformative power of empathy. Engaging clients requires more than clinical interventions: it demands a heart that understands, feels, and heals.

Transitioning from this heart-centric approach, we will venture into the next segment, highlighting the nuances of resistance. What happens when clients show reluctance toward treatment? "Addressing Initial Resistance to Treatment" will delve deep into strategies and insights, ensuring that the journey to recovery remains unobstructed.

Addressing Initial Resistance to Treatment

The room had the slight chill of a medical facility. The pale blue walls carried the weight of countless stories. Among them were Joey and Jodie, survivors of addiction's ruthless claws, gazing apprehensively at their surroundings. The road to recovery can be grueling, and the first step–acknowledging the need for treatment–can be the most daunting.

Resistance to treatment is not a mere obstinacy: it is a tapestry of fear, misunderstanding, trauma, and deep-rooted beliefs (Miller & Rollnick, 2012). Joey once said, "It was not just the drugs. It was about the fear of facing a life without them." With pain in her eyes, Jodie added, "And facing the trauma all over again without anything to numb it." Their testimonies resonate with Van der Kolk's assertion that trauma reshapes both body and mind, influencing reactions and decisions (Van der Kolk, 2014).

Understanding this resistance is pivotal. Maté (2008) poignantly describes addiction as a complex interplay of emotional pain, past traumas, and the desperation to escape from those feelings. It is not about the drugs or alcohol in isolation, but what they represent: a refuge, a numbing agent, an illusion of control. Addressing resistance is not about pushing someone into treatment but understanding these intricacies and guiding them gently toward healing.

However, how do we successfully navigate these murky waters of initial resistance?

Empathy–a powerful yet underutilized tool. Goleman (1995) elaborated on emotional intelligence, emphasizing that the ability to resonate with another's emotions can create profound change. This is the very bedrock of the therapeutic alliance. As care providers, our task is not just guiding, but feeling, understanding, and then guiding again.

Take Joey, for instance. Beneath his tattoos and stern demeanor lies a boy who was bullied for years. He began using drugs as a shield against the bullying memories (Dube et al., 2003).

When he was introduced to the concept of trauma-informed care, it was like a light piercing through the darkness. Through empathic care, Joey was not just another "addict." He was a survivor, fighting battles on multiple fronts. "For the first time, someone got it," he whispered, tears streaming down his face.

Jodie's journey echoed Joey's. Her descent into addiction was precipitated by early traumas and a need to self-medicate, a pattern identified by Khantzian (1997). She recollected a counselor who sat with her, sharing her pain, validating her experiences, and helping her find hope in the seemingly endless void of addiction. This empathy, Jodie asserted, was the turning point for her.

Empathy requires both emotional connection and informed action. One strategy that's shown promise is MI, a client-centered approach that seeks to evoke personal motivation for change from the individuals themselves (Miller & Rollnick, 2012). It is not about imposing change but facilitating an environment where individuals like Joey and Jodie can see the silver linings of their pasts and the potential in their futures.

Peer support, too, is invaluable (White, 2009). When Joey was introduced to a support group led by someone who had been through the hellish corridors of addiction and escaped it, he found hope. Jodie's recovery was also bolstered by group sessions where she met others who shared her struggles, experiences, and aspirations (Tracy & Wallace,

2016). Their shared experiences, the communal resilience, were tangible testaments that recovery was possible.

Despite the effectiveness of empathy, it is crucial to acknowledge that resistance is not easily melted away. It's intertwined with past traumas, societal stigma, and deeply ingrained habits (Livingston et al., 2012). Yet, as Harris and Fallot (2001) noted, envisioning a trauma-informed care system where empathy is at its core can lead to a paradigm shift in addiction treatment.

Remember Joey's tattoos? They were not just artistic expressions; they were milestones of his recovery journey. Every tattoo represented a challenge he had overcome, a silver lining from his past.

Within the intricate web of Jodie's life, her recovery journey shimmered like a golden thread, each strand woven with raw emotion, pain, hope, and a deep-seated determination. Every dawn she greeted was not just another day; it was a testament to her grit and a challenge she met head-on, her spirit unwavering even on the most treacherous days.

The moment Jodie was tapered off her medicated-assisted treatment (MAT) methadone, she was emotionally charged. It wasn't merely a step in medical detoxification but an emotional and spiritual cleansing. As she held her first "clean time key tag, feeling a moment of joy" her fingers brushed against a symbol of her invincible spirit, a tangible proof of her harrowing journey. It wasn't just a token but a phoenix feather representing her rise from the ashes of addiction.

At the twelve-step meetings, as Jodie observed others marking their "clean time," her heart swelled with a complex mix of awe, hope, and earnest aspiration. Each shared story wasn't just about numbers: they were intimate tales of redemption, resilience, and rebirth. The fiery determination she witnessed in their gazes, the narratives of battles won, and the shared bond of survivors invigorated her soul. It instilled in her a fierce longing to achieve, thrive, and stand tall among these warriors.

Jodie's inner world was a whirlwind of thoughts and emotions, ever-churning, seeking meaning and solace amidst the chaos. This relentless pursuit of clarity and purpose was her compass, guiding her toward the luminous beacon of a life untouched by the shadows of addiction.

The journey from resistance to acceptance is not linear. It's paved with ups and downs, hopes and despairs. But with empathy as our compass, we can ensure that every Joey and every Jodie feels understood, valued, and empowered to change.

As we peel back the layers of addiction, trauma, and resistance, we find a desperate call for understanding, care, and hope at its core. As we transition into Chapter 3: The Medical Foundation of Trauma and Addiction, we explore further into the biological mechanisms underpinning these emotions and how understanding them can further bolster our approach to treatment.

CHAPTER 3

The Medical Foundation of Trauma and Addiction

Neurochemical Implications of Trauma and Addiction

Whispers and Words isn't just a sanctuary of stories and a knowledge repository. Just past the cafe and beyond the nooks dedicated to personal experiences, one corner of the bookstore is painted with intricate hues of medical literature. Here, the ambiance becomes more focused, where steaming mugs give way to detailed illustrations and intricate scientific texts.

Among the organized chaos, Jodie stands engrossed, tracing the intricate pathways on a neuroscientific blueprint that maps the convergence of trauma and addiction. With its tangled web of circuits, this neural roadmap speaks of the dance between memory, emotion, and the chemicals that bind them. At the point where pain meets craving, euphoria dovetails with despair.

Joey approaches, his eyes also drawn to the chart's profound revelations. "It's an intricate weave of science and soul, right?" he reflects, trying to fathom the depths of human neurology intertwined with raw emotions.

Jodie responds, her voice echoing both awe and understanding, "This is where emotion meets molecule. It's the anatomy of our experiences."

As the resonance of past introspections from earlier chapters still echoes, this chapter's truth awaits. Together, they are poised to dive into the profound medical intricacies that bind trauma's emotional toll to the haunting seduction of addiction, emphasizing the imperative for a comprehensive approach to healing.

Jodie and Joey stand captivated in the corner of a bookstore where intellect and empathy converge. They are social workers who have transcended the death grip of addiction to become living testaments to resilience. Here, amongst medical literature, they find a visual tale of their own journeys—neuroscientific blueprints that depict how trauma and addiction meet at the crossroads of human vulnerability.

"Understanding this," Jodie says, gripping the chart, "is the first step toward revolutionizing recovery. We are not just looking at synaptic connections here, but the biographies of countless people trapped in the snare of trauma and addiction."

The neuroscience of addiction and trauma is not just about firing neurons or chemicals swarming, but the constant negotiation between emotional upheavals and physiological responses. In this tug-of-war, neurotransmitters like dopamine and serotonin become heroes and villains (Van der Kolk, 2014; Maté, 2008).

"When trauma happens," Joey adds, his voice tinged with a haunting resonance, "the brain secretes stress hormones like cortisol. These hormones imprint the traumatic experience into our memory. It is as though the brain is saying, 'This experience is important; do not forget it.'"

"And then comes the craving," Jodie continues. "To obliterate the pain or even to feel a semblance of normalcy, substances often become the go-to. The brain, already primed to seek pleasure and avoid pain, releases dopamine when we engage in substance use. It fools us into believing we have found the solution." However, the solution morphs over time into the problem (Najavits, 2002).

However, even in this gloomy interaction of chemicals and memories, there are glimpses of what can only be described as 'silver linings.' Joey, for instance, attributes his profound understanding of empathy to his past addiction struggles. "I remember feeling so isolated, as if I was stuck in an endless loop of despair. However, that pain opened my eyes to the suffering of others. It made me a better social worker, someone who could sit with another's pain without flinching."

Similarly, Jodie found her calling by going through years of substance use, coupled with undiagnosed PTSD. She recalls, "When I finally received trauma-informed care, it was as though someone had given me a new lens to look through. I could finally see that I was not broken; I was hurt. I carried that realization into my peer support. My suffering became my greatest asset in connecting with my clients."

The work of Harris and Fallot (2001) and White (2009) corroborates these life-altering insights. Their research asserts that trauma-informed care is not just about medical interventions but the compassionate presence of another human being who has walked the path of recovery.

Although neurochemical alterations due to trauma and addiction might sound like irreversible life sentences, they are not. Joey and Jodie are examples of the neuroplasticity that can ensue through effective treatments like CBT for PTSD and harm reduction approaches for addiction (Kar, 2011; Marlatt & Witkiewitz, 2002). Miller and Rollnick (2012) underline the transformative power of MI, another technique that has shown promising results.

"Knowing the biology of addiction and trauma is a double-edged sword," Joey concludes. "On one hand, it is a glimpse into the depth of human suffering; on the other, it illuminates the path towards genuine recovery. Moreover, sometimes, articulating your struggle in the language of neurotransmitters and brain circuits can be empowering. It is as if you are reclaiming agency over your body and life."

Jodie nods, deeply affected by their sense of collective responsibility. "But this is just one layer of the complexity," she sighs. "When we talk about addiction and trauma, we cannot ignore the psychiatric co-morbidities that often accompany them. Anxiety, depression, bipolar disorders—they all interact with trauma and addiction in a convoluted dance that is difficult to untangle."

As they look at the chart again, a mingling of medical jargon and lived experiences, they realize their mission is far from over. The road to recovery is not just about mending broken spirits; it involves addressing psychiatric complexities that often co-exist with trauma and addiction. And so, they brace themselves to delve into another layer of human complexity, knowing well that understanding is the first step toward healing.

This segues to our next focal point—"Psychiatric Co-morbidities"—where we will explore the intricate interplay between mental health disorders and the complex relationship between trauma and addiction.

Psychiatric Co-Morbidities

Sitting across from one another in a nondescript office, filled with soft lamps and motivational posters, Joey and Jodie appeared just like any other healthcare professional—focused, competent, empathic. However, these social workers wore their histories not just on their sleeves but embedded in their very DNA—a history tinged with addiction and colored by trauma.

Joey's eyes, although kind, bore the mark of someone who had been through hell and back. "When I was deep in my addiction, I could not see past the haze of my next high," he said. Jodie nodded, adding, "And for me, addiction was like a frantic answer to a question I could not even articulate—a maelstrom of confusion, guilt, and constant unease."

As survivors of addiction who now work hand in hand with addiction medicine physicians and nurses, Joey and Jodie are living proof of what Van der Kolk emphasizes: "The body keeps the score" (Van der Kolk, 2014). They ingested substances into their bodies and emotional and cognitive frameworks, fundamentally altering their responses to stress, happiness, pain, and almost every other sensation.

Psychiatric co-morbidities are common in the realm of SUDs. In simple terms, co-morbidity is the presence of one or more disorders and a primary disease (Krystal et al., 2004). Addiction recovery often involves mental health conditions like anxiety, depression, or PTSD. The relationship between trauma and addiction is symbiotic, toxic, and deeply complex (Najavits, 2002; Dube et al., 2003).

Jodie, for instance, was not just battling opioid addiction; she was also wrestling with PTSD from emotional and physical abuse—a haunting experience that she had tried to numb with substances but only served to exacerbate. "In trying to treat my emotional wounds myself, I had unknowingly worsened them. It is like putting a Band-Aid on a wound that needs stitches and then wondering why it is not healing," she reflected.

For Joey, it was chronic anxiety and depression that threaded through his years of substance abuse, a relentless hum in the background of his mind. "I thought I was self-medicating," he recalled, "but I was self-mutilating emotionally" (Khantzian, 1997).

Yet, these psychiatric co-morbidities are not just additional problems; they are, in many ways, keys to a holistic treatment approach. To deal effectively with addiction, it becomes crucial to recognize and treat these co-morbid conditions (Moos, 2007). Joey and Jodie found that their journeys to sobriety gained traction only when they began to address their co-occurring psychiatric disorders through cognitive-behavioral therapy and MI (Miller & Rollnick, 2012; Kar, 2011).

The silver lining? Joey discovered an unparalleled empathy that could only come from his own suffering. Jodie found a resilience she never knew she had—each acting as a beacon of hope for their clients navigating similar mental health and SUDs. In some strange way, their scars have made them adept at spotting the signs of psychiatric co-morbidities in others, giving them a unique ability to deliver trauma-informed care (Harris & Fallot, 2001).

Moreover, Joey and Jodie often find themselves drawing upon the harm reduction philosophy in their work, recognizing that not every individual is ready for complete abstinence. For some, reducing harm is a realistic and honorable short-term goal (Marlatt & Witkiewitz, 2002).

In working with their clients, Joey and Jodie are the personification of Maté's notion of the "Hungry Ghosts"—those who seek comfort from an external source, only to find themselves entrapped (Maté, 2008). But they also symbolize the enormous human potential for change, for turning scars into stars.

"In our field, every strategy we adopt is not just theory; it is a page from our own life," Jodie mused. Joey nodded. "Our co-morbidities, our past, make us clinicians and living testimonials to the power of holistic healing."

As they have illustrated so vividly through their own lives, tackling addiction without addressing psychiatric co-morbidities is akin to pulling weeds while leaving the roots untouched. The following section examines another crucial aspect of this complex healing journey: "The Role of Medications in Treatment."

The story of Joey and Jodie challenges us to reframe the narrative surrounding addiction and mental health. It nudges us to recognize that the path to recovery is not just medical—it's profoundly human.

The Role of Medications in Treatment

Jodie sat at her desk at the COE (Center of Excellence), haunted by the memories of life before recovery. She vividly recalled the guilt and emptiness that plagued her as she snuck away to use, chasing a fleeting but necessary high in her eyes. Joey, on the other side of the COE, shared her memories. He, too, had witnessed the horrifying ravages of addiction—first in his life and then in the lives of those he now helped as a social worker.

Both were keenly aware of a transformative truth: medication had been a lifesaver for them, in the most literal sense. No longer an abstract medical jargon, terms like "medication-assisted treatment" (MAT) and "pharmacotherapy" had deeply personal, almost sacred, meanings for them. Moreover, their experiences mirrored the scientific literature, substantiating that medications can be highly effective, especially when paired with behavioral therapies and peer support (Moos, 2007; Tracy & Wallace, 2016).

Jodie had been on methadone, a medication approved for opioid use disorder treatment. It helped normalize her brain chemistry, allowing her to think beyond the next fix (Krystal et al., 2004). She felt like she could breathe again and participate in life rather than merely surviving it. "It was as if a heavy fog had lifted," Jodie described. "And for the first time, I could see the sun peeking through." The methadone did not make her "normal": it simply gave her the chance to seek normality, the space to engage in therapy, and build coping skills (Maté, 2008).

Joey had a parallel journey. Struggling with opiate use disorder, he had taken a chance on buprenorphine, a medication that can also help with OUD (Marlatt & Witkiewitz, 2002). It was not a magic bullet but a tool in a more comprehensive strategy that also included trauma-informed care (Harris & Fallot, 2001).

Although medications played a vital role, Jodie and Joey also wanted their clients to understand that this path was not entirely smooth.

Medications can come with stigma, side effects, and, sometimes, a hefty price tag (Livingston et al., 2012). Joey remembered the sneers from acquaintances who believed that using medication was merely swapping one addiction for another. They were echoing a stigmatizing societal viewpoint, uninformed by science or empathy.

But science tells a different story, emphasizing neurochemical imbalances and their potential correction through medication (Kreek et al., 2005). Yes, medications have their limitations, but they also offer a medical response to a medical issue: addiction as a brain disease, deeply interwoven with trauma (Van der Kolk, 2014; Heilig et al., 2022).

Silver linings were not scarce in their journeys. Jodie fondly remembered her first Christmas on MAT, partially facilitated by medication that kept her cravings at bay. She had reconnected with her estranged family, while her younger sister, Cynthia offered a model of resilience and recovery. Joey recalled his first recovery anniversary; he had climbed a mountain, metaphorically, and planted a flag with his "clean" date written on it.

There is a philosophical shift in how we start to see medications: not as crutches but as bridges that lead to a better quality of life. At the COE, Jodie and Joey work hand in hand with addiction medicine physicians and nurses, deciding what MAT modality is best for their clients. They are living testaments to the benefits and complexities of combining medications with other forms of support and treatment (White, 2009; Miller & Rollnick, 2012).

A pill or a shot is not a singular solution, but for many, it is an indispensable part of a larger tapestry of recovery that also includes therapy, social support, and, yes, the painful but ultimately cathartic confrontation with past trauma (Najavits, 2002; Davidson et al., 2012). "It is not just about surviving; it is about thriving," Joey often tells his clients. "Medications gave us the foundation, but we built the house."

As we move forward, we cannot afford to be myopic. The conversation on addiction recovery is evolving, and it must include the complex but critical interplay between mental health and substance use. After all, the two are often two sides of the same coin, and the coin is a person—a human being seeking not just to heal but to flourish.

The Interplay Between Mental Health and Substance Use

In the world of recovery, medication, and therapy often play starring roles, but beneath the spotlight lies a symbiotic relationship less spoken about: the interplay between mental health and substance use. Joey and Jodie, both social workers and survivors of addiction, know this all too well.

Two Sides of the Same Coin

"Remember our long talks in the evenings?" Joey said to Jodie, as they left the coffee house. "We talked about how our traumas were like invisible scars, directing our actions without us even knowing."

Jodie nodded, her face reflecting the weight of recollection. "Trauma molds us, but it also reveals facets of our character that we never knew existed. I would have never tapped into my resilience without confronting my past traumas."

According to Maté (2008), trauma often fuels the cycle of addiction, serving as the initial trigger and continuing as the ever-persistent catalyst. From the medical standpoint, conditions such as depression, anxiety, and PTSD make individuals more vulnerable to substance abuse and compound the recovery challenges (Van der Kolk, 2014; Najavits, 2002).

Healing the Mind to Heal the Body

Joey and Jodie are strong advocates for a multi-pronged approach. They work closely with addiction medicine physicians, counselors, and psychiatrists. "You cannot simply treat the addiction and ignore the co-occurring mental health disorders," Joey explained. "That is like putting a bandage on a festering wound; it might look okay from the outside, but inside, it is still rotting."

This sentiment echoes the consensus in the scientific community. Harris and Fallot (2001) have emphasized that service systems must be designed with a trauma-informed approach. A comprehensive evaluation often reveals that substance abuse is interlaced with mental health issues; failing to address both can result in treatment setbacks (Heilig et al., 2022; Moos, 2007).

Silver Linings From the Abyss

But amidst the complexity of intertwining mental health and substance use, there is hope—often in places where you'd least expect it. For Joey, it was his crippling anxiety that led him to the art of mindfulness. "Meditation and breathing exercises did not just help my anxiety, they became indispensable tools in my sobriety tool kit," he replied.

Jodie found her silver lining in support groups that were not only for addiction but also for survivors of abuse. She recognized her own strength through the stories of others, providing her with a dual lens to view her recovery (Tracy & Wallace, 2016). "There is an insidious relationship between my past abuse and my addiction. They feed off each other. Nevertheless, I also know how tackling one can positively impact the other."

The Brain Behind the Behavior

Kreek et al. (2005) posited that genetic predispositions could make certain individuals more susceptible to mental disorders and addiction. This susceptibility does not necessarily lead to a dead-end but rather underlines the importance of early intervention and tailored treatments. For instance, CBT effectively treats mental health conditions and addiction (Kar, 2011).

"Understanding the neuroscience behind my behaviors was empowering," said Jodie, reflecting on her journey. "I was not 'broken' or 'weak.' My brain was responding to a set of conditions it was never prepared to handle."

Towards a New Horizon: A Holistic Medical Perspective

As we venture deeper into understanding the complex medical underpinnings of trauma and addiction, what becomes clear is the inseparability of mental health and substance use. Joey and Jodie's stories are not just individual narratives: they are testaments to the fact that comprehensive, trauma-informed, and person-centered care is not just a medical recommendation—it's a human necessity.

Their experiences underscore the need for a holistic medical perspective in treatment, one that does not compartmentalize mental health and substance use but rather views them as interlinked chapters of the same complex story—a story where the next chapter holds the promise of even more profound understanding and more effective interventions.

This leads us to our next critical discussion: How does a holistic medical perspective come into play in the realm of addiction and mental health? How can we incorporate medical, psychological, and social aspects into an integrative approach to treatment? Because to understand addiction, we must understand the human being experiencing it—in all their complexity and nuance.

A Holistic Medical Perspective in Treatment

In the labyrinth of addiction and trauma, Jodie and Joey found an exit sign that read "Holistic Medical Treatment." Both survivors of near-fatal addictions transformed their pain into a calling, becoming social workers and serving as living examples of how trauma-informed care can rekindle the dying embers of a life engulfed by SUDs. Their collaboration with addiction medicine physicians and nurses breathed life into the ideal of holistic medical treatment.

Holistic care transcends the singular approach of merely treating symptoms. It is a concept as intricate as the neural pathways that are disrupted by addiction, and it is every bit as revolutionary. Medical research often isolates specific problems to tackle; yet, as Van der Kolk emphasizes, the body keeps an integrated score of every experience and trauma (Van der Kolk, 2014). A holistic medical perspective, therefore, becomes imperative in treating addiction, not just as a disease but as a symphony of cognitive, emotional, and physiological imbalances.

"Drug use was just a part of it," Jodie remembers, her eyes the silent narrators of the invisible scars she still carries. "The core of my addiction was an incessant mental turmoil stemming from past traumas. I was using substances to self-medicate." This is not uncommon. Khantzian's self-medication hypothesis elaborates on how individuals use substances to temporarily alleviate the distress arising from their emotional pain (Khantzian, 1997).

Joey agrees, "Addiction was not just a bad habit for me; it was a coping mechanism gone wrong. Holistic care allowed me to address the root of my problem: my trauma." Indeed, according to Maté's work, addiction often manifests as an adaptation to emotionally intolerable states, often originating from unresolved traumas (Maté, 2008).

Understanding the role of trauma in addiction is essential, and a one-size-fits-all approach can be perilous. Trauma alters brain function, contributing to impulsivity and risk-taking behaviors that can lead to substance abuse (Kreek et al., 2005). These neurobiological alterations necessitate interventions that extend beyond detoxification and include mental health treatment, emphasizing the need for a holistic medical perspective in addiction treatment.

A sense of hope comes into play here. The stories of Jodie and Joey illuminate how holistic approaches, when supplemented with trauma-informed care, can foster resilience. At the COE, they were introduced to MI, a method that kindles the internal motivation to change (Miller & Rollnick, 2012). CBT for trauma, coupled with effective medications, can further equip the individual to manage cravings and confront deeprooted emotional triggers (Kar, 2011).

But it doesn't stop there. A genuinely holistic treatment plan also envelops the social context of an individual. As Heilig and colleagues point out, social factors like isolation and stress strongly influence the brain's addiction circuitry (Heilig et al., 2022). Peer support and community connections are crucial. The couple's peer support creates an ecosystem of mutual support, inspired by the scientific evidence advocating the efficacy of this modality in addiction treatment (Tracy & Wallace, 2016; White, 2009).

Perhaps the silver lining in their journeys was the discovery that addiction, no matter how grave, does not define them. Realizing they are more than the sum of their traumas and past choices was profoundly liberating. "We found a strength we never knew we had, in a place we never thought to look, inside ourselves," Joey shares, a flicker of triumph lighting up his eyes.

While it is crucial to note that holistic medical treatment is a blend of the scientific and the subjective, it is equally important to remember that every individual's pathway to recovery is unique.

The beauty of a holistic medical perspective lies in its versatility: whether it is incorporating harm reduction approaches to alcohol use (Marlatt & Witkiewitz, 2002) or implementing trauma theory in service systems

(Harris & Fallot, 2001), it can be adapted to serve the individual needs of each patient.

Jodie and Joey's stories are living testaments to the transformational power of holistic medical care, steeped in scientific rigor and elevated by human experience. The interplay of mental health and substance use is intricate, but understanding that they are entangled threads in the same assortment of human suffering brings us one step closer to more compassionate and effective treatment.

As we move toward Chapter 4: Pillars of Trauma-Informed Care in Addiction Treatment, remember that the journey toward understanding and treating addiction is not a straight path but a spiral. We revisit old patterns and problems, but each time, if guided by a comprehensive understanding and a holistic approach, we circle them at a different level—a level that brings us closer to the heart of healing.

CHAPTER 4

Pillars of Trauma-Informed Care in Addiction Treatment

Core Principles of Trauma-Informed Care

The atmosphere in Whispers and Words once again takes a subtle turn. Where there once lay tables for coffee and cozy reading nooks, towering bookshelves now stand, each laden with texts focusing on holistic healing and care principles. The room bathes in a gentle glow reminiscent of dawn's first light, suggesting hope, new beginnings, and a brighter approach.

In the heart of this section, a grand display captures attention: four prominent pillars emerge, each etched with core tenets of trauma-informed care. They stand as testaments to a more profound, more compassionate method of addressing addiction.

With a scholar's precision, Joey studies each pillar, acknowledging their monumental role. Ever the empath, Jodie gently touches the engraved principles, absorbing their essence. "These aren't just words," she murmurs, her voice brimming with emotion. "They're the heartbeat of true healing."

Drawn to their insight, visitors of the bookstore cluster around, eager to grasp the profound significance of these tenets. As Joey and Jodie share tales and testimonials, the principles come alive, resonating with experiences, challenges, and triumphs.

As you prepare to navigate this chapter, realize you're on the cusp of an evolution in understanding addiction treatment. Here, amidst the pillars, the approach shifts from mere protocols to a sanctuary of genuine empathy and awareness. With Joey and Jodie as your guides, you're set to journey into the transformative world of trauma-informed care.

In the transformative space of Whispers and Words, standing beside pillars of wisdom, Joey pauses and looks at Jodie. They both have been survivors—survivors of addiction, trauma, and themselves. They had wandered through the dark labyrinth of despair only to discover these pillars as their north star. Joey, analytical yet sensitive, realized that knowledge was their shared currency. Ever the intuitive empath, Jodie resonated with the emotional wavelengths of every word etched on the pillars.

"Remember when we used to think it was all about willpower?" Joey muses, reflecting on a time that seemed both another life and just yesterday. "If we just tried harder, we would not need substances."

Jodie looks at him, her eyes wet with a complex cocktail of sorrow and understanding. "The nights I would cry myself to sleep, thinking I was broken, were the moments I wish I knew about this." She gestures toward the first pillar: "Safety."

Safety

Safety is not just a physical construct but profoundly emotional and psychological (Van der Kolk, 2014). Joey and Jodie remember feeling like prisoners in their bodies, shackled by an overwhelming sense of insecurity and threat. This perpetual state of unsafety led them to seek refuge in substances, falsely believing that the numbness would act as sanctuaries (Maté, 2008).

They stress the importance of establishing a sense of safety with every client they encounter. It is not just about secure facilities or detox protocols but about helping people find a psychological space where they do not feel judged or ostracized (Harris & Fallot, 2001). "For us," Joey explains to his clients, "the first taste of real safety was in accepting the reality of trauma and understanding that our addictions were symptomatic of deeper wounds."

Trustworthiness and Transparency

"Trust is the lifeline of any therapeutic relationship," Jodie often told her clients. She and Joey knew all too well the erosion of trust accompanying addiction—distrust in oneself, distrust in loved ones, and a pervasive cynicism toward the world at large (Najavits, 2002). Regaining that lost trust is like navigating a minefield of past disappointments and betrayals.

However, here, transparency plays a pivotal role. Joey and Jodie advocate for open, honest communication in their discussions with clients. They share their journeys to inspire trust, turning their painful pasts into silver linings that foster connection and hope (White, 2009).

Peer Support

"We never have to go it alone," Joey once told Jodie during the early days of their recovery. Peer support was their secret weapon—people who had walked the fiery paths of addiction and emerged, if not unscathed, stronger and wiser (Tracy & Wallace, 2016). Now, they offer themselves as living testaments to the transformative power of peer relationships, weaving a tapestry of shared experiences and mutual empathy (Mead et al.; L., 2001).

"You are not just a case or a statistic," Jodie assures her clients. "You are a human being, deserving of support and connection."

Collaboration and Mutuality

There is a reciprocity in healing, Joey and Jodie found. The top-down authoritarian treatment models were often counterproductive, reinforcing feelings of powerlessness and inadequacy (Miller & Rollnick, 2012). Instead, they foster a collaborative atmosphere where clients feel like active participants in their recovery journeys.

This principle emanates from a shared struggle, a common humanity. It is not just about clinicians administering treatment; it is about creating a partnership in healing, understanding that everyone in the room brings something of value to the table (Marlatt & Witkiewitz, 2002).

Empowerment and Choice

Finally, but most crucially, is the principle of empowerment. Empowerment for Jodie was reclaiming her body and voice. For Joey, it was the freedom to make choices rooted in self-respect rather than desperation. They instill the same sense of empowerment in their clients, shifting the dialogue from "What is wrong with you?" to "What has happened to you?" (Abuse, S., 2014).

"We all have a choice," Joey emphasizes. "Sometimes it does not feel that way, but part of healing is recognizing that we can choose a different path."

The atmosphere in the room felt like a sanctified space, where words were not mere vibrations of air but chords of a soulful melody. Those listening felt a symbiotic rhythm between Joey and Jodie, a rhythm that echoed the more profound harmonies of their lived experiences. Their narratives were not just testimonies but sacred scriptures of trauma-informed care, illuminated by the pillars they stood beside.

As you turn the page, prepare to explore the ways in which these core principles can seamlessly integrate into the very fabric of addiction treatment. Because trauma is not just a chapter in the past; it is a language that permeates the present, and understanding this language is the first step in rewriting the story of recovery.

Integrating Trauma Care Into Addiction Treatment

Walking into the behavioral health agency group room, Jodie and Joey could feel their hearts pounding. They had been here many times before, as patients grappling with their addictions and as social workers, but today was different. Today, they were being introduced to a new trauma-informed approach that can be used in addiction treatment. The emotional weight was palpable yet imbued with a sense of urgency and potential for transformation.

As survivors of life-threatening addictions, Joey and Jodie knew firsthand how trauma acted like an insidious undercurrent flowing beneath the surface of SUDs. They had spent years being treated for the symptoms of their addictions—namely, the physical dependence on substances—but the deeply embedded trauma perpetuating the cycle had often been ignored. "The Body Keeps the Score," Van der Kolk tells us (Van der Kolk, 2014). The human, emotional, and intellectual selves are sites of scar tissue from past traumas that cannot be separated from the journey of addiction recovery.

The Indivisibility of Trauma and Addiction

It is crucial to recognize that addiction is rarely, if ever, an isolated issue. Most individuals with substance use disorders have experienced some form of trauma, whether from childhood neglect, physical or sexual abuse, or complex emotional dysfunction within families (Dube et al., 2003; Topitzes et al., 2012). Gabor Maté notes in *In the Realm of Hungry Ghosts* that addiction attempts to solve a problem—emotional pain, overwhelming stress, lost connection, and diminished self-regard (Maté, 2008). "When we were addicted," Jodie often said, "we were fleeing our traumas without realizing that we carried them within us."

A Personal Journey Towards Integrative Care

Joey and Jodie come from families that appeared promising from the outside but were rife with a lack of emotional connection and dysfunction. However, the silver lining in their recovery was a growing awareness that they could use their lived experiences to guide their approaches to treating others. For example, Joey recalled the transformative power of MI, an empathic, non-confrontational style of counseling that helped him voice his traumas (Miller & Rollnick, 2012). Jodie resonated with the therapeutic nature of peer support groups, a haven where she could share her story without judgment and feel the validating echoes of shared experiences (White, 2009; Tracy & Wallace, 2016). These seemingly small elements were what kept them both alive and clean. It gave them hope that they could bring about the exact change in their clients.

The Interdisciplinary Model: Collaborating Across Fields

Joey and Jodie collaborated closely with addiction medicine physicians and nurses at the COE, striving to infuse trauma-informed care principles, like safety, into the medical treatments offered while on medicated-assisted treatment (MAT). It is an approach supported by Najavits's *Seeking Safety* model, which insists on integrated treatment for PTSD and substance abuse rather than treating them as separate entities (Najavits, 2002). "It is like treating a person with diabetes and a heart condition by addressing both issues simultaneously," Joey explained. "You cannot neglect one condition without exacerbating the other."

This integrated model combined MAT with evidence-based psychological therapies tailored to address trauma. For instance, CBT for PTSD is an effective modality that can be integrated into addiction treatment (Kar, 2011). At the same time, this comprehensive approach also had room for harm reduction strategies, emphasizing patient autonomy and empowerment over moralistic judgments or punitive measures (Marlatt & Witkiewitz, 2002).

Navigating the Emotional Landscape

Perhaps one of the most transformative aspects of integrating trauma care into addiction treatment is the cultivation of emotional intelligence, both for the care providers and the patients (Goleman, 1995). "We must be attuned to the emotional undertones—the shame, the guilt, the dread—that accompany the medical symptoms of addiction," Jodie emphasized. She drew upon her ability to read and navigate emotional landscapes, a skill she had honed as a defense mechanism growing up in a dysfunctional family.

The Future is Holistic

Jodie and Joey understood that this transformation would not happen overnight. "It is a revolutionary shift requiring a profound change in how we conceptualize and address addiction," Joey said. The treatment model they were advocating for was not just about medications or clinical practices; it was about a paradigm shift—envisioning a trauma-informed service system as a vital pathway to healing (Harris & Fallot, 2001).

Integrating trauma care into addiction treatment is not just a "good-to-have" but a life-and-death imperative. If we want to address the root causes of addiction, we must dig deep to confront the traumas that often fuel it. This approach, while complex, offers a more authentic, human, and ultimately effective way of helping people recover.

We will explore how this integrative model has challenges as we move on. The following section, "Overcoming Potential Pitfalls in Treatment," will delve into these complexities, providing insights into navigating the risks and barriers in this intricate but necessary approach.

Overcoming Potential Pitfalls in Treatment

Navigating the labyrinthine path of addiction recovery is fraught with complexities, and when intertwined with the equally intricate maze of trauma, the challenges amplify. "Navigating these issues is like walking through a minefield," Joey often said. "One wrong step, and it can all explode." However, if anyone could guide people through that minefield, it was Joey and Jodie.

The Emotional Quagmire: Dual Diagnosis and Treatment

The co-occurrence of trauma and substance use disorders, often termed "dual diagnosis," renders treatment challenging. The persistent presence of PTSD symptoms can trigger relapses, further exacerbating trauma (Najavits, 2002). For Joey, the recurring nightmares thrust him back into opiate addiction, as each flashback acted like a detonator. Likewise, Jodie's intense anxiety often led her back to the numbing yet destructive arms of opioids.

"These are not just medical symptoms; they are deep emotional whirlpools that pull you under," Jodie said, her voice tinged with a mix of desperation and hope. "The key is to find the right balance between treatment modalities for trauma and addiction," Joey added. It was in finding that balance that they could truly begin to heal, and it became their mission to bring this awareness to their professional practice.

Medication Treadmills: The Risks of Pharmacotherapy

MAT has shown immense promise in treating addiction but could be perceived as merely another form of dependence (Kar, 2011). A crucial juncture in Joey's recovery was recognizing the essential but limited role that medications like methadone and naltrexone played. They were the life buoys that kept him afloat but did not pull him ashore; that required human connection and emotional insight from counseling and peer support (White, 2009).

Emotional Overload in the Therapeutic Space

Even the most promising therapeutic interventions, like MI, come with challenges (Miller & Rollnick, 2012). When a session explores deep into past traumas, there is a risk of retraumatization. "I remember feeling emotionally violated after one particularly intense session," Jodie recalls. "But that violation became a lesson—a lesson in setting boundaries and respecting the patient's emotional tempo." Learning from such experiences was not just a silver lining for Jodie; it became a golden rule in her peer support work.

The Perils of Peer Support Groups

Peer support is generally a boon, but it has its pitfalls. For instance, some support groups can inadvertently become echo chambers for negative experiences, perpetuating rather than alleviating the trauma (Davidson et al., 2012). Joey's turning point was when he noticed a group member continually justifying substance abuse as an inescapable consequence of trauma. Joey knew right then that the group needed a more structured, trauma-informed approach to remain beneficial (White, 2009).

Countering Stigmatization and Rebuilding Self-Identity

Another substantial challenge is the stigma associated with addiction and mental health disorders, which could hinder recovery (Livingston et al., 2012). Both Jodie and Joey felt this acutely, not just from society at large but also from their dysfunctional families who outwardly seemed so perfect. Yet, they turned this experience into an opportunity to focus on rebuilding self-identity as survivors and helpers rather than victims. "In a world that often sees labels, we teach our patients to see their unique selves," Jodie said.

Addressing the Complexity of Trauma Origins

Trauma's roots are complex and intertwined with biological, psychological, and social aspects (Kreek et al., 2005; Dube et al., 2003). Joey reflected, "While I was the only one grappling with addiction in our middle-class family, our collective dysfunctions only scratched the surface." Despite the healthcare advantages his family's status provided, pervasive societal stigmas around addiction persistently posed challenges to his recovery journey. This understanding, however, offered Joey a sense of enlightenment, emphasizing that his circumstances were not a measure of his character but a culmination of multiple overlapping factors (Khantzian, 1997).

The Ethical Considerations:
Patient Autonomy and Harm Reduction

Lastly, the ethical dimensions of treatment must be considered. Patient autonomy must be upheld, even when it clashes with the provider's notion of "best care." "We must remember that our role is not to force a roadmap onto our patients but to guide them as they create their own," Joey insists. This perspective aligns well with harm reduction models, prioritizing patient choices and autonomy over punitive or moralistic approaches (Marlatt & Witkiewitz, 2002).

Forward Momentum

As Jodie and Joey work side by side to revolutionize trauma-informed care in addiction treatment, they are well aware of the potential pitfalls. Yet, they see every challenge as an opportunity for growth—for themselves and their patients. Joey sums it up best: "In this complicated journey, the road may be strewn with obstacles, but each one is a stepping stone, not a stumbling block."

In overcoming these potential pitfalls, the true essence of individualized, patient-centered care is revealed. As we transition to the next section, "Tailoring Interventions to Individual Needs," we will explore the art and science of customizing this holistic approach to fit each patient's unique life experiences and needs.

Tailoring Interventions to Individual Needs

Joey vividly recalled the rough hands gripping his arm, syringe-ready. They had been in this place before—the sterile room, the cookie-cutter interventions. However, the impersonal approach of "one size fits all" never seemed to fit his contours. He remembered his frustration morphing into despair, a longing to flee from the very place meant to heal him.

Jodie had similar memories. She was always a little different, her brain circuitry attuned to the whispers of the world—thanks to a tumultuous past ripe with a lack of emotional connection (Dube et al., 2003). Traditional approaches never quite grasped her nuances, leaving her emotionally exposed and vulnerable to relapse.

Joey and Jodie knew the inefficacy of a monolithic approach to addiction treatment. When they became care navigators, teaming up with addiction medicine physicians and nurses, they took it upon themselves to preach the gospel of individualized recovery based on the framework of trauma-informed care principles.

Gábor Máté's influential work on addiction emphasizes how emotional pain, stemming from past trauma, forms the crux of addictive behavior (Maté, 2008). In line with this, Joey often mentions to his clients that recovery did not start for him until his therapists recognized the extent of his emotional wounds, which had been deeply embedded since childhood. A one-size-fits-all model would have overlooked entirely his deeply entrenched trauma and his desperate attempts to "self-medicate" (Khantzian, 1997).

Jodie, a fierce advocate of trauma-informed care, often quotes Van der Kolk: "The body keeps the score" (Van der Kolk, 2014). Her treatment approach harmonizes with her lived experience, favoring therapies like Seeking Safety, which is explicitly designed for PTSD and substance use disorders (Najavits, 2002).

Individualization goes beyond merely recognizing the unique origins of one's addiction; it encompasses a profound understanding of a person's life rhythms, emotional fluctuations, and even their social context (Heilig et al., 2022). Joey recalls how MI (Miller & Rollnick, 2012) was particularly effective for him because it met him where he was emotional. The therapists could tune into his internal narrative, demystifying his fears and aspirations, ultimately steering him toward change.

Jodie's approach is tinged with the hard-won wisdom of her past. She knows firsthand that harm reduction approaches, including relapse prevention strategies tailored to each individual's triggers and coping mechanisms, are essential (Marlatt & Witkiewitz, 2002; Gorski, 1990). She shares her story openly, making her a living testament that overcoming addiction is not a linear path but a complex journey, uniquely challenging and rewarding for everyone.

The role of peer support is another component that cannot be generalized. According to White's "Peer-based Addiction Recovery Support," not everyone responds to peer-led groups similarly, and some may even find them triggering (White, 2009). Joey and Jodie, drawing from their struggles, always assess a client's suitability for peer-based interventions, understanding that individual emotional thresholds vary considerably (Tracy & Wallace, 2016).

The silver linings of their past lives lend an irreplaceable authenticity to their work. Joey sometimes muses how his years of grappling with addiction gave him the patience and emotional intelligence to guide his clients through the darkest days (Goleman, 1995). Jodie feels her struggles equipped her to give voice to the unsayable to mend emotional fragments that many could not even perceive (Lieberman & Van Horn, 2009).

However, individualizing care does not mean neglecting evidence-based treatments. On the contrary, it calls for a nuanced application of such treatments, each modulated according to the unique needs of an individual. For instance, CBT can be customized to target specific anxieties or traumatic memories that trigger relapse (Kar, 2011).

In essence, individualized, trauma-informed care acknowledges the beautiful complexity of human beings. It honors each person's unique array of experiences, emotions, and needs, weaving interventions around them rather than forcing them into a pre-defined mold (Harris & Fallot, 2001).

The power of tailoring interventions to individual needs is transformative, not just for the person receiving care but also for the system delivering it. However, this is only one pillar in the complex architecture of trauma-informed care in addiction treatment. The next pivotal element in this structure is understanding and navigating the diverse treatment modalities to achieve the best outcomes, an area where the conventional models often fall short. Let us delve deeper into that, shall we?

Navigating Treatment Modalities for Optimum Outcomes

Navigating treatment modalities for optimum outcomes is no mere walk in the park; it is a journey through a labyrinth, intricate and fraught with choices that can make or break the quest for healing. Each step holds a potential lesson and misstep alike—a lesson Joey and Jodie knew too well.

The atmosphere in their offices was always brimming with a sense of urgency and empathy. At the COE, they sat with a team of addiction medicine physicians, nurses, and other navigators reviewing cases. Joey often referred to a quote by Bessel Van der Kolk, "The body keeps the score," which emphasizing the need to understand the physiological aspects of addiction and trauma (Van der Kolk, 2014). In doing so, he was quick to suggest incorporating yoga, remembering how his own body had carried the weight of his addiction, something that melted away gradually through holistic healing. His mentor, trauma expert, Cheryld Emala, MSW, LCSW, taught him the importance of that type of care.

Jodie, a fierce advocate for a client's self-determination, often researched the efficacy of meeting a client where they are at in their treatment and recovery while suffering from PTSD symptoms and substance use disorders (Kar, 2011). She felt a personal connection with this modality. As a young girl, she had lived in a household where silence was the norm, a cacophony that reverberated inside her long after she had left home. Not having enough healthy coping methods, it was hard to navigate the stormy seas of her emotions and come out on the other side.

"The journey is not a straight line, you know? It is a spiral. You go through the same loops, but each time you are a little stronger, a little better," she often says to her clients.

The labyrinthine path to recovery also has forks where different directions beckon. Harm reduction is one path that Joey and Jodie felt could be valuable, especially for those who were not yet ready to take the plunge into abstinence (Marlatt & Witkiewitz, 2002). Joey benefited from such approaches; as a former heroin addict, he had started on Suboxone before he found himself ready to abstain. This incremental step saved his life and made him less judgmental about the journeys of others.

Another critical dimension was peer-based recovery support. Drawing from William White's work, both advocated for the vital role of community and shared lived experience in treatment (White, 2009). They believed in the power of support groups, in being there to lend an understanding ear or share a hard-won insight. Sometimes, empathy makes the difference when clinical interventions reach their limits (Tracy & Wallace, 2016).

Jodie reflected on these silver linings during her client MI sessions (Miller & Rollnick, 2012). As she examined the unique motivations driving each individual, she was reminded of her own battles. She had been at death's door multiple times due to a mix of bad choices and harmful substances but clawed her way back each time. These episodes taught her the value of resilience and the potency of willpower, something she integrated into her therapeutic approach.

Joey, too, had his own silver linings. Despite falling in and out of recovery several times, he eventually found stability and purpose through integrating multiple treatment modalities, including pharmacotherapy and psychosocial treatments. His experiences served as testimonies, dispelling myths and inspiring those who were caught in the vicious cycle of relapse and despair (Gorski, 1990).

But no matter how many modalities one incorporates, the core of any treatment remains rooted in its ability to be trauma-informed. Ignoring the role of trauma is akin to treating a gunshot wound with a Band-Aid (Harris & Fallot, 2001). As Joey and Jodie crafted each individualized plan, they kept in mind the words of Gabor Maté: "Not why the addiction, but why the pain?" (Maté, 2008).

Both believed that recognizing and validating each individual's unique lived experience, including their traumas, is the cornerstone of effective treatment. This approach does not just aim to treat the symptoms but seeks to heal the afflicted human.

Thus, as they navigated through this maze of options, strategies, and interventions, Joey and Jodie remained anchored by their shared history, their scars, and, most importantly, their stars—the shimmering moments of triumph that propelled them to keep fighting, both for themselves and for their clients.

As the day ended and they prepared to leave, the couple paused to reflect on their journey so far. They knew all too well that the labyrinth of addiction and recovery was far from linear and was fraught with endless complexities. But it was a labyrinth they had walked themselves and one they were now guiding others through. Their eyes met, and in that silent exchange, both knew that their lived experiences were their greatest assets, which would be explored in greater depth in the next chapter. Joey's personal journey in recovery awaited a vivid testament to the value of experience in revolutionizing the approach to trauma and addiction.

CHAPTER 5

Life Experience:
The Precontemplation Bridge

Joey's Personal Journey in Recovery

Within the walls of Whispers and Words, the ambiance transforms once more. Between towering bookshelves laden with memoirs and tales of transformation, a radiant bridge unfolds, bridging the gap between one's past hesitations and future hopes. This bridge, bathed in a soft golden hue, symbolizes the preliminary steps in acknowledging the need for change, tainted by the shadows of doubt.

Holding a worn diary detailing his personal journey, Joey stands hesitantly at this bridge's onset. His past struggles, resistance, and denial all echo in the space behind him. At the other end, holding a beacon of hope, Jodie waits with arms open wide, representing the potential and transformative magic of acceptance and recovery.

Their voices intertwine in a heartfelt duet. Heavy with vulnerability, Joey confesses, "Life experiences aren't just past events; they're the guiding stars that navigate us through the tempestuous seas of recovery." Jodie's soothing balm voice replies, "They are the bridges we must cross, from the shadows of yesterday to the luminous promise of tomorrow."

As you venture into this chapter, Joey's raw, lived journey will become your guide. Walk with him across this precontemplation bridge, and with Jodie's insights, realize the profound power of personal experiences in illuminating the path of recovery.

Joey pauses, one foot lingering over the threshold of the metaphorical bridge he is about to cross. His worn diary in hand, each page an imprint of his past struggles and life lessons, feels heavy—almost as if it carried the weight of his years of addiction and ensuing recovery. It is a moment drenched in contemplation and hesitant hope.

Deep breaths, he thinks, *just like in therapy.*

Joey's journey into the abyss of addiction was not an isolated descent but an intertwined web of genetics, environment, and emotional voids (Kreek et al., 2005; Dube et al., 2003). Raised in a loving but dysfunctional family, the home environment had been chaotic. The trauma theories of Harris and Fallot (2001) would later help Joey understand how this chaos planted the seeds of his vulnerability to SUD.

He first turned to substances to numb the overwhelming emotions he could not understand or articulate, a common phenomenon described as self-medication (Khantzian, 1997). The euphoria and detachment felt like an out-of-body experience where he could momentarily abandon his angst and confusion.

However, the "Realm of Hungry Ghosts," as Maté (2008) so aptly describes it, is an unforgiving world. Joey's transient sense of relief was replaced by an all-encompassing craving, a never-ending hunger that could only be satiated with more substances. The substance did not discriminate; it took away as easily as it gave. Friends, family, job, and health all dissolved into a haze.

The turning point came in a sterile hospital room where Joey found himself after an overdose. As he lay there in bed, a nurse offered him medical intervention and human connection. This interaction, though brief, was the first "real" moment he had experienced in years.

Later, he would learn about the neuroscientific underpinnings of addiction (Heilig et al., 2022), how trauma affects the body and the brain (Van der Kolk, 2014), and how CBT could help him heal (Kar, 2011). After seeing someone for the first time who cared, Joey embarked on a long journey toward recovery.

The road was not smooth. He grappled with relapses, confronting the triggers Maté (2008) and Gorski (1990) discuss in their works. Marlatt & Witkiewitz (2002) call this harm reduction—a practical approach focusing on minimizing damage rather than the often unachievable concept of immediate, complete abstinence. This helped Joey adopt a realistic perspective on his own recovery, a crucial attitude change that Miller & Rollnick (2012) describe as vital in their MI model.

However, Joey's salvation was not just in the theories and models but in the raw, emotional journey of self-discovery and acceptance. Here lay the silver linings of his tumultuous past. His lived experience gave him unique insights into the complex realm of addiction, which he later used to fuel his advocacy and counseling endeavors. He would share his story with others, providing both a cautionary tale and a beacon of hope, exemplifying what White (2009) terms peer-based recovery support.

After marriage, Jodie and Joey continued working together at the COE in the mental health and SUD field. Joey's history gave him a compassionate understanding and an emotional intelligence (Goleman, 1995) that could not be taught but had to be lived. His experience illuminated for his clients not only the harsh realities but also the possibilities for redemption and change.

But the most transformative aspect of Joey's recovery journey was its ability to foster genuine connections—first with Jodie and others. As a survivor of addiction himself, he could relate to the emotional and physical turmoil that his clients were going through. This lived experience was not merely a chapter in his past but became the bridge leading him to the present moment, where he could look back without despair and look forward without delusion.

Joey had yet to realize how powerful these connections could be—not just for his own recovery but also for the recovery of others. The bridge he was now standing on symbolized his personal journey and the collective journeys of everyone he would touch.

As he takes the final steps toward Jodie, who stands on the other end of the bridge holding a beacon of hope, he knows that their shared experiences have transformative powers that could illuminate the paths of countless others. The intertwined voices of Joey and Jodie sing the lullaby of hope, resilience, and collective healing.

As they embrace, a new realization dawns on Joey. Life experiences ware not just the building blocks of one's personal history; they can also be the cornerstones of someone else's future.

While Joey and Jodie's journeys began as solitary expeditions, they converged into a shared path, signaling a deeper understanding of recovery—one that transcends individual experiences and touches the very core of human connection. As we traverse further into this chapter, we delve into the transformative power of shared experiences, not as isolated incidents but as collective journeys that amplify the promise and potential of recovery.

The Power of Shared Experiences

As Jodie sat in her dimly lit office, absorbed in case files, a knock on the door jarred her back to reality. It was Joey, her husband and fellow survivor in the battle against addiction. His eyes met hers, and a whole universe of unspoken understanding passed between them at that moment. They were both care navigators who had managed to find meaning and purpose by guiding others through the labyrinth of mental health and SUD.

This story is not just about Jodie and Joey. It is about the undercurrent of shared experiences that makes them so effective in their roles. They are survivors, but their survival is not a solitary chapter. It serves as a well of empathy and understanding they dip into each day, watering the parched souls they encounter.

Van der Kolk points out that the body keeps score—every experience we have, traumatic or not, gets embedded in our nervous system (Van der Kolk, 2014). Jodie and Joey carry the stories of their past not as burdens but as badges of resilience. They understand intimately what it feels like to be gripped by addiction, shrouded in despair, and snared in the cycle of relapse and recovery (Maté, 2008).

They also understand the transformational magic of "getting clean"—the intense vulnerability, the emotional fluctuation, and the slow, painful crawl toward daylight. Their lived experiences are their credentials, bolstering their academic qualifications and professional training.

It is easy to dismiss addiction survivors' raw, authentic experiences in favor of sterile, clinical solutions.

But Jodie and Joey do not just offer textbook solutions; they engage in trauma-informed care, a holistic approach that acknowledges their clients' emotional and psychological needs (Najavits, 2002; Harris & Fallot, 2001). Their past lives as addicts provide them with a wealth of real-world knowledge, allowing them to approach clients not as case numbers but as human beings seeking safety and empathy.

Joey, for instance, attributes his recovery partly to the sense of community he found in peer-based addiction recovery groups (White, 2009). He recalls the empowerment he felt when sharing his story and listening to others, fostering a sense of belonging and emotional safety that conventional therapy had failed to provide (Tracy & Wallace, 2016). Joey brings this perspective into his counseling sessions. "There is healing in shared narratives," he often says.

On the other hand, Jodie found strength in understanding the connection between her trauma and substance abuse (Dube et al., 2003). Knowledge served as her gateway to recovery. She tirelessly promotes MI and harm reduction approaches, appreciating their capacity to empower individuals to take control of their substance use and associated behaviors (Marlatt & Witkiewitz, 2002; Kar, 2011).

Despite their unique paths, there are silver linings that Joey and Jodie consistently highlight when they meet with their clients. The first is the incredible resilience they discovered within themselves through their recovery journeys. They have come to value life in a way that only someone who has skirted close to losing it can. The second is their relationships. Although both came from dysfunctional families, their trials have enabled them to build personally and professionally authentic connections.

Most importantly, they share the epiphany that the experience of addiction is not a life sentence but a part of a journey toward a richer, more nuanced existence (Moos, 2007).

"Your addiction is just a chapter in your life, not your whole story," Jodie tells her clients.

Furthermore, Joey chimes in, "A broken crayon still colors."

The mutual experiences of Jodie and Joey are a bridge—what we can term the "Precontemplation Bridge"—that enables them to connect with their clients at a profoundly human level. While clinical expertise is essential for effective addiction treatment, the power of shared experiences is a crucial, often underutilized tool in the recovery toolbox (Miller & Rollnick, 2012).

These lived experiences serve as an example of hope, resilience, and relatability, offering both a mirror and a window for those striving to create new narratives for their lives.

Moreover, as we transition into the core of this chapter, it is critical to emphasize that shared experiences are not just for creating rapport; they are a platform for engaging clients using relatable narratives. It is not just about having a shared story; it is about leveraging that common ground to foster meaningful change in the lives of those still ensnared in addiction. This is where the real work begins.

To truly appreciate the effectiveness of Jodie and Joey's approach, it is essential to investigate into how they engage their clients using resonating narratives. In the forthcoming sections, we will explore how they weave the threads of their pasts into the patchwork of their clients' futures, creating a quilt of empathy, understanding, and, ultimately, recovery.

Deepening Connections: Beyond Shared Moments

In the dimly lit community center, where the scent of fresh coffee mingled with the subtle notes of worn wooden chairs, Jodie and Joey sit across from a group of people bound together not by blood but by an experience—trauma and substance use disorder. Jodie and Joey have come a long way as social workers and survivors. The room changes when they share their stories; the air grows denser yet lighter simultaneously. It is a paradox that only those who have walked through the fire can fully understand.

Jodie often reminisces about her youth, a picturesque landscape disrupted by a tornado of family dysfunction. While her parents provided her with a materially comfortable life, emotionally, she was like a flower waiting for rain that never came. Joey, likewise, grew up in an environment where material riches were present, but emotional poverty was the norm. As Gabor Maté articulates, addiction is often less about the substance and more about soothing a pain that finds its roots in emotional or psychological soil (Maté, 2008).

Jodie's addiction almost claimed her life at thirty-three. She distinctly recalls the numbness that swallowed her when she used it, a stark contrast to the agony of her emotional existence. Joey was in a similar situation; his substance use had become a lifeboat in a turbulent sea of emotional chaos, but a lifeboat sinking. Although their families were heartbroken, they were ensnared in their own dysfunctions, proving what Maté illustrates—that addiction is not just an individual crisis but often a systemic one (Maté, 2008).

For Jodie and Joey, their turning point was a moment of "shared suffering." Both went to twelve-step support meetings, sharing quite often to each other, acknowledging—as Van der Kolk argues—that "the body keeps the score" (Van der Kolk, 2014). When Jodie met Joey, they recognized something intangible in each other—a flickering light in a cave of darkness, a commonality that went beyond their addictions. In clinical terms, this shared experience aids in "precontemplation," a stage in recovery when the individual has yet to recognize the gravity of their situation but is subconsciously yearning for change (Miller & Rollnick, 2012).

Studies indicate that peer support is remarkably effective in treating addiction and can act as a catalyst in the contemplative stage of recovery (Tracy & Wallace, 2016). Jodie and Joey became each other's peer support, albeit unofficially. The "silver lining" of their painful pasts became the cornerstone of their recovery and, later, their life mission. As they navigated their journeys, they found they could connect deeply with clients by sharing their experiences—moments where their vulnerabilities became their most significant strengths (White, 2009).

The weight of sharing is by no means trivial. Jodie and Joey were cautious not to re-traumatize themselves or their clients. Following a trauma-informed approach, they exercised the principles of "safety, trustworthiness, choice, collaboration, and empowerment" (Harris & Fallot, 2001).

It was a balancing act, akin to tightrope walking, but they managed by constant communication with addiction medicine physicians and mental health practitioners who supervised their work. Najavits suggests that this collaborative approach between lived experience and medical expertise creates a more effective recovery environment (Najavits, 2002).

However, for all the trauma and pain they had endured, their narratives were not just about suffering; they were also about resilience, the courage to confront one's demons, and the strength to move forward (Gorski, 1990). This embodiment of resilience gave their clients hope and substantiated the treatment paradigms they were presenting, making it easier for clients to trust the process.

Moreover, their stories also de-stigmatized addiction within the community, creating a ripple effect. Livingston et al. argue that combating stigma is crucial for effective treatment (Livingston et al., 2012). By sharing their lived experiences openly, they were unwittingly participating in a form of activism, creating a safer and more accepting environment for others to seek help.

Shared experiences are immensely potent in the field of addiction and mental health recovery. They transform clinical terms into relatable narratives and statistical data into real-life stories of defeat and triumph. As Heilig et al. advocate, including social context in addiction treatment is crucial, and what better way to bring in a social context than by sharing lived experiences (Heilig et al., 2022)?

The irony is not lost on Jodie and Joey; the very experiences that almost killed them became the bridge that not only led them back to life but also became the lifeline for others. Furthermore, as we move forward, we must consider how these authentic, relatable narratives can serve as a precontemplation bridge for clients yet to begin their journeys.

This leads us to our next point—how do we harness the power of these shared stories in a clinical setting? More importantly, how do we navigate the complexity of engaging clients using relatable narratives without undermining the rigor of scientific methods in treatment? It is a delicate balance but one that is essential for a holistic approach to recovery.

Engaging Clients Using Relatable Narratives

Joey stopped for a moment outside the main entrance of the COE, glancing over at Jodie. Even though they both worked in separate offices at the COE, their shared experiences in MI and harm reduction bound them together. They weren't facilitating groups but instead focused on one-on-one peer support sessions. Sometimes, Joey would visit Jodie's office, offering assistance and support.

Jodie took a deep breath. "Ready for another day?"

Joey smiled gently, his eyes reflecting a depth of understanding. "Always," he replied.

As they separated to their respective offices, both were driven by the same purpose—to guide others through their journeys. They had evolved from their personal challenges and used their training to help others make positive changes.

During one of Jodie's sessions, she shared, "It's incredible to be here, discussing this with you. I remember a time when I needed the guidance I'm offering you now."

From across the hall, Joey, having stepped into Jodie's office to help out, added, "And I felt the same. We've been there, but we learned that change is possible." He looked directly at a young woman named Lena, who seemed to be holding onto a world of internal struggles. "Even when it feels impossible, there's always a glimmer of hope."

In using their lived experiences, Jodie and Joey brought the most authentic version of MI into the therapeutic space, one charged with emotional resonance (Miller & Rollnick, 2012). This strategy was not merely a technique but a bridge to the world of the precontemplative—a world characterized by denial or ignorance of the problem.

Shane, eyes still wet, asked, "How did you find a way out of that place?"

Jodie paused and looked at Joey. "Well, one thing that helped us were the small but significant moments of clarity. Like when I overdosed and somehow survived, waking up to the realization that maybe, just maybe, I was saved for a reason. Alternatively, Joey here, discovered a love for writing during his darkest days and used it as a conduit to express his unspoken fears."

"And that is the point," Joey interjected. "These are not just stories; these are life vests. Tools like these can be your steppingstones, not just strategies ripped out of a manual."

The power of narratives as tools for healing is not merely anecdotal; a plethora of evidence supports it. According to Maté (2008), addiction often lies in the realm of hungry ghosts, souls eternally hungry, seeking something outside themselves to fill the emptiness within. The narrative can provide the context for understanding that emptiness and shedding light on the ghosts haunting the client. Clients can start the journey toward healing by recognizing the underlying trauma, often exacerbated by childhood adversities (Dube et al., 2003).

Jodie took over the discussion. "Sometimes, the stories you share do more than just make you feel heard. They can serve as a mirror to others in their journey. A mutual recognition of pain, and more importantly, of the possibility of survival, fosters a sense of community and shared resilience" (Tracy & Wallace, 2016).

One must recognize the impact of shared experiences on neurobiology itself. The emotional resonance created by relatable narratives activates the release of oxytocin, a hormone associated with social bonding (Heilig et al., 2022). This is particularly vital for clients often marred by a disrupted attachment system and a heightened stress response (Kreek et al., 2005).

"But remember," Joey leaned in for the final note, "there is a thin line between using your story as a tool and becoming a prisoner of your past. That is where trauma-informed care comes in (Harris & Fallot, 2001). It is about navigating your narrative without re-traumatizing yourself. Moreover, sometimes that means knowing when to step back and seek help, not just offer it."

Jodie nodded in agreement. "That is why it is a bridge— a transitional point to something more, something better. Our stories were our bridges to you; perhaps yours can be the bridge for someone else tomorrow."

As Jodie and Joey left the room, the weight they felt was different; it was not one of sorrow but of significance. As they prepared for the next part of their day, the thought lingered about what they had overcome and what lay ahead—more lives to touch, more narratives to share, and more bridges to build.

With that, we understand that while the power of relatable narratives is irrefutable, its fullest potential is realized when it evolves into peer-led initiatives, a theme we explore, as we journey further into this transformative path of recovery.

The Value of Peer-Led Initiatives

Joey felt warmth when stepping into the COE, not just from the heater on a chilly winter morning. It was the warmth of familiarity, shared experiences, and a bond that most outside this circle could not fathom. Joey and Jodie exchanged knowing glances, ready to meet clients for peer support. Their eyes spoke volumes, for they both knew too well that the people they were about to help were mirrors of their own pasts—a past drenched in the icy waters of addiction but thawed by the heat of recovery.

No amount of academic training can impart what Joey and Jodie bring to the table. The concept of "lived experience" is not just a resume point; it is a soul-bearing narrative that makes the road to recovery a journey of shared steps rather than a lonesome trudge (White, 2009).

Relatable Narratives as Medicine

Van der Kolk writes, "Being able to feel safe with other people is probably the single most important aspect of mental health; safe connections are fundamental to meaningful and satisfying lives" (Van der Kolk, 2014. When Joey shares his story of finding a makeshift family in the dark corners of drug dens and how those connections made him feel momentarily "safe," there is an almost palpable sigh of relief in the room. Everyone knows what it is like to seek safety, even in dangerous places.

Jodie complements Joey's narrative with her own tale. It is a tale of addiction masked by a veneer of normalcy. She had a good family and an excellent education but a hollow core that she tried to fill with substances. The façade of her "functional addiction" crumbled eventually, as facades often do. "I was fortunate," she says. "I hit rock bottom but bounced back because my family, though dysfunctional, at least recognized the value of medical intervention. Not everyone is that lucky."

A Bridge of Understanding

One of the most potent aspects of peer-led initiatives in SUD and mental health is the concept of "being understood" (Mead et al., 2001). Joey and Jodie's clients do not just want treatment; they yearn for understanding. It is hard to be truly understood by someone who has not waded through the same murky waters as you. Medical professionals treat the symptoms, but peer-led support addresses the gaping emotional and existential wounds often accompanying addiction (Tracy & Wallace, 2016).

According to Harris & Fallot, designing trauma-informed service systems necessitates understanding the "lived experiences" of the people being served (2001). Joey and Jodie not only understand trauma but have lived it. Their words do not stem from clinical detachment but from the empathy of personal experience, offering a real-world application of harm reduction approaches (Marlatt & Witkiewitz, 2002).

Silver Linings and the Gifts of Desperation

For all the gut-wrenching narratives, Joey and Jodie always weave in the silver linings—the "gifts of desperation," as they call them. Jodie's addiction drove her to living, but on those very streets, she found her first mentor, a recovered addict who guided her toward recovery. It is a dark paradox where the disease also leads her to the antidote.

Joey's silver lining came wrapped in a moment of devastating clarity. He almost committed suicide, which became his turning point. "If I had not experienced the full circle of addiction—right from the first ecstatic high to the lowest pits of despair—I could not have understood the value of life as I do now," he reflects.

Transitioning to Action:
Overcoming the Precontemplation Stage

As the session winds down, Joey and Jodie know their work is not just about storytelling. It is about instilling hope and facilitating the transition from precontemplation to contemplation and eventually to action (Miller & Rollnick, 2012).

So, what makes their shared narratives different from cautionary tales? The difference lies in the outcome—the living, breathing proof that recovery is possible, that trauma can be integrated, and that life, with all its scars and stars, can indeed go on.

The room empties, but the atmosphere of cathartic liberation lingers. As Joey and Jodie prepare to see their next clients, they realize that each shared story, each unveiled truth, and each revealed trauma is not just a therapeutic exercise but a radical act of human connection.

In our next segment, we explore the critical process of "Overcoming the Precontemplation Stage," the first step toward any meaningful change. It is a juncture where many falter, but with the right kind of support—peer-led or otherwise—the barriers may be surmountable.

Overcoming the Precontemplation Stage

Nestled in a quiet office, with walls adorned by credentials and mementos of triumphs and losses, Joey and Jodie faced yet another life teetering on the brink. The individual in front of them was named April. She looked weary, her eyes sagging from the weight of denial, self-loathing, and a crushing dependency she could not yet admit to. April embodied the precontemplation stage—a point where the mere consideration of change feels foreign or even hostile (Miller & Rollnick, 2012).

In this space, Jodie and Joey found their callings. However, to reach someone like April, they needed to break through their own precontemplation stages first, a journey that required scaling mental barricades and navigating emotional minefields.

Jodie's descent into addiction began subtly. She was from a "good family," but dysfunction was the undercurrent that pulled her into a realm she had not anticipated. Her relationship with heroin began as an escape, a salve for her untreated trauma and emotional wounds. Van der Kolk's "The Body Keeps the Score" articulates how trauma is not just mental but manifests physically in the body, affecting our relationship with substances (Van der Kolk, 2014). It took domestic abuse for Jodie to recognize the gravity of her situation. However, it was also in those darkest corners that she found a glimmer of light—she discovered her innate ability to empathize with others. This silver lining became the bedrock of her recovery and, eventually, her career as a social worker.

Joey, equally a survivor, found solace in opioids. They presented an illusion of control in a world where his family's dysfunction made him feel powerless. Nevertheless, like Jodie, Joey's journey to overcoming the precontemplation stage was punctuated by moments of insight. The deeply entrenched trauma that served as an accelerator for his addiction also made him intuitively understand the trauma of others (Harris & Fallot, 2001). For Joey, the silver lining was his ability to translate his lived experience into a language that could heal, educate, and empathize.

"Your past does not have to define you, April. It can refine you,"

Joey's words punctuated the heavy silence. His statement was not just a cliché but the crystallization of years of battling internal demons and societal judgments. The scars from their battles with addiction were not just physical or emotional; they were educational. Jodie and Joey knew the science and the human element; they knew the feeling.

It is one thing to understand the neural pathways that contribute to addiction: quite another to feel your pulse quicken, your hands shake, and your mind create a labyrinth of justifications for "one more hit" or "one more drink." They knew the discomfort of confronting ugly truths head-on, without the veil of substances to blur the jagged edges (Maté, 2008).

That human element, the visceral reality of addiction, cannot be discounted. For many, it is not a lack of information but an abundance of raw, often contradictory feelings that hampers progress from precontemplation to contemplation and, ultimately, to action (Najavits, 2002). Emotional intelligence becomes as critical in this journey as any scientific understanding (Goleman, 1995).

"Remember, our bodies have a profound wisdom. They remember every experience, every emotion," Jodie added, echoing a blend of Van der Kolk and personal wisdom. "But we can learn new ways of coping, healthier ways to respond."

This idea is not just an optimistic narrative; it is substantiated by numerous studies highlighting the role of emotional and cognitive strategies in treating substance use disorders (Moos, 2007; Kar, 2011). Moreover, like what Jodie and Joey provide, peer support has demonstrated measurable benefits in treating addiction (Tracy & Wallace, 2016; White, 2009).

If precontemplation is a bridge, then crossing it requires more than just willpower; it demands a sort of alchemy. One where the scars from the past can indeed become the stars that guide us toward a brighter, sober future (Heilig et al., 2022).

Both Jodie and Joey serve as beacons that it is possible not just to cross that bridge but to construct a new one, with stronger foundations built on the meshing of lived experience and empirical evidence. A bridge is more resilient to the storms of doubt, relapse, and societal stigmatization (Livingston et al., 2012).

April left the office that day, her steps slightly less burdened. For the first time, the idea of change—of crossing that terrifying bridge—did not seem like a threat but a possibility—a beginning for her.

In our next chapter, we transition from the existential crisis encapsulated in the precontemplation stage to a theme that will guide the practicalities of this journey: "The Essence of Harm Reduction." Stay tuned as we explore the symbiotic relationship between harm reduction and long-term recovery, offering a lifeline and a blueprint for sustainable change (Marlatt & Witkiewitz, 2002).

CHAPTER 6

Harmony in Harm Reduction

The Essence of Harm Reduction

Inside Whispers and Words, the atmosphere undergoes yet another metamorphosis. A tranquil alcove materializes amid a sea of books chronicling individual challenges and redemption. Resembling a secluded garden pond, its waters hold the stillness of time, reflecting the vast expanse of the cerulean sky above. An ornate harp rises at its center, its strings seemingly woven from stories of heartache and hope alike.

Drawn to its magnetic aura, Joey and Jodie find themselves standing before the instrument. With every gentle touch, the harp releases melodies, each encapsulating the ethos of harm reduction— the principles that champion understanding, compassion, and acceptance.

Caressing a silken string, Jodie notes, "Every vibration, every tone, tells a tale of seeking understanding, of yearning for a world that chooses to care rather than condemn." Joey, deeply engrossed, chimes in, "Together, they create a harmony that resonates with the essence of trauma-informed care, intertwining seamlessly with harm reduction."

Embarking on this chapter, readers are set to navigate the intricate interplay between harm reduction and trauma-informed care. As the tales unravel and tunes play, the journey ahead promises an immersion into the symphonic union of these principles—a harmonious blend that crafts a more compassionate roadmap to healing and recovery.

Joey and Jodie stood beside the ornate harp, its strings still vibrating with melodies that conveyed more than any human words could capture. The room around them, suffused with light and echoes, felt like a sanctuary—a far cry from the rooms they once found themselves in, rooms that were corners of torment, enclaves of misery.

"Can you hear it, Jodie?" Joey's voice was quivering with emotion. "Can you hear the music saying it's okay to be you, wherever you are in your life, in your recovery? It's like a touch that doesn't judge."

Jodie nodded. "Yes, Joey. To me, the music sings of the essence of harm reduction—a philosophy that resonates so deeply with our lived experiences. A philosophy that extends a compassionate hand rather than a judgmental finger."

In the realm of mental health and SUD, Joey and Jodie were well-versed in the spectrum of treatment approaches available. They appreciated the foundational, abstinence-focused methods that many find invaluable and effective, recognizing that what works wonders for one may not resonate with another. Joey's journey, without spelling it out, leaned toward these foundational methods, while Jodie's path was distinct. Despite being born into families with means, both grappled with the tempest of complex emotions, vicarious traumas, and the pull of addictive substances often linked to such backgrounds. Their education and social standing offered some protection but not a solution; they were enmeshed in a web of emotional turmoil and dependency.

Maté (2008) elucidates that addiction often serves as a coping mechanism for deep-seated pain and trauma, a realm of "hungry ghosts" where the longing for relief turns into a vicious cycle of consumption and anguish (*In the Realm of Hungry Ghosts*). As Van der Kolk (2014) further describes, the body "keeps the score," accumulating the emotional and physiological scars of past traumas (*The Body Keeps the Score*).

"Remember when we used to share needles with the people we used with?" Joey's somber but not remorseful words cut through the musical ambiance.

"I do," Jodie replied, her face a mirror of contemplation. "And yet, even in those days, I remember we would clean the needles with bleach. It was a small act but harm reduction in its most elemental form. We didn't know what we were doing, but our intuition guided us toward minimizing harm, toward something that felt humane."

"Exactly," Joey exclaimed, recognizing a silver lining in their troubled pasts. "Even then, we weren't trying to destroy ourselves. We were trying to survive, to mitigate the harm, the risk. That bleach was our first gesture toward self-compassion, though we didn't realize it at the time."

This intuitive gravitation toward harm reduction reflects what Marlatt and Witkiewitz (2002) call a "health promotion, prevention, and treatment" approach (Harm reduction approaches to alcohol use). Instead of punitive measures that amplify the shame and stigma associated with addiction—a cycle confirmed by Dube et al. (2003) to correlate with childhood abuse and neglect (childhood abuse, neglect, and household dysfunction)—harm reduction provides a non-judgmental and evidence-based framework that prioritizes safety and personal choice.

"I remember," Joey continued, "how those needle exchange programs felt like islands of sanity in our insane lives. The nurses there didn't judge us; they educated us. I felt seen, perhaps for the first time, as a person and not just a 'user.'"

Najavits (2002) emphasizes the importance of such safe spaces in her treatment manual for PTSD and substance abuse, asserting that *Seeking Safety* is not just an intervention but a universal need (*Seeking Safety*).

Jodie's eyes met Joey's. "The essence of harm reduction is not just about lessening damage or risk. It's an act of empowering the individual, a form of love, a type of human connection. That connection counteracts the isolating, debilitating nature of addiction. Just as harm reduction doesn't condemn people for their choices, trauma-informed care recognizes that our choices often stem from life experiences beyond our control."

With their hands almost touching the harp strings again, Joey and Jodie could feel a new tune beginning to form, a melody that captured their next thought in perfect pitch.

"Jodie," said Joey, "it's almost as if the strings of harm reduction and the chords of trauma-informed care are waiting to play in unison to create a new harmony that takes healing and recovery to a level of depth we've never seen before."

Jodie nodded in agreement. "Yes, and this symphony can transform the entire landscape of addiction treatment, redefining how we approach those in their own battles, bringing a more nuanced, compassionate lens to our practice."

Both sensed they were on the cusp of something monumental, something transformative that could reshape their field and save lives. As they paused to contemplate, the room seemed to hold its breath as if waiting for the first note of a groundbreaking composition.

"In our next journey," Joey concluded, "we explore how this harmony can be achieved. How can the empathic, accepting philosophy of harm reduction align seamlessly with trauma-informed care to create a holistic, truly compassionate roadmap to healing and recovery."

Aligning Trauma-Informed Care With Harm Reduction

Joey's hand was rock-steady as he held the syringe, an act performed countless times in what seemed like another life. But today was different. The syringe contained not heroin but Naloxone, and he was administering it to a young man who had just overdosed.

Joey's heart pounded in his chest, mingled emotions of fear and hope permeating the air as palpably as the antiseptic scent. For him, the moment was a full-circle journey—from the pits of his own addiction that nearly took his life to a place of recovery and empowerment.

Beside him, Jodie watched with a gaze that was equal parts clinical and compassionate. She knew all too well the weight of what they were doing. Years before, she had found herself on the other side of the needle. When the young man finally gasped for air, eyes fluttering open, the room filled with a collective sigh that almost whispered, "You're safe now; you are seen."

The very act of harm reduction, encapsulated in this moment, was recognizing humanity, vulnerability, and the complications of life that often get overlooked in more traditional "just say no" addiction treatment methods (Marlatt & Witkiewitz, 2002). However, harm reduction alone is not enough. Understanding trauma's role in addiction can inform more empathetic, effective, and human-focused treatments.

"It is not just the substance. It is the why," Joey said later in a group session. "Why did we turn to drugs in the first place?" This question, loaded with emotional gravitas, brought him back to his past—fraught with family dysfunction despite normality, a history of emotional neglect, and disguised traumas (Dube et al., 2003).

Jodie nodded, adding, "Often, people focus solely on the substance use, ignoring the traumatic experiences that frequently accompany, and sometimes even foster, addictive behaviors." Their point was buttressed by an overwhelming body of evidence linking trauma to substance use disorders (Van der Kolk, 2014; Maté, 2008).

Trauma-informed care integrates an understanding of the pervasive impact of trauma and creates a safe environment where individuals can build a sense of control and empowerment (Harris & Fallot, 2001). Jodie and Joey, in their roles as navigators but social workers at heart, do more than dispense medication; they help build supportive networks, bolster self-esteem, and impart coping skills rooted in self-understanding (White, 2009).

Their journeys toward recovery had been marked by multiple relapses, an often-stigmatizing feature of substance use disorder that, in their case, was driven mainly by unaddressed traumas (Gorski, 1990).

While Joey found solace and self-acceptance through CBT designed to treat post-traumatic stress disorder (Kar, 2011), Jodie was significantly helped by peer-support groups that acted as a therapeutic space to vocalize her internalized trauma (Tracy & Wallace, 2016).

And it is not just the individual journey that matters. Joey and Jodie recognized that systemic changes were imperative for trauma-informed care to align with harm reduction strategies effectively. "It is about changing the entire service system," Joey said, referring to Harris & Fallot's insights on designing trauma-informed service systems (2001).

Yet, the silver linings from their past life experiences in addiction were tangible. Joey had cultivated an incredible emotional intelligence (Goleman, 1995), his own tribulations enabling him to resonate with his clients' emotions in a way few could. In a similar vein, Jodie discovered her innate capacity for MI, leveraging her lived experience to help people believe that change was possible (Miller & Rollnick, 2012).

Above all, the emotions woven by Joey and Jodie's own histories enhanced their abilities to navigate the intricate human dimensions of addiction treatment. Through their eyes, clients were not seen as cases but as complex individuals, often battling demons born from their pasts. Their empathy was their strength, and their scars were their wisdom.

Wounded healers are said to be the best clinicians (Maté, 2008). Joey and Jodie embodied this principle, leveraging their own histories of trauma and addiction not as liabilities but as sources of strength and insight. As we venture further into this chapter, we will see that harmonizing trauma-informed care with harm reduction is not just a clinical imperative but a human one.

As powerful as the stories of Joey and Jodie are, they point to a more extensive conversation that's evolving in the addiction treatment landscape. We need to shift from isolated interventions to a more integrated approach. An approach where harm reduction and trauma-informed care coexist, not as competing paradigms but as complementary strategies that speak to the complex realities of human experience. This leads us to our next essential topic: the transition from abstinence-only models in addiction treatment to more nuanced, compassionate strategies.

The Transition From Abstinence-Only Models

Jodie and Joey, both social workers and survivors of a grim addiction battle, leaned against the glass walls of their office, coffee mugs in hand, watching as April, one of their clients, walked away after a counseling session. A tranquility in April's gait made Joey recall a time when peace felt like a foreign concept.

"It is unbelievable how much April has improved since we switched from abstinence-only to harm reduction," Joey said, reminiscing about their past.

Jodie nodded. "And to think we grew up in an era that insisted on abstinence as the only route to recovery. It is a miracle we made it out alive, let alone work on the other side of the battlefield."

Like countless others, their lives had been ensnared in the trap of SUDs. Yet, in their struggle, they had stumbled upon a silver lining—wisdom. Wisdom guided them into merging trauma-informed care with the modern tenets of harm reduction.

Abstinence-only models, while traditional, underscore the significance of total commitment and discipline in the path to recovery. Rooted in the idea that individuals can find the strength to abstain, they serve as a testament to the human spirit's resilience. As Jodie often mentions, "While addiction might not always be a choice, our commitment to breaking free from it certainly is" (Maté, 2008). Though it's essential to consider the underlying trauma that might perpetuate addiction, abstinence-only models prioritize a clear, steadfast approach to healing.

It is paramount, however, to recognize that every individual's journey to recovery is unique. Therefore, while some might succeed with the rigorous discipline of abstinence-only models, others might need different approaches. We should strive for an open-mindedness that seeks the best fit for each person. After all, the goal is holistic recovery, understanding, and compassion for all those battling addiction.

The Intersection of Trauma-Informed Care and Harm Reduction

Jodie and Joey discovered that their personal and familial dysfunctions contributed to their addictive behaviors (Dube et al., 2003). Jodie was a victim of a loss of autonomy, while Joey had a history of years of being bullied. They recognized that trauma-informed care could not be an afterthought—it had to be an integral part of the recovery process (Harris & Fallot, 2001).

The trauma-informed approach does not just address the "what" of substance abuse and the "why." This shift in focus aims to understand and address the underlying issues, often related to trauma, which lead to harmful behavior (Najavits, 2002).

Harm reduction is an umbrella term for interventions aimed at reducing the adverse effects of health behaviors without necessarily extinguishing the problematic behavior entirely (Marlatt & Witkiewitz, 2002). Harm reduction allows for more achievable and immediate goals, such as safer drug use or moderated drinking, as steppingstones toward long-term recovery.

The Emotional Weight of Transition

"Remember when we thought that a drink would numb the pain away or that a hit would make us forget? How naive we were," Joey sighed, his eyes misty but not quite teary.

"Yeah," Jodie said softly. "But look at us now. Those scars led us to find our stars—our purpose and calling."

Joey nodded, wiping away a single tear. "We understand addiction not just from textbooks but from lived experiences, from the shame, the degradation, the agony, and the crippling fear. And now, we can guide others through the gloomy labyrinth of recovery, holding up a lantern of empathy and compassion."

They both knew that their holistic approach was making a real difference; April was just one example. "We have come to appreciate that one size does not fit all, haven't we?" Jodie added.

The Silver Linings

The vulnerability of their past lives offered Jodie and Joey a unique prism to view the world. They recognized that abstinence-only models, while well-meaning, often lacked the scope to address the intricate collage of human suffering that often underpins addiction. Their own experiences had taught them that understanding one's trauma and integrating that understanding into treatment could open the gateway to more enduring recovery.

"People like April remind us that the blend of trauma-informed care and harm reduction is not just theoretical—it is life-changing," Jodie said, clutching her mug as if holding onto hope.

Joey nodded, adding, "It is more than that. It is lifesaving."

They looked at each other, realizing they had found a method that does not merely "manage" addiction but reshapes the entire recovery trajectory. They had found harmony in harm reduction—a harmony that respected the individual's journey and did not mandate a single, rigid path for all.

As we have observed through Jodie and Joey's lens, integrating trauma-informed care and harm reduction promises a more humane and effective strategy for tackling addiction. The real-world applicability of this novel approach does not just end in clinical settings or theoretical debates; its ripples are felt in the lives it touches, turning inevitable scars into constellations of stars. In the next section, we delve deeper into the practical applications and case studies that underpin this harmony in harm reduction, illuminating its transformative potential for those walking the rocky path of recovery.

Practical Applications and Case Studies

Joey adjusted his reading glasses and looked up from his tablet. On the screen were graphs and treatment pathways, a science-backed puzzle he was fervently piecing together. But in front of him sat Carl, a twenty-four-year-old with a mild opioid addiction and a lifetime of experiences that led him there. Joey felt the weight of his responsibility and an overwhelming sense of familiarity. He remembered a similar emotional landscape—his own—filled with despair and a longing for something beyond the reaches of self-constructed barriers (Maté, 2008).

"Carl, I see that you have been through a lot, and it is okay. We will help you figure this out, step by step, without judgment. No big leaps, just small manageable steps," Joey said.

The wariness in Carl's eyes flickered for a moment, replaced by something softer, maybe hope. Joey knew that look. It was his look when he met Jodie, his wife and colleague, in the battle against addiction.

"Have you heard of Naloxone?" Joey began embracing the science to counteract the stigma that often accompanies SUDs. "It is a medication designed to reverse opioid overdose rapidly. Carrying one could be a lifesaving measure for you and someone you might encounter."

This was a classic harm reduction technique—acknowledging the risks of the existing behavior and taking concrete steps to mitigate it (Marlatt & Witkiewitz, 2002). It is not an end solution but a crucial step toward a safer life.

Meanwhile, Jodie was having a peer-support session with women who had histories of trauma and were in various stages of recovery from addiction. The room was a sacred space filled with vulnerability and strength. Today's topic was "Understanding the Body's Response to Trauma" (Van der Kolk, 2014).

"Your body keeps a score," Jodie began. "But knowing that score, understanding how trauma is stored in the very sinews and cells of your being, can be the first step in reclaiming your life."

She introduced grounding techniques to help manage triggers. Jodie felt a resonating pride as she watched the women slowly breathe, centering themselves. It was far from the empty sensation of euphoria she had once chased; this was a feeling that sprang from the depths of her soul.

When Jodie and Joey regrouped at the COE, they discussed the recent peer-support cases they had overseen. There was Erin, a girl who had turned to substance abuse after experiencing emotional abuse.

They facilitated her getting into an outpatient group focused on her addiction and traumatic experiences (Najavits, 2002). There was Lee, a war veteran struggling with PTSD, OUD, and alcoholism. His treatment plan included medication and exposure therapy in outpatient, a multi-pronged approach recognizing his disorders' interconnectedness (Kar, 2011).

In these instances, the emotional weight was like a torrential rain, unpredictable and heavy. Nevertheless, Jodie and Joey found solace in knowing they provided more than just umbrellas; they constructed fortresses.

They both understood that the practical application of trauma-informed care in the realm of addiction was not just about intervention strategies; it was about redefining what treatment and recovery could look like (Harris & Fallot, 2001). It was about creating a healing space that acknowledged not just the medical symptoms but also the emotional, psychological, and social aspects of addiction.

Their approaches integrated evidence-based engagement, led by their mentor Cheryld and case-by-case adaptations. Sometimes, that meant incorporating MI to help with engagement. Other times, it meant bringing family into the treatment equation, accounting for the complicated dynamics that often contribute to SUDs (Dube et al., 2003).

For Jodie and Joey, their own scars were their greatest tools in helping others find their stars. These scars, the remnants of histories almost lost to addiction, were testaments to the power of resilience, serving as both cautionary tales and inspiring beacons. As they looked at their clients—each a mirror reflecting different facets of their pasts—they were reminded of their arduous journey. A journey that validated their belief in second chances and the transformative power of understanding one's trauma (Harris & Fallot, 2001).

"It is almost like we are turning scars into constellations, right?" Joey pondered.

Jodie smiled. "Exactly, but constellations that guide not just us, but everyone lost in this endless night."

In the symbiotic relationship between trauma-informed care and harm reduction, Jodie and Joey found professional callings and personal redemption. Their lived experiences, echoing in the corridors of their shared pasts, were no longer mere memories but fuel for a revolutionary engine of change.

These real-world applications and case studies serve as strong pillars, validating the marriage between trauma-informed care and harm reduction. However, the keystone in this arch is the lived experience of those who administer these programs. Next, we explore the potent, often underestimated, value of incorporating lived experiences into harm reduction strategies, laying bare how this integration can serve as both a balm and a catalyst for enduring recovery.

CHAPTER 7

The Power of Motivational Interviewing

Basics of Motivational Interviewing (MI)

Within Whispers and Words, the ambiance subtly transforms again. Amidst bookshelves laden with wisdom from eons past, a secluded alcove emerges. Its walls are adorned with intricate scrolls and parchment, reminiscent of dialogues between sages and seekers of yore. The gentle cadence of purposeful conversations reverberates, illustrating the nuances of the spoken word.

At the alcove's heart, two regal armchairs face one another. Joey occupies one, the very embodiment of patience and intent. Seated across is a silhouette, representing every soul yearning for clarity amidst the cacophony of life. A waltz of words ensues between them, capturing the essence of MI.

From a cozy corner, Jodie observes, "It's a craft of deep listening and deliberate questioning. It's about guiding the spirit to unearth its buried truths and aspirations." Joey, his eyes reflecting a myriad of emotions, adds, "Every dialogue is a dance, every response a step, leading toward revelation and realization."

In this chapter, immerse yourself in the world of MI—a therapeutic dance designed to amplify the inner voices often muted by external tumult. Traverse the labyrinth of inquiry and reflection, fathom its synergy with trauma-informed care, and appreciate the potent transformations evoked by the art of genuine conversation. Venture forth and experience the rhythmic revelations of dialogue.

The alcove reverberates with a silence that isn't empty but full—full of potential, aspirations, and undisclosed turmoil. Joey feels the weight of this silence as his eyes meet those of the silhouette sitting across from him. These eyes have seen the depths of despair, traversed the landscapes of addiction, and are now searching for a glimmer of hope, a path to redemption.

"Where do we go from here?" the silhouette finally murmurs, breaking the silence.

"We begin by knowing that there's a journey ahead—a journey of change," Joey responds, the corners of his mouth lifting in a subtle smile.

Jodie, who's been observing this intimate exchange, recalls her own battles with substance abuse. Her skin was once a canvas of bruises, her veins infiltrated by the drug that momentarily filled her emptiness, only to widen it further. But that's not who she is now. "Addiction was my crucible," she muses. "It broke me, but from that rupture sprouted the me who exists today: healed, or healing still, and helping others heal."

What Joey and Jodie know profoundly is the power of MI to catalyze this sort of transformation. Born from the psychotherapeutic theories developed by Miller and Rollnick, MI is a client-centered counseling style for changing behavior by helping clients explore and resolve ambivalence (Miller & Rollnick, 2012).

The elegance of MI lies in its respect for the individual's autonomy, while gently guiding them toward self-discovery. It doesn't argue or admonish but instead empathizes and evokes. The substance user isn't viewed as a "problem to be solved" but as a person with strengths and resources who can choose to change (Harris & Fallot, 2001).

MI's core rests on four interlinked principles: expressing empathy, developing discrepancy, rolling with resistance, and supporting self-efficacy. The therapist uses skillful open-ended questions, affirmations, and reflective listening to elicit "change talk" from the client. This is not mere conversation; it's a nuanced orchestration to help the client listen to their inner selves, to let them hear their own arguments for change.

"It's so important to hold space for someone's complexity, for their multitude of emotions—guilt, sorrow, hope," Joey says, recollecting his own history of substance abuse. Born into a good family, although dysfunctional, Joey's addiction wasn't an "act of rebellion" but a search for solace. In his tumultuous journey from addiction toward recovery, MI was the lighthouse guiding him through the thick fog of his conflicting emotions (Maté, 2008).

Likewise, Jodie identifies MI as instrumental in helping her accept her past traumas deeply entrenched in her addictive behaviors. Science tells us that childhood experiences like neglect or abuse significantly elevate the risk of substance abuse later in life (Dube et al., 2003). For Jodie, MI was the therapeutic scaffold upon which her fractured identity could be reconstructed. It empowered her to face her traumatic past, illuminated by the awareness that "The Body Keeps the Score" (Van der Kolk, 2014).

Joey and Jodie owe a great deal to MI for bringing them back from the brink and equipping them with the skills to help others. "When we share our lived experience with our clients," Jodie notes, "it serves as a testament that change is possible. MI can be that catalyst."

You might wonder how MI harmonizes with trauma-informed care. The answer is that MI adds depth to the trauma-informed approach, making it sensitive and action-oriented. MI and trauma-informed care are like two dancers in perfect synchrony, each amplifying the grace of the other (Najavits, 2002).

A skeptic might question the efficacy of "just talking" in treating something as visceral as addiction. Yet, the beauty of MI lies in its simplicity. In a realm where medication and intensive therapy play undeniable roles, the power of a genuine, empathetic conversation can often be underrated. But as anyone who has been through the grinder of addiction will tell you, sometimes the first step to salvation is as simple and complicated as wanting to change.

And that's where we find Joey and Jodie today—social workers and embodiments of resilience, using MI to guide their clients through the labyrinthine paths of their internal worlds. They know from lived experience that the recovery journey is arduous but not impossible. Their scars are testimonies of battles lost and won; their lives, the radiant stars illuminating the path for those still engulfed in darkness.

As the alchemy of MI continues to reverberate through Joey and Jodie's alcove, let's delve deeper into its role in engaging clients—our next compass point in understanding the rhythmic revelations of dialogue.

MI's Role in Engaging Client

As Jodie sat across from Lee, a middle-aged man grappling with alcoholism, she could almost see the wall he had built around himself. It was a fortress of defense mechanisms, rationalizations, and deeply embedded guilt. He wore a tough exterior but seemed like an empty shell. His eyes searched for something—perhaps a glimmer of hope or a safe harbor. And she knew that feeling, having been on the other side of that desk, battling her own demons, clinging to a bottle like it was her life support.

Jodie's husband and colleague, Joey, a fellow survivor of SUD, watched from the next room. He understood that the walls people built were not always out of bricks and mortar but often out of pain, guilt, and trauma. He knew it well; his past was checkered with trials that nearly ended him. Jodie, a blended case manager (BCM) now, and Joey, a clinical supervisor and certified recovery specialist (CRS) in the mental health and SUD field, had come a long way from their old lives. They had a unique gift: the ability to channel the turmoil and chaos of their past into helping others navigate their own stormy seas.

MI was a keystone in their practice, an approach that was less about giving advice and more about listening, understanding, and evoking change from within the client. It was not a one-size-fits-all, prescriptive method but a form of communication that considered each person's unique emotional and psychological landscape (Miller & Rollnick, 2012).

"People need more than just advice," Jodie would often say. "They need to feel heard, and MI gives them that voice."

The process was akin to how Jodie and Joey found their own way through their struggles; the similarities were uncanny. In their days of addiction, both had been locked in a battle with what Maté (2008) describes as "hungry ghosts," those relentless cravings that eclipse all logic and reason. Yet amidst that maelstrom, there had been moments—fleeting as they were—when they questioned their paths, pondered their choices, and touched the edges of change. Those moments were often facilitated by an empathetic ear, a compassionate gaze, or a non-judgmental space where they felt safe. Van der Kolk (2014) puts it best: "Being able to feel safe with other people is probably the single most important aspect of mental health."

Today, while working for a large behavioral health agency, Jodie and Joey incorporate MI techniques to provide safety and enable a collaborative journey into the client's thoughts and feelings. For instance, when Jodie recognized Lee's hesitance, she leaned back, providing him with physical and emotional space. Then, in her gentle voice, she asked, "Lee, what's important to you about changing your relationship with alcohol?"

This simple question was a hand reaching out, inviting Lee to step over his own barricades. Observing this, Joey was reminded of his own path to getting "clean"—a path where the most meaningful changes had been internal, nudged along by individuals who engaged him emotionally. It's a modality that Najavits (2002) calls the "treatment alliance," where a clinician and client form a partnership grounded in mutual trust and respect.

The ultimate power of MI lies in the paradox that the more you step back and allow people to find their reasons for change, the more likely they are to change (Miller & Rollnick, 2012). For Jodie and Joey, this involved more than just well-placed questions; it involved sharing snippets of their own lives, the silver linings of their dark times, to illustrate the resilience of the human spirit. Joey would talk about the importance of peer support in his journey, resonating with research indicating its benefits in SUD treatment (Tracy & Wallace, 2016). Jodie would share her own experiences of trauma and recovery, emphasizing how trauma-informed care helped her turn her life around (Harris & Fallot, 2001).

Sharing these fragments of their own journeys was their way of saying, "We've walked a path, and while we can't walk yours for you, we can certainly walk beside you."

Emotions and feelings are at the core of human experience and are inextricably linked to the challenge of behavioral change. MI makes space for these emotions: it respects them, honors them, and, most importantly, uses them as catalysts for transformation. Jodie and Joey understood that what they were engaging with were not just symptoms of a disorder, but human lives shaped by myriad influences—some heartbreakingly painful, others profoundly enlightening.

As we look deeper into this nuanced landscape, we arrive at the nexus where MI meets trauma-informed care. Here, the walls people erected are not obstacles but rather pieces of a complex puzzle—a mosaic of bitter and sweet life experiences. As noted earlier, it's a place where we don't just ask, "What's wrong with you?" but rather, "What happened to you?"

And so, as we transition to exploring how MI can be augmented by integrating it with trauma-informed care, let us keep in mind that we can genuinely revolutionize recovery by amalgamating these approaches.

Combining MI With Trauma-Informed care

The emotions that wrap itself around the lives of Joey and Jodie is a testament to the resilience of the human spirit. They sit together in their house, adorned with artworks that tell stories of struggle and triumph and resemble their own journeys from addiction to recovery. Their faces bear the patina of experience, tempered by years of working in the SUD and mental health fields. They are not just survivors; they are warriors.

But being a warrior involves more than just surviving. It's about understanding the battle within and outside oneself. MI has proven to be a game-changing technique in the complex mental health and substance use arena. But what elevates this approach, as Joey and Jodie have found, is the seamless integration of MI with trauma-informed care.

"Remember Alexis?" Jodie asks Joey one day after work, recalling a client whose demeanor was like a constantly closing door. "She was skeptical about sharing her history, and rightfully so. She'd been through so much, trauma layered upon trauma."

Joey nods, his eyes clouding with the understanding that it only comes from having seen darkness himself. He, too, remembers Alexis and the dozens like her. "You know," he starts slowly, "MI helped us chip away at that wall, but trauma-informed care lets us rebuild her from within. It wasn't about persuading her to change but giving her the tools to create her own sanctuary."

Trauma-informed care requires a foundational understanding that a person's behavioral issues are not isolated instances but are often the echoes of past suffering (Van der Kolk, 2014; Harris & Fallot, 2001). It's an acknowledgment that trauma often lies at the heart of substance abuse and other forms of self-destructive behavior. MI allows professionals to dig deeper, guiding the client's own verbal expression toward discovering their reasons for change (Miller & Rollnick, 2012).

For Jodie and Joey, the fusion of MI and trauma-informed care has been instrumental in the successful treatment of their clients. With their lived experiences of past addiction and trauma, both understand the crucial role of emotional safety in effective communication. "When you've been to hell and back like we have, you know that the last thing someone wants is to be 'talked at,'" says Jodie, her voice tinged with emotion.

The beauty of MI is in its empathic nature and client-centered approach: it's about asking, listening, and mirroring back. Jodie and Joey view it as a form of emotional architecture, scaffolding built on trust and understanding. MI becomes an even more potent healing force when overlaid with the principles of trauma-informed care—safety, trustworthiness, peer support, collaboration, and empowerment (Abuse, 2014).

Trauma complicates the substance use landscape and illuminates the path to more effective treatment (Najavits, 2002). "It's like holding a lantern in a dark room," says Joey. "And that lantern is not us or any of our techniques. It's the client's own will."

This insight is deeply embedded in their work ethos. Joey recalls his darkest days, clouded with substance use, as a journey through an endless tunnel. "But even in that gloom," he reflects, "I found some power. My will to survive. It was buried, but it was there. I believe that everyone has that seed within them. Our job is to water, nurture, and let it sprout."

These silver linings from their pasts and the uncanny ability to find a beacon in despair make Joey and Jodie uniquely poised to help their clients. They consider their experiences as their most significant burden and their most potent weapon. "The scars we carry make the stars shine brighter," says Jodie.

"The combination of MI and trauma-informed care offers us a navigational tool," adds Joey. "A compass that not only helps us in understanding where the client is coming from but also in helping them chart out where they wish to go."

In a complex, interconnected web of psychological, social, and biological factors (Maté, 2008; Kreek et al., 2005; Heilig et al., 2022), this blended approach helps professionals and clients navigate the labyrinth of emotions and circumstances. It paves the way for individualized treatment plans that address the symptoms and underlying emotional wounds.

With the wisdom they've gained, Joey and Jodie are well aware that their role is not to "fix" someone but to serve as partners in the recovery journey. They understand that combining MI with trauma-informed care isn't merely an approach: it's a philosophy that recognizes the intricate textures of human suffering, the hidden resilience, and the boundless possibilities for change.

As we prepare to explore the next layer of this subject, we are led to a compelling point—the power that comes from lived experiences. Joey and Jodie's journeys have molded them and added unique layers to their professional personas. The marriage of MI with their lived experiences is not just a clinical amalgamation; it's a humane fusion that resonates on an emotional, existential level. We are thus led to ponder: Can lived experiences further enrich the techniques of MI? Let's explore this as we look deeper into the powerful MI narrative.

Lived Experiences Enhancing MI Techniques

Jodie leans back in her office chair, taking a sip of her lukewarm coffee as she writes her notes from the current week. Her eyes meet Joey's, who is engrossed in his own paperwork, while visiting Jodie's office and helping her with a client. They exchange a knowing look, a subtle communication that only those who have been to hell and back could comprehend.

"You know, Joe," Jodie starts, her voice muffled by the emotion filling the room, "This case made me think of my prior experience. It hit me like a brick wall. My journey's suffering has become my strength, a lens through which I connect with our clients."

Joey, putting aside his papers, leans forward. "It's like Van der Kolk says, 'The body keeps the score.' Our bodies remember trauma, but so do our souls. It's in the fabric of who we are, and it informs how we connect with others" (Van der Kolk, 2014).

In the sea of methods and modalities for treating substance use and mental health issues, lived experiences create a unique undertow. For Joey and Jodie, the emotional resonance stemming from their own past addictions, near-death experiences, and family dysfunction adds a layer of raw authenticity to their practice. It's like another tool in their therapeutic arsenal; they wield it carefully with precision and vulnerability.

"I remember feeling like the medical staff saw me as just another number," Joey recalls, "but the moment a counselor spoke to me with a shared understanding, it was like someone had turned on a light in a very dark room."

Tactile Empathy: The Essence of Emotional Translation

Empathy in MI isn't just a professional skill; it's a human capacity to understand someone else's emotional landscape (Miller & Rollnick, 2012). While MI alone can facilitate change by eliciting clients' reasons for change, Jodie and Joey bring something more: tactile empathy. This is empathy that doesn't just "understand"—it "feels."

Jodie elaborates, "Being part of good families steeped in dysfunction taught me the paradox of love and harm. Clients often resonate with that. It's not just about asking open-ended questions; it's about asking them in a way that taps into the heart of the matter."

This nuanced emotional translation is akin to what Maté refers to as "close encounters with addiction" (Maté, 2008). The emotional touchpoints derived from lived experience offer a therapeutic mirror reflective of the clients' spoken words and their unspoken emotional dialect.

Emotional Safety Nets: Creating Spaces of Shared Vulnerability

Jodie and Joey often recount their journeys of how they went from the edge of the abyss to being the safety net for others. It's not just their credentials that build trust; it's their visible scars.

Joey remembers how he almost lost his life and lay in a hospital bed, wondering if the fight was worth it. "I was touched by the unconditional support of medical professionals who saw my humanity, even when I couldn't," he says, his voice thick with emotion. "But I needed more. I needed someone who had navigated the same churning emotional waters."

"For me, it was my therapist who had also struggled with substance abuse," Jodie chimes in. "That shared experience created an emotional safety net that clinical acumen alone couldn't offer. She was a living example of recovery, just like we are to our clients today."

The authentic emotional connections they form with their clients serve as a live testament to what is often termed as "Peer-based Addiction Recovery Support" (White, 2009). This reciprocal emotional ecosystem fosters a supportive therapeutic environment and personalizes evidence-based techniques, like MI, to resonate deeply with the individual client.

Lived Experience as an Anchor

Jodie recalls a moment when a client teared up during an MI session. "You understand me because you've been there," the client had whispered. And at that moment, Jodie had felt the lived experience anchor itself into the MI technique they were using.

Their lived experiences aren't badges of past hardships but emblems of resilience and humanity. They serve as anchors, grounding the professional techniques in the real human experience of suffering and recovery. When Jodie and Joey talk about "harm reduction" or "safety planning," it's not just a theoretical concept (Marlatt & Witkiewitz, 2002; Najavits, 2002). It's a lived reality, vivid and palpable.

Concluding Thoughts: The Seamless Fusion

In their emotionally charged but fulfilling journey of helping others, Jodie and Joey have found a confluence where MI and lived experiences meet, enriching each other in a seamless dance of empathy, authenticity, and skilled intervention. Their story exemplifies how MI can be imbued with the depths of shared human experiences to create a powerful therapeutic alliance. This is not just Motivational Interviewing; it's Motivational Interviewing elevated by the profoundness of the human experience.

As we ponder the deeply rooted emotional complexities that therapists and clients bring into the therapeutic space, it becomes evident that lived experiences are not just supplemental to MI but complementary and often instrumental. This brings us to our next crucial point: How does this blend of technique and lived experience manifest in real-world scenarios? To answer that, let's examine case studies that showcase the compelling efficacy of MI in the chapters to come.

Case Studies Showcasing MI's Efficacy

Case 1: Becky—The Ghosts of Childhood Trauma

Becky had deep-set eyes that seemed to harbor years of secrets. When she first met Jodie, her words stumbled over each other, barricaded by fear and doubt. What was apparent was her love for her two children and her desperation to emerge from the shadow of opioid addiction that had gripped her since her late teens.

Jodie gently applied MI techniques, knowing that the wound of addiction was deeply tied to past traumas (Najavits, 2002). But there was something more. Jodie shared a story from her own life—how she had faced the abyss and clawed her way back. It was risky to open up that much, but she sensed Becky needed that human connection. When Jodie mentioned her dysfunctional but loving family, Becky's eyes filled with tears. It was a nod to their shared universe of love marred by trauma.

"We're not just survivors, Becky. We're warriors," Jodie told her, applying the principles of "trauma-informed care" (Harris & Fallot, 2001). This single statement became a turning point. Becky felt understood and saw a future where she could be more than her addiction and past traumas.

Case 2: Luke—The Spiral of Relapse

Luke had been through the revolving door of rehab clinics and hospital visits. Joey remembered the eeriness in Luke's voice when he said, "You can't possibly understand how hard it is." But Joey did. He remembered the cold grip of substances and how close he had come to losing himself entirely.

This experience guided him as he used MI to explore Luke's motivations (Miller & Rollnick, 2012). Joey's approach differed from the textbook techniques; it was deeply personal. As Luke revealed a recent relapse, Joey shared his own story about almost succumbing to his addiction after a year of sobriety. Luke was stunned. "You've been where I am?"

"Yes," Joey nodded. "Relapse isn't the end; it's a bend in your journey. And every bend offers a new perspective, a new lesson" (Gorski, 1990).

This connection served as a catalyst for Luke, who gradually learned to see relapse as part of the recovery journey and not a sign of perpetual failure. The blend of MI and lived experience made Luke receptive to the idea that each relapse offered growth and self-reinvention opportunities.

Case 3: Mindi—Unseen Scars and Hidden Pain

Mindi had a history of self-harm and drug use rooted in emotional abuse during her childhood. This manifested in her teenage years as an addiction to prescription drugs, a coping mechanism that doubled as a cry for help (Dube et al., 2003).

Jodie saw Mindi's scars as battles fought against inner demons, scars similar to those she bore in a different way but had never shown. She used MI to allow Mindi to express her internal pain, guiding her to articulate her fears and hopes (Maté, 2008).

"I remember feeling that the world was against me," Jodie shared, "that no one could see beyond my flaws and addictions. But the world began to change when I saw myself through compassionate eyes. Can we try that perspective shift together?"

Mindi started to break down her walls, eventually moving to a path of medication-assisted treatment combined with trauma-focused therapies (Van der Kolk, 2014; Kar, 2011). The tender, empathetic, and informed MI technique opened the door for Mindi to enter a healing space.

Case 4: Robbie—The Stigma of Masculine Silence

Robbie was a war veteran suffering from PTSD and alcoholism. When Joey met him, he was withdrawn, cocooned in the stigma that men should not speak about their emotions (Livingston et al., 2012).

Joey used MI to unearth Robbie's hidden motivations and fears but with an additional layer—the lived experience of overcoming societal expectations. "In my darkest days, the hardest part wasn't admitting I had a problem. It was admitting I needed help," Joey confided.

The revelation drew Robbie out of his shell. "You mean, it's okay not to be okay?" he asked.

"Yes," Joey said softly, "And the bravest thing you can do is take the first step, even when it feels like a leap."

This single conversation shifted Robbie's perception, paving the way for a more specialized approach combining MI and trauma-focused therapies, allowing him to embrace vulnerability as a strength, not a weakness (Van der Kolk, 2014; Harris & Fallot, 2001).

What we see in Becky, Luke, Mindi, and Robbie are not just cases but human stories—each one teetering on the edge of despair and hope. Through MI, infused with Jodie and Joey's own lived experiences, their clients find more than a clinical approach; they find a human touch that reaches deep within their soul, pulling them back from the abyss (White, 2009; Mead et al., 2001).

This leads us to our next exploration in Chapter 8: how this rich collage of clinical acumen and personal vulnerability forms a symbiotic dance that transcends traditional therapeutic boundaries, reaching something more profound and human. Because when clinical meets experience, the possibilities for authentic healing are not just increased—they're revolutionized.

CHAPTER 8

Clinical Meets Experience: A Symbiotic Dance

The Marriage of Clinical and Personal Perspectives

The setting shifts once again in the heart of the Whispers and Words bookstore. A makeshift dance floor emerges between towering bookshelves filled with academic books and personal memoirs. Half of it is adorned with well-defined patterns, representing the clinical intricacies. The other half remains untouched, symbolizing the raw, unpredictable path of personal experiences.

As the room's gentle hum morphs into a classical melody, clinical practitioners gracefully glide across the floor, their moves sharp, well-practiced, and refined. Then, another group steps forth from the coffee shop's cozy corners. Their dance, less structured but deeply expressive, tells of personal trials, tribulations, and triumphs.

In this beautiful chaos, Joey and Jodie come together. Their dance is unique—a melding of clinical precision with the emotive swirls of lived experiences. Their movements make the message clear: True understanding stems from merging structured learning with heartfelt narratives.

Lost in the moment, Jodie reflects, "Knowledge offers guidance, but it's the real stories that provide depth and color." Joey, twirling her, adds, "When these worlds intertwine, they paint a holistic picture of healing." Journey with this chapter into the transformative blend of clinical insights and genuine life experiences. Witness how this symbiotic dance redefines the paradigm of holistic recovery.

In the healing space where clinical science and lived experience intersect, a vibrant mosaic unfolds, each thread contributing to a complex and compassionate recovery narrative. At the heart of this nexus are Joey and Jodie, social workers whose expertise extends beyond their degrees to the indelible marks of their own encounters with addiction. Their trajectory has been a mosaic of despair and revival, emotional vacuums filled with the wisdom textbooks can't convey.

"Medication-assisted treatment is a pathway," Joey says as he examines the chart of a client with opioid use disorder. "But it's not the only path. We must tailor the treatment to the individual."

Jodie nods in agreement. "Exactly. One size doesn't fit all. Van der Kolk emphasized the impact of trauma on the body and mind (Van der Kolk, 2014). Many of our clients' addictive behaviors stem from untreated traumatic experiences."

The gravity of her words weighs heavily on Joey. In his early twenties, his addiction consumed him like wildfire, forcing him to disconnect from family, education, and his sense of self. It had all begun as a coping mechanism for the physical abuse he faced at school. His clinical knowledge—valuable as it is—doesn't capture the shame he felt when his father called him worthless or the guilt that welled up when his mother cried over his deteriorating condition.

The silver lining? Joey's past has made him exceptionally attuned to the emotional landscape of his clients, understanding their resistance to treatments that can feel impersonal and intimidating.

Jodie carries her own history stitched into her memory like a collection of lessons she's gleaned over the years. Raised in a family where she felt alone, though she was not alone at all, she took solace in substances that dulled her emotional pain. Years later, as she navigates the challenges of being a social worker in many roles, Jodie always remembers her loneliness and desolation. It makes her a better listener and communicator, sensitive to her clients' unspoken fears and hopes.

"There's also the issue of harm reduction," she says, remembering Maté's research (Maté, 2008). "It's crucial we implement strategies that don't demonize the person for not being able to quit entirely. The journey toward recovery is non-linear."

Joey's eyes meet hers. They both understand the immense value of meeting people where they are and of adopting approaches like seeking safety, an integrative treatment designed to improve PTSD and substance abuse simultaneously (Najavits, 2002). He reflects on how their clinical training in MI (Miller & Rollnick, 2012) gains depth and richness when infused with their own memories of hitting rock bottom and scraping their way up.

"Have you ever noticed," Joey starts, "how our clients respond when we share a sliver of our own stories? It's as if a light goes on. It's the moment when clinical jargon gives way to human connection."

Jodie nods, her mind darting to the literature on the benefits of peer support in addiction treatment (Tracy & Wallace, 2016; White, 2009). "It's one of the purest forms of validation. And as you've always said, validation can be a powerful catalyst for change."

As they sift through complex case files—each a unique blend of environmental, genetic, and psychological factors (Kreek et al., 2005)—they find themselves continually grateful for the second chance they've been given. Their past experiences, dark as they were, now serve as beacons of hope for others. They can speak not just to the clinical aspects of addiction—withdrawal symptoms, comorbidities, and medication—but also to the crippling emotional disarray, the loss of identity, and the torturous path to reclaiming oneself.

"We often underestimate the resilience of the human spirit," Jodie says softly. "Each day, I see clients fighting battles many can't even comprehend, and their courage is awe-inspiring."

"And that's why we must foster a trauma-informed care approach," Joey adds, alluding to Harris and Fallot's work (Harris & Fallot, 2001). "We need to understand the root causes, recognize the signs of trauma, and create an environment that champions not just medical treatment but emotional and psychological healing."

Their symbiotic dance—clinical expertise coupled with the wisdom of lived experience—creates a therapeutic dynamic that transcends the sum of its parts. As they continue to work in tandem, they understand that they are revolutionizing the field not through medication alone or psychotherapy in isolation, but through a holistic approach that recognizes the dignity and worth of every life story.

As the chapter unfolds, we'll dig deeper into the undeniable benefits of this combined approach, from providing a richer context for intervention strategies to reducing stigma and enhancing long-term recovery outcomes. Because, as Joey and Jodie have realized, true healing doesn't just address the symptoms; it seeks to understand and nurture the whole person. And so, the dance continues, a graceful and ever-evolving testament to the power of a unified approach to addiction recovery.

Benefits of a Combined Approach

The COE was always busy, where Jodie and Joey had spent years absorbing facts, talking to clients, and treatment options. Yet, despite the chaos, it was also a sanctuary—a place where their clients could begin to make sense of their fragmented lives.

Jodie and Joey had a rare synergy in their professional roles, amplified by a sense of camaraderie from their harrowing pasts. They were survivors of addiction, steeped in the essence of the struggles they now aim to heal. Their survival wasn't a testament to their own strength alone but an intricate ballet between clinical knowledge and lived experience.

"Science can give us the 'what' and 'how' of addiction, but it is lived experience that gives us the 'why,'" Joey would often say. His words weren't just poetic flourishes but rooted in a complex reality. Clinical and experiential approaches are pivotal in trauma-informed care, but when united, they create an unparalleled formula for recovery.

Understanding the Intersection

Clinical wisdom asserts that trauma can often be at the root of addiction. The neurobiological pathways prove how trauma can manifest in self-destructive behavior (Van der Kolk, 2014). Yet, the numbers, percentages, and neural circuits are just a prelude to a richer, more complex narrative. Joey knew this firsthand. His "good family" was also an epicenter of dysfunction—a paradox that left scars hidden deep beneath the surface. Joey managed to detoxify his system through therapy and medications, but his lived experience offered others the context the real sense of "I've been there."

Jodie had a similar story. She had used substances as a coping mechanism, a way to fill a hollow void that had been excavated by a lack of emotional connection and complex trauma. Science labels this phenomenon as the self-medication hypothesis (Khantzian, 1997). But science couldn't encapsulate the feeling of sheer emptiness that substances falsely promised to fill, an emptiness Jodie could articulate in a way that clinical language could never encapsulate.

The Emotional Quotient

It's essential to realize that lived experiences bring emotional richness into the clinical environment, transforming it into a space of empathy and deep understanding (Goleman, 1995). Jodie and Joey had a gift—the gift of empathy, fortified by the scars of their past. When they spoke to clients about withdrawal, relapse, or family dysfunction, they weren't quoting textbooks or rattling off statistics; they were sharing a part of themselves.

The Silver Linings

You could say that Jodie and Joey's addictions almost killed them, but you could also argue that it saved them, not physically, but in a way that allowed them to fully grasp the humanity behind the addiction cycle (White, 2009). Their pasts were rife with moments where they had straddled the line between life and death—a vantage point that offered unique insights into harm reduction approaches (Marlatt & Witkiewitz, 2002). Their ability to frame the benefits of MI (Miller & Rollnick, 2012) and the importance of seeking safety (Najavits, 2002) was informed by the haunting but enlightening days when they were the clients, not the caregivers.

Bridging the Gap

Moreover, their lived experiences bridged the gap between clinical treatment and long-term recovery support, an alliance crucial for effective treatment (Tracy & Wallace, 2016). They were the living epitome of a trauma-informed approach, adhering to the guidelines set forth by SAMHSA (Abuse, 2014) but also expanding its scope through their personal narratives. Their story wasn't just theirs; it became a shared journey for everyone who walked through the COE's door—a tangible, vivid sight that clinical language could never fully capture.

The dance between clinical understanding and lived experience is symbiotic, each filling the gaps the other leaves, forming a fuller, richer blend of care. It's a mutualistic relationship where science gains a human face, and lived experiences are substantiated by empirical evidence. Neither could stand alone, but together, they can revolutionize how we approach recovery in mental health and SUD.

As we move forward, we explore into specific case studies that outline the successes and challenges of this combined approach. The proof, after all, lies in the outcomes, in the lives saved and the souls understood—a testament to the miraculous transformations that happen when clinical meets experience in a harmonious dance.

Case Studies: Successes and Challenges

In the dim-lit room of the COE, adorned with inspirational posters and tastefully potted plants, Joey could feel the tension as he sat across from April, a young woman struggling with opioid addiction. April's feet were restless, her fingers drumming on the chair's armrest. Joey recognized that restlessness, the frenetic energy barely contained beneath the surface. "You're not alone, April. You might feel like it, but I promise you're not," he said softly, leaning forward to make eye contact.

Similarly, Jodie encountered Sam, a middle-aged man battling alcoholism. In his glazed eyes, she saw a reflection of her past struggles, the abyss she had stared into for years. "Your pain is your pain, Lee. But you don't have to walk the path out of it alone."

These moments represent not mere exchanges between a social worker and a client but embody a symbiotic relationship that combines clinical insight with lived experience. For Joey and Jodie, the scars from their past battles with addiction serve as a tangible testament to their clients—evidence that recovery, while arduous, is possible.

April's Success: The Role of Empathy and Evidence-based Treatment

April had been in and out of rehabilitation centers and tried methadone and suboxone, but something was missing. Joey suspected that her unresolved trauma was creating a block. Through sessions that involved MI (Miller & Rollnick, 2012), April felt genuinely heard for the first time. While linking her to an outpatient therapist, Joey combined this with evidence-based trauma-informed care, incorporating insights from seeking safety (Najavits, 2002).

His understanding of April's trauma, rooted in clinical knowledge and lived experience, created an emotionally charged connection. With time, April began to trust the process. Her family started to notice the difference—the silver lining emerged when she began to teach her younger sister strategies to cope with their dysfunctional home environment, drawing upon her own experiences in therapy.

Lee's Challenge: The Struggle with Stigma and Acceptance

Despite Jodie's earnest attempts, Lee was still struggling. He was plagued by internalized stigma, a common hurdle that impedes recovery (Livingston et al., 2012). Sensing the need for more support, Jodie referred him to a peer-support group, recognizing its proven effectiveness in addiction treatment (Tracy & Wallace, 2016). Lee's attendance was sporadic at first. However, Jodie noticed that their sessions would be noticeably more productive whenever he did attend. The setbacks were fewer; the smiles were more frequent. "You're allowed to fail, Lee. I did it more times than I can count. But each time, I found something worthwhile in the struggle each time," Jodie shared, recalling her own failures and lessons learned. Lee's journey isn't over, but those glimmers of progress are his silver linings, tangible bits of hope that Jodie knows to celebrate.

The Symbiotic Dance: Why it Works

What made these relationships particularly impactful were not just the clinical interventions employed but the way these interventions were infused with genuine empathy and understanding. Joey and Jodie brought a unique sensitivity to trauma's pervasive impact on addiction (Van der Kolk, 2014; Harris & Fallot, 2001).

Their lived experience added a layer of nuance to their understanding of SAMHSA's concept of trauma and guidance for a trauma-informed approach (Abuse, 2014). This "humanized" the clinical approach, generating a nuanced treatment plan that was emotionally resonant.

Moreover, they used their journeys to illuminate the strengths and resilience that their clients couldn't yet see in themselves. The past traumas and failures, the scars they still carry, are transformed into powerful anecdotes of hope and human will, thus enabling the so-called "hungry ghosts" within their clients to finally seek nourishment through trust, hope, and acceptance (Maté, 2008).

Challenges Ahead

While the power of combining clinical and lived experience cannot be overstated, it isn't a cure-all. Sometimes, the rawness of their own pasts made emotional boundaries blurry for Joey and Jodie, emphasizing the need for continuous self-monitoring and self-care (Heatherton & Wagner, 2011).

The dance of clinical and experiential wisdom is beautiful, but it isn't without complexities. The delicate balance between being a clinician and an individual who has faced the same battles is a tightrope that requires focus, skill, and humanity.

As we transition into discussing the potential pitfalls of these blended models, let's remember that the challenges outweigh the potential. They merely represent the hurdles that must be acknowledged, addressed, and integrated into this symbiotic dance, ensuring that the weave of clinical and personal recovery narratives is as nuanced as the lives they aim to restore.

Navigating Potential Pitfalls in Blended Models

Navigating potential pitfalls in blended models isn't just a clinical exercise; it's a deeply emotional one, and few understand this better than Joey and Jodie. Survivors of life-threatening addictions, their lived experiences offer a vital backdrop against which the shortcomings of both clinical and experiential methods are thrown into sharp relief. Together, they represent the epitome of the symbiotic dance between clinical understanding and lived experience in the mental health and SUD field.

One pivotal issue is the power dynamics often accompanying the clinical experience. For Jodie, who came from a good but dysfunctional family, entering a clinical setting initially felt like stepping into another hierarchy where her voice was diminished. "I felt like a statistic; I felt diagnosed but not seen," she confessed. Maté (2008) discusses this problem, describing how the clinical landscape can often turn into a realm of "hungry ghosts," where patients and healthcare providers navigate complex emotional needs and systemic constraints. It's a poignant example of how clinical settings can inadvertently stifle the individuality and unique trauma histories that patients bring with them, an aspect emphasized by Harris & Fallot (2001) in their work on trauma theory.

Joey faced a different challenge. The clinical approach was too reductionistic for him, not capturing the rich collection of emotional, psychological, and sociological factors that contributed to his addiction. This is a pitfall cited by Heilig et al. (2022), who argue for a more holistic, socially contextualized understanding of addiction. Joey felt the clinicians were "fixing the symptoms, not the person. They never really asked about the years of emotional abuse I had suffered or the coping strategies

I had adopted, however unhealthy they were." As Van der Kolk (2014) points out, our bodies keep the score of our traumas, and Joey felt that the clinical approach he initially encountered was not equipped to read that score, let alone address it.

Yet, it would be a disservice to disregard the significant benefits of clinical expertise. Joey, for example, credits medication-assisted treatment and CBT for giving him the "toolbox" he needed to manage his addictive behaviors (Kar, 2011; Moos, 2007). For Jodie, the structured environment and the evidence-based approach of her treatment center helped her turn a corner.

However, it was when they began to integrate their lived experiences with their clinical encounters that the magic happened. "I remember sitting in a peer-support group for the first time," Jodie says, "and realizing that my experiences had value, that they weren't just cautionary tales or statistical data points but real, lived experiences that could help others" (Mead et al., 2001; Tracy & Wallace, 2016). In the same way, Joey found his purpose when he began working as a social worker, using MI to connect deeply with his clients, a method he says is like "talking to my past self" (Miller & Rollnick, 2012).

However, the fusion of clinical and lived experience has its stumbling blocks. There are ethical considerations, the risk of overidentification with clients, and the potential to blur professional boundaries. "It's a balancing act," Joey admits. "You can't get lost in someone else's story, but you can't hold it at arm's length either." This represents a major pitfall: the risk of "empathic distress," which Goleman (1995) outlines in his work on emotional intelligence. It requires skill and self-awareness to navigate this space effectively, as Marlatt & Witkiewitz (2002) discuss in their harm reduction approaches.

But the beauty lies in how Joey and Jodie have turned their pain into their power. The abuse, neglect, and household dysfunction they faced, far from breaking them, became the crucible in which their resilience was forged (Dube et al., 2003). In their roles as social workers, they have been able to give voice to those who are often voiceless, in effect repairing the effects of trauma through human connection, a phenomenon that Lieberman & Van Horn (2009) describe as crucial for healing.

Despite the pitfalls, the blended model, represented so vividly in the lives and work of Joey and Jodie, holds enormous promise. It's akin to a symbiotic dance, where each step, each twirl, however risky, makes the ensuing movement more graceful and meaningful. But as we relish this intricate dance, our eyes must be set on the horizon. There is yet another step to be considered—taking us from the present paradigms and pitfalls to a future where these models are blended and integrated seamlessly.

And so, as we pivot on the balls of our feet, let's envision this integrated future of care—a future that takes the clinical and the experiential, the scars and the stars, and melds them into something greater than the sum of its parts. It is to this vision that we now turn.

Envisioning an Integrated Future of Care

As we take a step back and breathe in the world Jodie and Joey have created—a world layered with the complexity of clinical expertise and hard-fought lived experience—we find a model of care that promises to revolutionize how we approach addiction and mental health treatment. They testify to the transformative power of pain, resilience, and genuine empathy. They remind us that our "scars" don't just lead where we've been wounded; they show us where we have healed and hint at how we can heal others (Dube et al., 2003).

But what does the future hold? How can we integrate this symphony of science and story into a healthcare system that often appears monolithic, rigid, and intractable?

First, we must recognize the importance of dismantling hierarchical models of care that inadvertently perpetuate shame and stigma. Jodie still remembers walking into her first clinical setting, feeling like her voice, laden with years of unspoken trauma, was immediately reduced to a mere case file. "The trauma was still living in me," she confides. "And although the clinicians were kind, their medical gaze seemed only to penetrate skin deep" (Van der Kolk, 2014). The journey toward an integrated future starts with clinicians doing more than treating symptoms; they must aim to treat the human behind the symptoms. Harris and Fallot's trauma theory offers a lens through which a more empathetic, nuanced model can emerge (Harris & Fallot, 2001).

Similarly, Joey echoes that the clinical setting often missed the intricate web of social, psychological, and emotional factors that contributed to his addiction. "I had to tell them my addiction isn't just a gene gone wrong or a brain circuit malfunctioning; it's a failed attempt at solving a problem. It's a coping mechanism turned traitor," Joey recalls (Khantzian, 1997). Although immensely valuable, the neurological view needs to co-exist with a more holistic understanding of addiction (Heilig et al., 2022). In this future of integrated care, Joey imagines a synergy of MI, medication-assisted treatment, and shared stories of survival, creating a holistic treatment approach (Miller & Rollnick, 2012; Kar, 2011; Moos, 2007).

The silver lining from their pasts is rich and instructive. Jodie's harrowing journey through addiction has made her extraordinarily skilled in navigating the nuances of trauma-informed care. She can speak to its necessity not as an abstract theory but as a tangible reality, something she's lived and breathed (Najavits, 2002). Joey, too, found that his past became his greatest asset in the field. "My past gives me an intimate knowledge of the patient's pain," he says. "But my recovery gives me the intimate belief in their potential."

And this is where the patient experience comes in. "Our systems need to create room for patients to be partners in their care, not just recipients," says Jodie. The clinician's science and the patient's story are equally valid evidence in treatment planning (White, 2009). In such a system, the term "patient" might even become obsolete, replaced by "partner" or "participant" in a mutual journey toward healing.

Moreover, the stigma surrounding addiction and mental health must be combatted at both micro and macro levels. To do so, a future of integrated care would prioritize anti-stigma interventions as a core component of treatment, fostering a culture of acceptance and understanding (Livingston et al., 2012).

But let's not underestimate the complications. This symbiotic dance has its own pitfalls—ethical considerations, potential for over-identification, blurring of boundaries, and what Goleman describes as "empathic distress" (Goleman, 1995). Jodie and Joey agree that the fusion of clinical and lived experience can be potent and precarious. "If not balanced well, the empathic overload can cripple you," says Joey (Marlatt & Witkiewitz, 2002).

Yet, despite these hurdles, imagine a world where integrated care is the norm rather than the exception. Imagine a world where Jodies and Joeys don't feel like outliers but are woven into the fabric of mainstream healthcare. As Joey puts it, "Our work, stories, and healing—individually and collectively—form the tapestry of what healthcare can become."

As we pause and reflect on this vision, let's appreciate that every moment of growth and integration brings us closer to a model of care that honors the diversity of human experience. It's a vision worth striving for that marries science and story, brain and heart, scars and stars.

With this, we pivot toward another frontier that holds promise for the future of recovery: the role of peer supporters. It's time to look into how these non-degree workers, with their own unique tapestries of lived experience, are not just ancillary characters but pivotal players in the transformative narrative of healing and recovery. And that's where we'll pick up in Chapter 9: The Value of Non-Degree Workers in Recovery.

CHAPTER 9

The Value of Non-Degree Workers in Recovery

Role of Peer Supporters in Recovery

As the sun gently dips, painting the horizon with shades of amber and mauve, the Whispers and Words bookstore undergoes a transformation that feels almost magical. Nestled between towering bookshelves that carry tales of adventure, love, and mystery, a quaint stage emerges. Here, the real heroes are not those who pen tales but those who've lived them. Their stories are written not on paper but in the wrinkles of their foreheads and the spark in their eyes.

The comforting aroma of roasted coffee fills the air, harmonizing with the soft rustle of pages being turned. The room's ambiance follows a rhythm reminiscent of a slow, comforting ballad. Deep in reflection, an individual takes center stage, ready to share their personal odyssey of recovery. Their only diploma? The visible and invisible scars, potent memories, and lessons learned in the fiercest battles. This testimony underscores the theme of our next chapter: the incredible impact and relevance of those healers who don't boast formal degrees but embody experience.

Amidst the audience, Joey and Jodie find themselves gravitating closer, each heartbeat in tune with the cadence of the storyteller's voice. Joey, visibly moved, whispers, "This is purity and wisdom in its rawest form. It's like a song where life's trials and triumphs shape the notes." Jodie's eyes shimmer, and she replies, "These brave souls guide us through the complex maze of healing. Their knowledge isn't from textbooks but from the very essence of life."

Let this chapter take you on a lyrical journey, celebrating the invaluable role of peer supporters. These are the real-life heroes, often hidden in plain sight, who bring unparalleled empathy and profound insights. Immerse yourself in their melodies and narratives and recognize that in the vast concert of recovery, the heart's impassioned song often leaves an indelible mark.

In the warm cocoon of trust and empathy that envelopes the COE, Joey and Jodie navigate the labyrinth of human suffering and hope with an intimacy that only few can truly fathom. Their credentials don't flaunt academic degrees—at least not initially. Yet, their mastery in addiction recovery speaks of hard-earned wisdom, resilience, and an acute understanding of trauma-informed care.

The setting is clinical, but the atmosphere is anything but sterile. Joey, at the COE, and Jodie, a BCM, embody a synergy of professional expertise and lived experience. They work in tandem with addiction medicine physicians, therapists, and nurses, united by a joint mission: the holistic recovery of their clients. But what sets Joey and Jodie apart is the essence of their humanness—their scars, which have become their stars in a strange yet transformative way.

Joey recalls the days when opioids made him feel like a balloon, floating in a sky where responsibilities and pain were clouds too distant to touch. However, those fleeting moments of artificial joy were mere pauses in a tragic odyssey that nearly claimed his life. Jodie, on her part, remembers how substances once promised an escape from an emotional maelstrom but instead bound her in shackles of addiction that took years to break.

Their odysseys are not merely stories but reservoirs of raw emotional intelligence (Goleman, 1995).

Their narratives enrich their interventions far beyond conventional therapy. While clinicians are armed with valuable techniques from CBT or MI (Miller & Rollnick, 2012; Kar, 2011), Joey and Jodie bring a poignant, emotional resonance to the table. When they discuss harm reduction (Marlatt & Witkiewitz, 2002) or the multi-pronged challenges of dual diagnosis involving PTSD and SUD (Najavits, 2002), their words breathe life into theories and guidelines. They speak not just to the mind but to the heart; their transformative power lies therein.

Drawing upon Van der Kolk's seminal work, "The Body Keeps the Score," they understand viscerally how trauma lodges itself not just in the recesses of the mind but manifests in bodily symptoms (Van der Kolk, 2014). They embrace Maté's "In the Realm of Hungry Ghosts" to explore addiction as an intricate web of emotional pain, social disconnection, and neurobiological shifts (Maté, 2008). Their counseling sessions become sanctuaries where clients feel seen, heard, and profoundly understood (Harris & Fallot, 2001).

Peer support isn't merely ancillary to formal treatments; it's a cornerstone. Research on the effectiveness of peer-based addiction recovery elucidates the profound insights and unparalleled empathy that non-degree workers like Joey and Jodie offer (White, 2009; Tracy & Wallace, 2016). Sharing personal narratives creates a relatable connection that often makes a pivotal difference in recovery. This emotional rapport builds stronger, more durable bridges to treatment adherence and long-term recovery (Mead, S., Hilton, D., & Curtis, L., 2001).

Joey and Jodie are living proof of SAMHSA's concept of a trauma-informed approach, which emphasizes physical, psychological, and emotional safety and helps survivors rebuild a sense of control and empowerment (Abuse, S., 2014). Their work has a ripple effect—empowering clients, enriching the recovery community, and influencing policy. They have given voice to those who were once voiceless, imbuing the system with a vital paradigm shift toward understanding addiction not as a moral failing but as a complex interplay of biological, psychological, and social factors (Knight, K. R., Lopez, A. M., et al., 2014; Livingston, J. D., Milne, T., et al., 2012).

Joey and Jodie's ascent in the academic ladder—Joey almost completing his Doctor of Social Work and Jodie earning her Bachelor of Social Work—speaks volumes about their resilience and the evolving perspectives within the addiction recovery field. They were given a chance by two behavioral health executives, Kellie McKevitt, MSW, and Cheryld Emala, MSW, LCSW, who looked beyond traditional credentials to recognize the raw, transformative power of lived experience.

In their journey, Joey and Jodie show us that the most profound wisdom often comes not from textbooks or lecture halls but from the very crucible of life. As they continue serving as peer supporters, they remind us of the indispensable role that non-degree workers play in the recovery landscape—a role transcending academic labels and tapping into the core of our shared humanity.

As we move on in this chapter, let us transition to another profound truth: the indispensable importance of lived experience in treatment. In a world where emotional and mental challenges are increasingly complex, who better to guide us through the murky waters of recovery than those who have not only charted these waters but have also found their way to the shore?

Importance of Lived Experience in Treatment

In the walls of the COE, a sanctuary for opiate use disorder treatment, clinical supervisor Joey and BCM Jodie are living testaments to the power of resilience. Theirs is a love story woven through the tapestry of trauma, addiction, and recovery.

They both come from good families despite being dysfunctional, and neither held any formal degree when they began working in the field of addiction and mental health. Their journeys provide critical insight into the importance of lived experience in treatment, a concept often overlooked by traditional academia and bureaucratic systems.

As Van der Kolk wrote in *The Body Keeps the Score*, trauma imprints itself on both mind and body, leaving indelible marks that shape one's interactions with the world (Van der Kolk, 2014). Joey and Jodie understood this viscerally from their own lives, filled with moments that saw them dangling precariously between life and death due to addiction. Joey overdosed three times before age thirty; Jodie had faced PTSD and addiction. Their silver linings came from their lived experiences—the emotional memory and empathic understanding they could offer clients, building a bridge of trust that conventional therapy sometimes fails to construct.

Both believed the empathetic approach to treatment aligns well with the tenets of trauma-informed care. This methodology seeks to understand the patient beyond the scope of their medical symptoms (Harris & Fallot, 2001). They have seen firsthand how a one-size-fits-all clinical approach can overlook the deeply rooted psychological factors affecting their clients. As Gabor Maté elucidated in *In the Realm of Hungry Ghosts*, addiction is often an escape from emotional pain or trauma (Maté, 2008).

While formal education provides a structured learning environment to understand clinical diagnosis and treatment, the nuanced education Joey and Jodie received through their lived experiences is invaluable. They are aware of the factors contributing to addiction, such as bullying, neglect, and household dysfunction, all of which strongly correlate with the risk of illicit drug use (Dube et al., 2003). Both could resonate profoundly with their clients' struggles, sometimes without uttering a single word.

Joey remembered working with a young man in his early twenties battling heroin addiction. During a MI session (Miller & Rollnick, 2012), the young man broke down, sharing that he started using drugs after his mother passed away. Joey could relate, remembering his descent into addiction after losing a loved one. His eyes met the young man's, and without having to say anything, they both understood the depth of the pain. It was a moment that transcended academic training—a healing communion possible only through the mirror of lived experience.

Jodie had similar connections with many of her female clients. One woman, a survivor of sexual assault, found it challenging to trust health-care providers. Jodie's approach, grounded in trauma-informed care (Harris & Fallot, 2001) and her own experiences, helped the client feel seen and understood. With Jodie's support, the woman found the courage to participate in group therapy, later citing Jodie as the godsend peer-support specialist for feeling safe enough to share her story.

Kellie and Cheryld recognized the incredible value that Joey and Jodie brought to the treatment center. Their approach aligned with peer-based recovery support, demonstrating better outcomes for addiction treatment (White, 2009; Tracy & Wallace, 2016). While Joey and Jodie did not initially have academic credentials, their lived experience and the richness of emotional intelligence they brought to their roles were unparalleled (Goleman, 1995).

The couple often found solace in their shared mission, uplifting each other during challenging times. "You remember that lady we thought wouldn't make it?" Joey would ask. "She's in college now, studying to become a social worker." Jodie would smile, her eyes shining. "Yes, love, we've planted seeds. And they're beginning to sprout."

But it isn't all sunshine and rainbows; there are challenges, especially for non-degree workers like Joey and Jodie when they started their journey. Although their experience is a treasure trove of emotional and practical wisdom, it often clashes with the conventional medical model or colleagues with a more traditional academic background. This conflict sets the stage for our next discussion: non-degree workers' challenges in recovery.

Challenges Faced by Non-Degree Workers

The air in the COE is a blend of tension and hope; this mingles with the aroma of warm coffee brewing in the corner. For those who work here, there's a sense of urgency but also a sense of mission. Joey scans the faces in the morning meeting with his colleagues—each carrying the weight of human lives in their hands.

The phone rings; it's his wife Jodie, now a BCM in another job setting. Their initial silence is an unspoken pact: they know the road they've traveled and the daily stakes they face.

Before they found their place in the COE, Joey and Jodie were survivors of addiction that nearly claimed their lives. They were far from the conventional, degree-armed professionals one might expect to find in their current roles. Yet, their lived experience made them invaluable, complementing their academic credentials with authentic empathy and hands-on knowledge.

The Weight of Paper

In the United States, the escalating work shortage is especially pronounced in the human services field. There's a widening gap between the demand for qualified professionals and the number of degree-holding candidates available (White, 2009). This dilemma raises a profound question: Should academic qualifications be the sole criteria for hiring?

While academic rigor brings valuable skills and a theoretical foundation, it can't emulate the nuances captured only through lived experience. As Maté (2008) insightfully replies, addiction isn't just a clinical problem to be addressed; it's an emotional and psychological labyrinth only those who have navigated it genuinely understand.

The lack of formal credentials presented an uphill battle for Joey and Jodie. Their resumes wouldn't survive the first sift-through of a traditional HR department. Questions about their credibility were frequent, often laced with skepticism. "Can they adhere to evidence-based approaches?" some wondered, citing Marlatt & Witkiewitz (2002) or Miller & Rollnick (2012) to emphasize the importance of academic understanding.

The Power of Empathy

However, what couldn't be captured on paper was their exceptional emotional intelligence (EI) (Goleman, 1995). This EI, forged through their shared crucible of addiction, allowed them to approach their work with a nuanced, genuinely trauma-informed sensitivity (Van der Kolk, 2014; Harris & Fallot, 2001). As Najavits (2002) asserts in her work, treating SUD necessitates a trauma-sensitive approach. And who better to be trauma-sensitive than those who've personally experienced the stinging brunt of it?

They understood the unspoken. When clients are introverted, they sense the wall of shame or fear behind the silence (Livingston et al., 2012). They navigated conversations about substance use and mental health to reduce stigma, making them aware of how societal judgments can be internalized and exacerbate the problem (Tracy & Wallace, 2016). They engaged in MI, not merely as a clinical tool but as a personal communication style molded by their past of facing addiction.

The Silver Lining: Strength Through Struggle

Their previous addiction struggles were not disqualifications but rather essential assets. The skills and insights they gained were aligned with many evidence-based practices. For instance, they implemented the principles of peer-based recovery support, as delineated by White (2009), in a manner that was intuitively resonant with their clients. The couples' degrees were testaments to their capacity for professional growth and depth. Still, their most valuable contributions could not be graded or framed. They were the human elements of compassion, empathy, and understanding, refined not in classrooms but in the darkest corners of life.

Chief Executives of a large behavioral health agency, Kellie and Cheryld saw the untapped potential in Joey and Jodie. They understood that academic degrees are a part of the puzzle but not the complete picture. As Moos (2007) noted, the active ingredients of effective treatment for substance use disorders are often non-specific factors, such as the quality of the therapeutic relationship and client engagement—qualities that Joey and Jodie exemplified.

Bridging the Gap

Joey and Jodie's journeys are testaments to the untapped value that non-degree workers bring in addressing addiction and mental health crises, particularly in a labor shortage struggling to meet demand. Both come from families with their share of dysfunction, but their lived experience has filled them with wisdom that only adversity can teach. It's a wisdom they are now sharing to save other lives.

Their challenges have led to a broader discussion on the indispensability of such individuals in recovery. The invaluable role they play adds a human touch to the realm of addiction and mental health services. It is an exemplary model, leading us to the following crucial conversation—building bridges between professionals and peer supporters. The world needs both, as interconnected pieces of a complex puzzle, to usher in a truly comprehensive, empathetic, and effective system of recovery.

Building Bridges Between Professionals and Peer Supporters

In an era plagued by labor shortages across multiple sectors in the United States, particularly within human services, the role of non-degree workers in aiding recovery takes on an unprecedented gravity as clinical supervisors and BCMs at a behavioral health agency, like Joey and Jodie, stand as living testaments to the transformative power of lived experience, merged with formal education in mental health and SUD fields.

Their journeys, however, were not straight paths paved with academic milestones. They entered the field without degrees, armed only with life experience and the sheer will to contribute to recovery in their community. For them, each day at work doesn't just involve analyzing case studies; it's about understanding the soul-shattering depths of despair, the shuddering withdrawals, the gnawing emotional voids—because they've been there.

The gulf between clinicians and peer supporters can be as comprehensive as fraught, perpetuated by a system that traditionally places more value on academic credentials than lived experience. But as Maté (2008) elucidates in In the Realm of Hungry Ghosts, addiction isn't a condition that solely afflicts the body and mind; it ravages the soul, and who better to guide someone through that labyrinth than those who have navigated it themselves?

Kellie and Cheryld understood this potential for transformative empathy. Citing the trauma-informed approach suggested by Harris & Fallot (2001), they hired Joey and Jodie not despite their histories but because of them. A living theme for this approach is, "Addiction doesn't discriminate, and neither should our approach to healing." The duo's EI (Goleman, 1995), in relating to clients, surpassed what many of their degree-holding colleagues could offer. They were bridges between worlds.

For Joey and Jodie, their past experiences with addiction were not blemishes to be concealed but badges of resilience to be displayed. As Van der Kolk (2014) explains in The Body Keeps the Score, trauma has a way of encapsulating itself in the neural pathways, creating patterns of thought and behavior that are hard to break. Joey's struggle with opiates began as a misguided attempt at self-medication (Khantzian, 1997). Despite the odds, Joey saw his recovery as a "silver lining," leveraging his own experiences to validate and inspire his clients. As Mead, Hilton, & Curtis (2001) emphasize, he discovered that peer support is a two-way street, often giving the supporter as much of a healing experience as the supported.

Jodie, too, harnessed her past into a beacon of hope for others. Having dealt with addiction and trauma (Dube et al., 2003) and its emotional reverberations, she practiced what Najavits (2002) proposes in Seeking Safety: the dual treatment of PTSD and substance abuse. Her addiction was less about the high and more about filling an emotional chasm. Recovery was both physical, emotional, and psychological, a multifaceted approach (Marlatt & Witkiewitz, 2002) that she enthusiastically applies in her work today.

Clinical knowledge and lived experience have been revolutionary for their clients. In Joey's MI sessions (Miller & Rollnick, 2012) or Jodie's trauma-informed case management, they utilize professional techniques without erasing the human touch. In doing so, they subconsciously challenge the stigmas around addiction (Livingston et al., 2012), making their clients feel less like "cases" and more like human beings struggling with complex issues.

Yet, a question remains. In a country where professional shortages persist, how can we afford to ignore such a potent pool of human resources? A 2016 study by Tracy & Wallace suggests that peer- support groups in addiction treatment have significant benefits. So why are we not leveraging this more? To overlook the transformative potential of non-degree workers, particularly those with lived experience, is a missed opportunity and a glaring oversight in an industry desperate for change.

Joey and Jodie serve as proof that when we embrace diverse talents, the benefits reverberate far beyond the individual, fostering a richer, more nuanced fabric of care. They remind us that in the labyrinthine journey of addiction and recovery, sometimes the most reliable guides are those who have walked the path themselves.

This leads us to ponder the enormous potential and the future of peer-led initiatives in recovery. As we venture further into this evolving landscape, we must ask, "What would it look like to genuinely institutionalize the wisdom born from struggle and weave it into the fabric of our treatment models? This will focus on our discussion: "The Future of Peer-Led Initiatives in Recovery."

The Future of Peer-Led Initiatives in Recovery

Joey glanced across the desk, locking eyes with his wife, Jodie. The air was charged, not with tension but with a shared sense of purpose. Their past flashed before his eyes for a fleeting second—the crippling cycles of addiction, the broken promises, and the importance of existential dread that had bound them. Yet, even in that dark journey, they had found silver linings: raw, valuable experiences that became their foundation in aiding others to heal.

They had traveled this road, deeply pitted with dysfunction from their seemingly perfect families, but this very tumultuous path had fortified them as agents of change. At the COE, Joey felt a tinge of gratitude. Jodie, although having moved on to another agency as a BCM, was still his unwavering partner in this mission.

According to Van der Kolk, trauma remains stored within the bodily self, affecting the brain and body's capacity to engage with the present (2014). But Joey and Jodie understood this at a gut level long before they read about it. They lived it.

When Joey talks about MI to assess a patient's readiness to change, he isn't simply quoting Miller and Rollnick (2012); he's revisiting his own pivotal conversations with Jodie. Conversations that shifted the odds for them.

Jodie felt the same way. She uses Najavits's *Seeking Safety* model to deal with PTSD and substance abuse (2002) but supplements it with the wisdom gained from her own path to sobriety. The ability to weave lived experience with evidence-based approaches gives their methods an indefinable quality of authenticity that a degree alone couldn't provide.

Peer-led initiatives like theirs have started to be recognized as potent tools in the recovery arsenal. White (2009) stated the historical significance and scientific validation of peer-based addiction recovery support. In practice, Joey and Jodie have taken this a step further by incorporating a trauma-informed approach into their peer-support framework, acknowledging Harris and Fallot's vision for trauma-sensitive service systems (2001).

While degrees and formal education provide a theoretical grounding, the pair are walking testimonies that recovery is also an emotionally charged journey. They understand the layers of stigma, validated by Livingston et al. (2012), which many of their clients feel because they have felt it themselves. Their families, though well-intentioned, perpetuated a form of ignorance that Gorski (1990) identified as a risk for relapse.

But this ignorance is not impossible. A combination of lived experience, emotion, and science can shatter it. Joey and Jodie have experienced how trauma, family dysfunction, and substance abuse can form an interlinked chain, described by Topitzes, Mersky, & Reynolds (2012). Yet they are living proof that these chains can be broken.

The efficacy of peer-led initiatives is not just in the advice or counseling given, but in the transformational emotional exchange that occurs. When Joey speaks, his words are imbued with vulnerability and resilience that can only come from being there. When Jodie listens, she does so with a sensitivity to unsaid emotions, validated by Lieberman & Van Horn (2009) that can only be honed by her own unspoken traumas.

Amid all this, their past addiction experiences offer silver linings that make the path to recovery tangible for those they help. Joey recalls the solace he found in art during his darkest days, a positive outlet he recommends to others. Jodie remembers the strength she drew from the community, a lesson she uses to encourage participation in group therapy sessions.

So, what does the future hold for peer-led initiatives in recovery? To answer that, look no further than Joey and Jodie. Their work, merging empirical wisdom with the irreplaceable value of lived experience, is set to continue and expand. Tracy and Wallace (2016) affirmed that peer-support groups are pivotal in treating addiction. Joey and Jodie are amplifying this truth by humanizing it, by giving it a face—two faces, to be precise, deeply etched with scars but shining like stars.

Yet, as we celebrate these lived-experience workers, it becomes increasingly important to question why formal education is often considered superior in treatment scenarios. This leads us to a much-needed discussion on the status quo of valuing degrees in treatment, which we will explore in Chapter 10: Reevaluating Worker Value Beyond Degrees.

CHAPTER 10

Reevaluating Worker Value Beyond Degrees

The Status Quo of Valuing Degrees in Treatment

The familiar hum of Whispers and Words greets early risers, as the cafe side begins brewing its first cups of the day. By the window, an elderly craftsman, fingers showing signs of years of dedication, is engrossed in a conversation with a young scholar, her desk littered with textbooks and academic journals.

Their animated exchange draws in patrons. The craftsman speaks of life's raw lessons, while the scholar cites researched theories. To the onlookers, it's a compelling dance between the world of academia and lived experience.

From their cozy corner, Joey and Jodie watch this interaction unfold. Jodie's eyes trace the contours of the scholar's books and muses, "Knowledge from institutions is like a guiding star." Joey adds, looking at the craftsman's hands, "Yet the stories etched in the lines of those hands, they form constellations of their own."

This chapter beckons readers to a more profound realm of understanding, challenging the traditional emphasis on formal education. As you turn the pages, ponder on this: In the ever-evolving narrative of recovery, shouldn't the wisdom of the streets harmonize with the lessons of the classrooms? Join us on a journey where every voice, degree-clad or not, enriches the symphony of healing and hope.

As Joey and Jodie sat, musing over the interplay between academic prowess and the lived experience they had just witnessed, they could not help but relate it to their journeys. Both of them had come a long way from the throes of opiate addiction—transformed souls and now change-makers in addiction recovery. Joey, a licensed social worker (LSW), and Jodie, a BCM, were walking proof that recovery was not just possible but could pave the way for fulfilling lives.

However, their paths were not garnished with the gleaming Ph.D. or Psy.D letters, yet. Those were tracks they deeply respected but did not tread. As Maté's *In the Realm of Hungry Ghosts* delineates, the labyrinth of addiction is complex, often stemming from trauma, pain, and systemic dysfunction (Maté, 2008). It is not an academic degree but rather the scars that bind Joey and Jodie to their work.

As they watched the sun rise higher, they realized that their lack of formal degrees often left them feeling marginalized in the recovery ecosystem. There was an overwhelming sense of the valuation of a degree over lived experience, leaving some of the most transformative stories and practical methods on the outskirts of mainstream treatment approaches.

Joey reflected on his time in the COE, recalling how he had read about many clinical theories but was not formally trained in them (Najavits, 2002). He remembered how skeptical some clinicians were with him, primarily because Joey did not come from a background rich in academic studies. "There is a tinge of irony," Joey mused, "for it is often those scars that allow us to connect so deeply with the people we serve, that let us glimpse into their unspoken pains and traumas."

Jodie nodded, her mind drifting to the families she had worked with—families that looked so much like her own, well-intended but dysfunctionally toxic. She thought about the principles of trauma theory and how essential it was to recognize and respond to the effects of all types of trauma (Harris & Fallot, 2001). "Sometimes, the healing journey is not about what we have learned from textbooks, but about understanding the language of trauma stored within the body" (Van der Kolk, 2014). That language, she thought, could sometimes be best interpreted by those who had spoken it themselves.

Their conversations about degrees, or the lack thereof, were not merely musings; they carried a real heaviness, a sense of diminished value. Joey would never forget when he was passed over for a promotion in favor of someone with a master's degree but less hands-on experience. As White's work on peer-based addiction recovery support suggests, the power of empathetic connection should not be underestimated (White, 2009). Joey knew he had that power. The silver lining, however, was that the rejection made him double down on his commitment. While working in his COE peer-support program, he grew, which had efficacy (Tracy & Wallace, 2016). This program allowed recovered addicts to use their lived experiences as a tool for change.

Moreover, despite her professional demeanor and the robustness of her programs, Jodie often found her proposals met with skepticism due to her lack of academic backing. However, she, too, found her silver lining. She channeled her disappointment into community education at the non-profit Club Serenity, drawing from research on stigma reduction (Livingston et al., 2012). She served in outreach events and other fundraisers that gave harm reduction principles a voice (Marlatt & Witkiewitz, 2002) with stories from her past, highlighting the crucial role of understanding trauma in addiction treatment (Van der Kolk, 2014).

At the time, they might not have had the certificates and diplomas that many others did, but their credibility was etched in the lines on their palms and the years of personal struggle and transformation they had endured. Their understanding of addiction went beyond neurotransmitters and circuitry (Heilig et al., 2022): it reached the emotional, social, and psychological realms (Khantzian, 1997).

So, as Joey and Jodie watched the craftsman and scholar finally part ways, each richer from the exchange, they returned to a realization that defined not just their relationship but their life's work: "In a field like ours, there should be room for both the scholar and the craftsman—for the book-learned and the life-taught. Because healing comes not just from one or the other, but from the intricate interplay between the two."

This sentiment leads us to our following crucial discussion: real-life impact versus academic credentials. When it comes to healing from the multifaceted experience of addiction, shouldn't we consider the symphony of approaches and backgrounds, the harmony of scholarly understanding and life-taught wisdom? In the following section, we will dig deeper into how these two forms of expertise coexist and can deeply enrich one another, painting a more nuanced picture of recovery and resilience.

Real-Life Impact vs. Academic Credentials

Meet Joey and Jodie, embodying resilience, compassion, and, most importantly, real-life experience in addiction treatment. Their names resonate with more authority than any alphabet soup of academic credentials trailing behind a surname. They have been through the crucible—once caught in the cyclone of addiction, they have emerged as bedrocks in the COE.

Joey's Journey

At the COE, Joey's past addiction experiences often serve as an informal credential, providing a tangible link to the recovering addicts he counsels. Once confined to the walls of despair and numbing doses of heroin, Joey survived the physical entanglements and the emotional and mental shackles. When Joey says he understands, it is not textbook empathy; it is the resonance of a man who has walked through the same hellfire.

His role is not just supervisory; it is transformative. The sentiments resonate with Van der Kolk's assertion that trauma leaves an indelible impact on the body and mind, requiring holistic healing beyond medications (Van der Kolk, 2014). Through his lived experiences, Joey often uses this whole-body approach to treat OUD clients.

Jodie's Light

Jodie, as a BCM, is another beacon of lived wisdom. She understands the realm of "hungry ghosts," the emptiness and ceaseless craving Maté speaks of (Maté, 2008). Her past life has given her an advanced degree in the emotional intelligence needed to guide patients through the intricacies of recovery. She comes across not as a distant clinician but as an empathetic mentor, integrating trauma-informed approaches in her service, aligned with the guidelines from SAMHSA (Abuse, 2014).

The Silver Linings

Joey and Jodie credit their recovery journey and the lessons learned for the remarkable success rate in their respective work positions. Their backgrounds do not come from dysfunction; they come from good families with their share of issues, like most families. However, they both struggled with childhood traumas and household dysfunction, elements well-documented as precursors to addiction (Dube et al., 2003). However, those experiences equipped them with harm-reduction strategies that textbooks seldom teach (Marlatt & Witkiewitz, 2002).

Joey remembers successfully navigating a critical situation involving a client on the brink of relapse, using his intuitive grasp of the client's emotional state. His understanding of MI (Miller & Rollnick, 2012) was not a lesson learned in college but amid his journey through addiction and recovery.

Jodie has had a similar trajectory. In her current role, she has helped several women transition back to social settings post-recovery, mitigating the effects of trauma and PTSD, guided by principles of MI (Kar, 2011) and trauma-informed care (Harris & Fallot, 2001).

Their past addictions taught them the values of peer-based recovery, which empowers individuals to participate in their healing actively (White, 2009; Tracy & Wallace, 2016). Joey and Jodie have become living proof that skills acquired through life's hard lessons can sometimes outweigh the teachings from any academic curriculum. They are tangible examples of education not confined to mortar boards and lecture halls.

The Reevaluation

What makes Joey and Jodie indispensable in the fight against addiction is their humanizing touch—something that resonates with patients on a level academic credentials often cannot reach. They are, in essence, practical applications of Najavits's *Seeking Safety* model, merging PTSD and substance abuse treatment through the lens of lived experience (Najavits, 2002).

So, when evaluating the worth of a worker in the addiction recovery field, it is time we look beyond academic qualifications. As evidenced by Joey and Jodie's profound impact, lived experience, training, and ongoing education can create the most effective agents of change. Credentials are essential, but they should be within the skills and passion professionals like Joey and Jodie bring.

Their stories force us to reevaluate worker value, challenging the traditional notions that underlie our definitions of "qualified." In the next chapter, we will dig deeper into how the most effective treatment is often a blend of skills and passion, transcending the limits of academic theory to reach the depths of human emotion and experience.

Highlighting Skills and Passion in Treatment

In the muted light of his office at the COE, Joey stares at his computer screen, flipping through electronic client files. As a clinical supervisor, his role carries a unique blend of administrative tedium and emotional gravity. In another setting, his wife, Jodie, engages with clients as a BCM. They have both journeyed far from their respective encounters with opioid addiction, both their own and each other's, and have lived to tell the tale.

A tangible, almost real sense of empathy emanates from Joey and Jodie; they bring an unspoken understanding to their work, enriching each client's recovery journey. This empathic connection is borne out of their lived experiences, a nuanced human element transcending the sterile aura of diplomas and certifications hanging on their walls. They know firsthand the cage of addiction, the howling loneliness, the festering guilt, the relentless gnaw of withdrawal.

Their clients can sense this. "I do not know how to explain it," a young man once confided in Joey, "but when I talk to you, it is like you get me, man. Like really understand what I am going through.» And Joey did. So did Jodie. This ability to connect emotionally is not something they learned from textbooks or college courses but from the grit and grime of their battles with addiction. As Maté (2008) poignantly noted in *In the Realm of Hungry Ghosts*, the essence of addiction is about filling a void, a gnawing emotional emptiness, often stemming from trauma or pain (Maté, 2008).

However, this field, addicted to qualifications, often overlooks the incalculable worth of lived experience. The human element is frequently sidelined in an industry obsessed with degrees, certifications, and methodologies. Nevertheless, as researchers like White (2009) have argued, peer-based addiction recovery support can offer something unique and invaluable (White, 2009).

Joey reflects on his darkest moments, years ago when he was wrapped in the cold embrace of opioids. The tunnel was bleak, but there were flickers of light. He remembers a support group facilitator—himself a recovered addict—whose genuine understanding provided Joey the lifeline he needed. The facilitator did not just recite protocols; he recognized the subtext of Joey's despair. He understood that the "body keeps the score, bearing the imprints of trauma that often underlie addiction (Van der Kolk, 2014).

Jodie, too, cherishes silver linings from her past, like her therapist, who encouraged her to share her feelings to help her release her pain.

They utilize MI, a technique expounded by Miller and Rollnick (2012), to tap into each client's intrinsic motivation to change (Miller & Rollnick, 2012). They also adopt Najavits's (2002) *Seeking Safety* model, focusing on coping skills and grounding techniques to address PTSD and substance abuse (Najavits, 2002).

Joey and Jodie emerged from families with their dysfunctions and complexities, further enriching their understanding of the social and familial dynamics often enmeshed in addiction (Dube et al., 2003). In the COE, they encountered individuals from myriad backgrounds, adding layers to their comprehension of how various stigmas, prejudices, and systemic issues play into addiction and recovery (Livingston et al., 2012).

So, when we reevaluate worker value in addiction recovery, let us look beyond the conventional barometers of academic degrees and clinical training. Joey and Jodie's lived experiences, their transformative journeys from scars to stars, offer professional expertise and the irreplaceable human touch, the essence of compassion and empathy. This calls for a broader, more inclusive lens in understanding the complex tapestry of qualifications that workers bring, especially in such a profoundly human field.

However, this is only part of the story. As we venture further into the realm of addiction treatment and recovery, we must also turn our focus toward another vital element. Beyond skills and passion lies another terrain: the transformative power of empathy and understanding.

The Transformative Power of Empathy and Understanding

What is the value of a human life? For Jodie and Joey, a married couple both surviving the throes of near-fatal addiction, this is more than a philosophical question; it is a daily affirmation that shapes their work in addiction recovery.

Joey and Jodie agree that their past experiences—no matter how painful—were their most significant assets in connecting with and helping their clients.

There is something profound about the way Joey talks to a new client. He has a kind of aura that fills the room—perhaps it manifests the emotional intelligence that Goleman (1995) expounded on. When he leans in, makes eye contact, and speaks, it is not just a clinical interaction; it is one human being reaching into the soul of another. Clients often find it startling, for Joey understands the intricate web of guilt, shame, and trauma that addiction weaves around a person's life in ways that most professionals simply cannot (Maté, 2008; Najavits, 2002).

In her setting, Jodie practices what could be described as a "trauma-informed approach" based on the principles of safety and empowerment (Harris & Fallot, 2001). When a client sits in her office, usually fidgety and nervous, she gives them space to narrate their stories. Jodie is not just listening; she is embodying empathy. She understands that, as Van der Kolk (2014) elucidates, "the body keeps the score." Her history with addiction has engrained a deep, emotional understanding of what trauma does to the mind and body.

The silver linings in Joey and Jodie's pasts are not just figments of hopeful imagination but tangible benefits they bring to their work. Joey recounts how he used to steal to fund his addiction. Now, that same sense of strategic cunning allows him to navigate the bureaucratic mazes that often prevent his clients from accessing care. Jodie, whose addiction isolated her from family and friends, uses her experience to forge connections with her clients. She knows what it is like to be stigmatized (Livingston et al., 2012), making her an effective advocate for those who are voiceless.

Joey and Jodie exemplify the power of peer-based addiction recovery support, as chronicled by White (2009). The wisdom of lived experience becomes a scaffold for building new lives (Mead et al., 2001; Tracy & Wallace, 2016). Their relational skills, refined through adversity, have become their most potent tools—more effective than any degree could ever confer.

The couple's journey also shines a light on the complexities and vulnerabilities that surround addiction. It is not just about substance misuse; it is about adverse childhood experiences (Dube et al., 2003), self-medication (Khantzian, 1997), impulsivity (Kreek et al., 2005), and often, a history of trauma (Kar, 2011). Understanding this, Joey and Jodie integrate harm reduction approaches (Marlatt & Witkiewitz, 2002) and MI techniques (Miller & Rollnick, 2012) into their practice, recognizing that every patient's path to recovery is uniquely theirs.

Significantly, they realize the need for a paradigm shift toward a trauma-informed service system in the broader healthcare landscape (Harris & Fallot, 2001). They are not just service providers but catalysts for systemic change, leading by example and forging a way for others with lived experience to follow.

This brings us to a pivotal point—an urgent need to reassess what "value" means in providing addiction and mental health care. Joey and Jodie's experiences resonate with an undeniable truth: Empathy, understanding, and lived experience are often more impactful than a barrage of degrees and certificates hanging on an office wall. In their eyes, the lessons learned from the school of hard knocks are just as credible, if not more so, than the lessons learned in lecture halls.

As we discuss broader acceptance, it is vital to recognize that while degrees and professional training offer essential knowledge and skills, they should not be the sole yardstick for measuring a healthcare worker's capabilities. It is time we give due respect and space to the transformative power of empathy and understanding qualities often forged in the crucible of personal experience. Thus, as we move forward, let us expand our perception of what it truly means to be a qualified and effective professional in addiction recovery.

A Call for Broader Acceptance in the Professional Sphere

A bleak, rainy afternoon cast a gray hue over the city skyline as Joey sat at his desk, surrounded by his clinical supervision files. Across the miles, Jodie, his wife and fellow survivor of addiction, reviewed her stack of case management notes. On the surface, they were merely professionals in addiction recovery, fulfilling their daily duties. However, underneath the polished façade, their shared past of addiction painted with struggle, resilience, and a profound understanding of what it means to recover.

We often assign value to professionals based on their educational credentials, overlooking the vital ingredient of lived experience that people like Joey and Jodie bring to their roles. Even in the most evidence-based paradigms of addiction treatment, degrees and diplomas cannot replace the empathy and understanding that come from surviving the very thing one seeks to treat. "To truly help someone, you must reach into your own experiences," says Maté (2008). Such experiences provide an unparalleled understanding of the complexities of addiction—a genuine embrace of its nuances and irregularities (*In the Realm of Hungry Ghosts: Close Encounters with Addiction*).

Joey and Jodie are no strangers to such complexities. Both came from good families with their own set of dysfunctions, environments where love and chaos often intermingled. For years, they stumbled down the rabbit hole of addiction, leaving them perilously close to losing it all. However, the darkest corners of their pasts were also the bedrock of their strength. In their shared journeys through recovery, the stumbles and falls became lessons, propelling them forward with an enhanced sense of self-awareness. These "scars" from their pasts have become their "stars," glistening with knowledge and empathy.

While the traumas of addiction left their mark—both physically and psychologically—Joey and Jodie found that "the body keeps the score," as Van der Kolk (2014) so astutely noted. The impact of trauma on the brain and body is profound, but so too is the human capacity for resilience (*The Body Keeps the Score: Brain, Mind, and Body in the Healing of Trauma*). When Joey speaks to a patient struggling with opiate use disorder, he taps into this resilience, offering not just a clinical perspective but a shared humanity, a mutual understanding that transcends medical terminology and enters the realm of real connection.

On her end, Jodie employs her role as a BCM to engage clients through the lens of "Seeking Safety," a concept presented by Najavits (2002). This is more than just a clinical approach for her; it is a way of life (*Seeking Safety: A Treatment Manual for PTSD and Substance Abuse*). Jodie knows what it is like to seek a safety that often feels elusive when wrestling with addiction and trauma, and this lends her a credibility that cannot be learned from textbooks.

Yet, despite their skills and the tangible impact they make daily, society still hesitates to accept the value of lived experience within professional settings. This gap is especially concerning because the foundations of a therapeutic alliance—a key factor for effective addiction treatment—are often grounded in empathy and shared experience (Miller & Rollnick, 2012; Tracy & Wallace, 2016). Isn't it high time we reconsider how we define qualifications and competency?

A wealth of scientific evidence supports the role of empathy, understanding, and shared experiences in addiction recovery. Harris Fallot (2001) discusses how designing service systems through a trauma-informed lens could be revolutionary (using trauma theory to design service systems). Studies have demonstrated that peer support can significantly increase the success rates in addiction recovery (White, 2009; Tracy & Wallace, 2016). Moreover, a trauma-informed approach that integrates understanding, empathy, and lived experience effectively treats addiction (Harris & Fallot, 2001; Abuse, S., 2014).

Today, a compelling example of broader acceptance in the professional sphere lies in the lives of Joey and Jodie. Both have always been frontline warriors in the field of social work. Joey, already licensed with an MSW, LSW, and CRS, is far from being confined to academic theories; he is on the ground, navigating the complicated lives of those he serves. Jodie, equally passionate, has her BSW and CRS and is also heavily invested in her daily interactions with clients.

They have decided to return to the classroom, not because they lack credibility or need more accolades, but because they seek to add more layers to their rich life experiences. Joey is pursuing a DSW, a journey to deepen his understanding of daily societal complexities. Jodie is on her way to a MSW, aiming to blend her coursework with her innate ability to connect with people.

These academic pursuits are not about fulfilling societal expectations; they are about enhancing their own life stories. Their degrees become more than mere credentials; they become an integrated part of their life narratives, enriching every decision they have made and will make.

For the two of them, the silver linings in their past experiences of addiction have always been the life lessons they now share with their clients. The insights they have gained, steeped in the cauldron of their trials and tribulations, offer a unique and invaluable perspective. They prove that scars can become stars, a beacon of hope for others.

And yet, the question remains: When will society at large acknowledge the critical importance of lived experience as an irreplaceable element of professional competency in addiction treatment? It is not just about diversifying our understanding of worker value but about enriching the fabric of healthcare and recovery services.

As we turn the page, let us delve deeper into what underlies the success of any therapeutic endeavor—the foundational aspects of a genuine therapeutic alliance, a subject that Joey and Jodie exemplify through their roles and lives.

Understanding the true value of professionals like Joey and Jodie is not merely an academic exercise; it is a fundamental shift that needs to happen for a more effective, empathic, and holistic approach to addiction treatment. The next chapter will explore how the foundations of a therapeutic alliance rest not only on academic knowledge but also on the human connections that underlie it all.

CHAPTER 11

Therapeutic Alliance: The Role of Empathy and Understanding

Foundations of a Therapeutic Alliance

In Whispers and Words, tucked away behind the bookshelves, a secluded corner forms the backdrop for an intimate scene. There, beneath the warm glow of a solitary lamp, a therapist with her refined scholarly wisdom sits across from a client whose eyes speak of tales not yet put to paper. Their exchange, filled with silent understanding, speaks louder than words, allying trust and empathy.

From a spot near the café counter, Joey and Jodie share a glance, their expressions mirroring past reflections and revelations. Taking a thoughtful sip, Jodie murmurs, "Between these bookshelves and amidst these coffee aromas, it is not just the theories that matter." Looking toward the duet, Joey adds, "It is the silent moments, the shared glances, the unspoken understanding–that is where true transformation brews."

This chapter invites you to experience the sublime dance of the therapeutic alliance, where the structured meets the spontaneous, and textbook knowledge blends seamlessly with heart-driven understanding.

As you explore deeper, recognize the sanctity of this relationship, which offers more than just therapy but serves as a beacon, illuminating the path of recovery with its soft, guiding light.

Step into a narrative where healing is not merely clinical but deeply personal, where empathy and understanding are the unsung transformation heroes.

Amidst coffee machines' hushed whispers and rhythmic hum, two souls sat adjacent in an isolated nook of Whispers and Words. Their environment resonated with therapeutic energy, an almost palpable force that encapsulated them, pulling them together.

As Van der Kolk (2014) beautifully articulated in The Body Keeps the Score, the human spirit can heal, even from the most deep-seated traumas. But the pivotal key lies in forming connections, re-establishing trust, and fostering mutual understanding. This scene, playing out in the dim light of the café, epitomized this very process.

From their vantage point, Joey and Jodie witnessed this therapeutic dance. Both had traversed the torturous terrain of addiction, a journey fraught with personal perils, underpinned by family dysfunctions and deeply rooted traumas. Joey, having been instrumental in the inception of the COE, was now its clinical supervisor. His lifelong partner, Jodie, had spread her wings to another agency, offering her insights as a BCM.

Their shared pasts were riddled with silver linings, which lent gravity to their perspectives. During their time at the COE, they realized a profound truth: there was an undeniable magic in the therapeutic relationship, which transcended the boundaries of mere clinical interactions. As Maté (2008) suggested in In the Realm of Hungry Ghosts, the unseen emotions, often buried deep beneath layers of pain and substance, fuel the recovery journey.

Joey recollected a poignant memory when the clutches of addiction almost defeated him. "I remember looking into my therapist's eyes," he whispered, the memory still fresh. "In that space, filled only with genuine empathy and understanding, I felt seen. I felt heard. It was the beginning of true recovery."

Jodie nodded, her eyes distant yet luminous. "Empathy is not just about understanding someone's pain. It is about feeling it with them." This sentiment mirrors Najavits's (2002) thoughts in Seeking Safety, where the mutual experience of pain and the shared journey toward healing are highlighted as cornerstones of trauma recovery.

White (2009) emphasized the importance of lived experiences in addiction recovery. Moreover, Joey and Jodie embodied this, leveraging their past battles with addiction to illuminate the path for others. Their intertwined journeys bore testament to the power of understanding and human connection, a living emblem of the healing capacity of a genuine therapeutic alliance.

However, it is vital to note that a therapeutic alliance is not a one-size-fits-all model.

Harris & Fallot (2001), in their book Using Trauma Theory to Design Service Systems, clarify that trauma-informed care should always be tailored to the individual's unique narrative. After all, everyone's journey with trauma and addiction is deeply personal, shaped by countless factors, from childhood adversities (Dube et al., 2003) to genetic predispositions (Kreek et al., 2005).

However, amidst the vast array of variables, a singular truth remains consistent: the healing power of empathy and understanding. As Joey and Jodie reflected on their experiences, this became abundantly clear. Though marred by pain and struggle, their pasts were also rich with instances where the sheer force of empathy transformed their trajectory. Be it the silent nod of acknowledgment from a fellow addict or the reassuring touch of a therapist, these seemingly small gestures accumulated to create profound shifts.

Goleman (1995), in Emotional Intelligence, asserted that the ability to understand and manage our emotions forms the heart of human relationships. In the realm of addiction and trauma recovery, this rings especially true. It is through the emotional lens that healing finds its path, and the therapeutic alliance is the vessel that facilitates this journey.

Drawing inspiration from their past experiences and the wisdom of countless experts, Joey and Jodie's message was lucid. The foundations of a therapeutic alliance are rooted in genuine empathy and deep-seated understanding. As the chapter unfolds, this central theme takes center stage.

But as foundational as these elements are, a deeper layer underpins the therapeutic alliance, empathy not just as an emotion but as the very cornerstone of therapy. The next chapter digs deeper into this, unraveling the profound intricacies of "Empathy as the cornerstone."

Empathy as the Cornerstone

In the transformative journey of healing, the most valuable currency is empathy. This seemingly simple emotion bridges anguish, acceptance, trauma, and transcendence within the vast mosaic of addiction and recovery. Joey and Jodie, with the scars of their pasts and the hope of a shared future, embody this principle profoundly.

Jodie recounts, "At the lowest point in my addiction, when the world saw me as just another statistic, Joey looked into my eyes and saw the human behind the pain." Van der Kolk (2014) often emphasized that the traumas we endure are held deeply within the body; they manifest in ways we cannot consistently articulate. Even before fully understanding the academic depths of this, Joey instinctively felt it with Jodie. Their shared experiences gave them an almost telepathic bond, helping them connect the dots of each other's pain (Van der Kolk, 2014).

Empathy is far more than a mere feeling. It is an understanding grounded in shared experience, and for Joey and Jodie, this was central to their journeys. The COE, where they once worked together, played an instrumental role in shaping this understanding. Maté (2008) describes addiction as an encounter with "hungry ghosts," ghosts of our past that drive our insatiable cravings. In the OUD program, Joey and Jodie confronted these ghosts together, illuminating their path with the light of empathy.

Joey, at the COE, recalls, "Every individual walking through those doors carries a story, a narrative filled with trauma, disappointment, and often regret. To truly help them, you must step into their world, feel their pain, and journey with them." This approach aligns with what White (2009) defines as peer-based recovery, emphasizing shared experiences' value in guiding others toward healing.

However, genuine empathy also requires an analytical depth of understanding. Jodie's move to a BCM introduced her to many complex cases, further enriching her perspective. Najavits (2002) underscores the intricate relationship between PTSD and substance abuse, often finding roots in early childhood trauma. Dube et al. (2003) also highlighted that childhood abuse significantly increases the risk of illicit drug use later in life. Jodie began recognizing these patterns in her role, without any formal clinical education, while connecting past traumas with present afflictions.

One of the silver linings from Joey and Jodie's past struggles was their innate ability to resonate with these pain points. While fraught with personal dysfunctions and challenges, their histories provided an authentic backdrop many could relate to. Jodie often shared, "Our past is like a mosaic of broken pieces. However, it can form a beautiful picture when pieced together, with understanding and love."

The story of Joey and Jodie exemplifies the power of connection and the necessity of trauma-informed care. Harris Fallot (2001) argues that a trauma-informed service system is beneficial and vital. By understanding the sources of trauma and tailoring interventions to cater to individual histories and needs, healing becomes a collaborative journey. It becomes a partnership where one's vulnerabilities are met with understanding and compassion, and not judgment.

Joey's emphasis on MI at the COE (Miller & Rollnick, 2012) further magnified this point. By actively listening and reflecting, he made the individuals feel seen and understood, validating their feelings and guiding them toward positive change.

Empathy also extends to acknowledging the socio-cultural dimensions of addiction. Topitzes, Mersky, & Reynolds (2012) highlight the gender-specific aspects of trauma and addiction. Joey and Jodie's dual perspectives offered a unique insight into these dimensions, fostering a more inclusive and comprehensive approach to healing.

The intertwining of their personal and professional journeys offers a touching testimony to the redemptive power of love, understanding, and empathy. As Goleman (1995) would put it, their emotional intelligence became their most significant asset, allowing them to navigate the tumultuous waters of addiction personally and in their caregiver roles.

However, the journey continues. While empathy is the cornerstone, building a therapeutic alliance presents its challenges. Understanding, compassion, and connection are pivotal, but how does one navigate the hurdles in building these alliances? Joey and Jodie's intertwining stories provide inspiration and valuable lessons for anyone looking to deepen their understanding of addiction, recovery, and the human spirit. As we explore further, we will explore the complexities and challenges of building such alliances, recognizing that empathy, while central, is just the beginning.

His opulent array of human emotions, interwoven with threads of experiences and beliefs, creates a rich backdrop against which therapeutic relationships unfold. In this intricate dance of trust-building, empathy and understanding are paramount. Through the lens of Joey and Jodie, we take a closer dive into the challenges faced in constructing these pivotal relationships and the opportunities they bring.

Their pasts were clouded with the chaos of addiction, but there was an undeniable silver lining–the shared empathy and compassion that emerged from their turbulent experiences. "I remember the cold nights at the COE, seeing the despair in clients' eyes. That feeling was all too familiar," Joey said, his voice heavy with the weight of lived experience. Having moved on to another agency, Jodie echoed, "It is like watching a reflection of our past every day, but with the knowledge that recovery is possible."

Navigating the intricate corridors of human emotions, especially when scarred by trauma, is no easy feat. In his seminal work, Van der Kolk states that trauma becomes embodied, with the body keeping a score of every painful memory and experience (Van der Kolk, 2014). The emotional and physiological responses tied to trauma can pose significant barriers to building trust, especially in therapeutic settings. As Joey and Jodie's stories unravel, the pivotal role of personal lived experiences in circumventing these barriers becomes evident.

Maté (2008) illustrates the haunting realms of addiction, depicting it as a painful echo of unmet needs unsatiated by the world. For those enveloped in its clutches, every relationship and every interaction is tinted with the mistrust birthed from past betrayals and pain. In such settings, the mere act of understanding, without judgment, is profoundly therapeutic. "When a client comes in, drowning in despair, sometimes all they need is to feel seen," Joey whispered, his eyes shining with unshed tears.

Drawing from their journeys, Joey and Jodie became the embodiment of trauma-informed care. Their empathic approach was grounded in the profound understanding that trauma often disrupts the very core of one's being, necessitating interventions tailored to individual needs (Harris & Fallot, 2001). The collage of their shared experiences became a beacon of hope for many, illuminating the path toward recovery.

Nevertheless, challenges were aplenty. While shared lived experiences facilitated understanding, they also brought back painful memories. Jodie often found herself overwhelmed, the boundaries between her past and her client's stories blurring. But with every challenge came a new opportunity. "It is a continuous journey of self-awareness and self-regulation," she shared, drawing inspiration from the cognitive neuroscience findings that underscore the pivotal role of self-regulation in managing emotions and behaviors (Heatherton & Wagner, 2011).

Another crucial facet in navigating these alliances was the significance of peer support. White (2009) stresses that peer-based recovery anchors on shared experiences, fostering understanding and resilience. The collective wisdom derived from Joey and Jodie's pasts, connected with the lived experiences of other survivors, became a sanctuary for many. This network of shared stories and mutual support became instrumental in the healing journey of countless souls.

However, the journey was not devoid of pitfalls. The emotional intensity of their roles and their pasts sometimes took a toll. They had to ensure they were not subconsciously attempting to self-medicate, a phenomenon Khantzian (1997) elaborates upon, highlighting how individuals often use substances to cope with overwhelming emotions.

Yet, amidst the challenges, the silver linings of their past addiction experiences shone brightly. Their shared histories, while painful, were also testaments to resilience, love, and the power of human connection. Joey often shared with his clients, "Our scars are proof of battles won, and they illuminate the path for others."

Drawing this segment to a close, it becomes evident that the foundation of a therapeutic alliance rests on the pillars of empathy, understanding, and genuine human connection. These connections transcend professional boundaries, entering the realm of shared humanity. The emotions, feelings, and stories interlace to form a guiding star in the recovery journey. As we transition to the subsequent section, we explore deeper into enhancing treatment through strong therapist-client relationships, further accentuating the role of shared empathy and understanding in the intricate dance of healing.

Enhancing Treatment Through Strong Therapist-Client Relationships

Navigators and clients met daily in the bustling COE to share, heal, and grow. But for Joey and Jodie, their meetings carried deeper nuances, for they were not just navigators. They were survivors, messengers of hope, and living testimonies to the power of therapeutic alliance. With roots in well-intentioned families marred by dysfunction, their journey through addiction, healing, and recovery was nothing short of a miracle.

Van der Kolk once wrote, "Being able to feel safe with other people is probably the most important aspect of mental health; safe connections are fundamental to meaningful and satisfying lives" (2014). Joey and Jodie, survivors of near-fatal addiction, understood this profound truth at a cellular level. They had been on the other side, having felt the weight of shame and isolation that often accompanies addiction. Now, serving at the COE, their lived experiences gave them unparalleled depth of understanding and empathy.

As Jodie would often share with her clients, "Addiction does not discriminate. It touches even the most loving homes." She would draw parallels from her own life, showing them that there was always a silver lining, even in the face of challenges. For Jodie, it was meeting Joey at a difficult juncture in her life.

On the other hand, Joey remembered the relief he felt when Jodie, with her shared experiences and empathetic touch, joined the COE. Together, they became beacons of hope for many.

Maté (2008) argued that this human touch is essential for those grappling with addiction. In his book, *In the Realm of Hungry Ghosts*, he passionately advocates for compassion as a primary tool in addiction treatment, noting that trauma often pushes people toward addictive behavior. Najavits (2002) also stresses the importance of trauma-informed care, emphasizing safety and stabilization as core treatment components. This care understands and integrates the widespread impact of trauma and offers recovery paths grounded in understanding the survivor's lived experience (Harris & Fallot, 2001).

Drawing from their pasts, Joey would often use anecdotes of their addiction journeys to highlight the importance of self-awareness. Recounting the days of their shared struggle, he would emphasize, "Every relapse, every stumble was a lesson. We learned more about our triggers, our weaknesses, but more importantly, our strengths." White (2009) and Miller Rollnick (2012) concur, emphasizing peer-based recovery and MI as tools to empower clients to explore and resolve their ambivalence.

Joey's ability to infuse such hope emanated from his understanding that addiction was a personal failing or weak character and a complex interplay of genes, environment, and personal experiences (Kreek et al., 2005; Khantzian, 1997). They both knew the importance of addressing underlying traumas, having seen firsthand the devastating impact of unprocessed traumatic memories. Gorski's relapse prevention model (1990) and the Adverse Childhood Experiences study by Dube et al. (2003) further strengthened their resolve to weave trauma care into addiction recovery.

However, why were Joey and Jodie effective in building solid therapeutic alliances? The answer lies in Goleman's concept of emotional intelligence (1995). They did not just understand their clients: they felt their pain, fears, and hopes. By sharing their personal stories and the silver lining that emerged from their struggles, they bridged the gap between therapist and client, embodying the principles of Mead et al. (2001) and highlighting the transformative power of peer support.

One day in a peer support session, a client replied, "When I talk to Jodie, I do not feel judged. I feel seen." Another shared about Joey, "His stories inspire me. I feel like if he could overcome his past, maybe, just maybe, I can too."

Such testimonials attest to the words of Tracy Wallace (2016), who found peer support crucial in addiction treatment. It fosters an environment of mutual respect, understanding, and shared responsibility. This bond, fostered by shared lived experiences, is the cornerstone of healing (Davidson et al., 2012).

As this chapter draws to a close, the emphasis on the unique insights and connections created by those with lived experience in addiction becomes even clearer. While harrowing, Joey and Jodie's journeys provided them with the tools and understanding to truly connect with their clients, enhancing treatment outcomes through a strong therapist-client bond. Their lived experiences are not just tales of survival but serve as testaments and motivation to others on similar paths. As we transition to our next focal point, we how these lived experiences, much like Joey and Jodie's, play a pivotal role in strengthening therapeutic bonds.

Lived Experiences Strengthening Therapeutic Bonds

Lived experiences are imprints that sculpt one›s worldview, emotions, and resilience. Joey and Jodie knew this firsthand. Survivors of an addiction that nearly claimed their lives, they were living testaments to the phrase "triumph over adversity." Their work in addiction had made them powerful allies for others on the journey to recovery, a journey they knew too intimately.

At the COE, Joey and Jodie had been the beacons for many, their stories echoing resilience and hope. Joey's position at the COE gave him an influential stance to guide and direct others. As a BCM, Jodie, had channeled her experience to provide personalized care, acknowledging that every addict's journey is nuanced, unique, and deserving of understanding.

Theoretical paradigms like trauma theory have always emphasized recognizing the past to craft better futures (Harris & Fallot, 2001). Joey and Jodie, with their familial histories peppered with dysfunction, could resonate with this. Yet, it was their lived experiences that granted them a unique empathy. As Van der Kolk (2014) poignantly writes in The Body Keeps the Score, trauma does not just affect the mind; it creates tangible, physical changes. Joey and Jodie bore the emotional and physical scars of their battles. However, like stars, they illuminated the paths for others, demonstrating that recovery was attainable.

They both bore witness to the convergence of trauma and addiction in their roles. According to Dube et al. (2003), childhood adversities such as abuse or household dysfunctions significantly increase the risk of illicit drug use. This correlation was not lost on Joey and Jodie. They had seen how the trauma of one's past could lead to the desperate embrace of substances, a self-medication strategy that Khantzian (1997) describes in his seminal work.

The silver linings in their narratives were undeniable. When Jodie shared tales of her past, she spoke of the darkness and the moments of light. The fleeting moments when a kind stranger offered her a meal, or she found solace in music during her most challenging days. On the other hand, Joey recollected times when he witnessed unparalleled kindness in the darkest corners of his addiction phase. These memories were not just retrospective glimpses; they became therapeutic tools, allowing Joey and Jodie to connect with their patients deeply.

Maté (2008), in In the Realm of Hungry Ghosts, speaks of the spiritual void that addiction often tries to fill. Jodie often quoted this in peer support sessions, emphasizing that understanding this void was crucial to crafting therapeutic bonds. Empathy was not just about listening; it was about feeling. Moreover, who better than those who have trudged the same path to offer this empathy?

Research has consistently highlighted the effectiveness of peer support in addiction treatment. Tracy & Wallace (2016) showcased the undeniable benefits of peer-support groups in addiction treatment. Jodie and Joey's personal experiences validated these findings. Raw and unfiltered, their stories bore the power to connect, console, and catalyze change.

MI, a technique where practitioners guide patients to voice their motivations and discrepancies concerning substance use (Miller & Rollnick, 2012), became even more impactful when employed by someone with a lived experience. With his personal history, Joey could navigate these sessions with genuine understanding. He knew when to push, when to pause, and when just to be present with a client.

However, their therapeutic alliance was not just about sharing their stories. It was about listening–genuinely listening. As Goleman (1995) emphasized in his work on emotional intelligence, true empathy was about attuning to others, understanding their emotions, and acting accordingly. Joey and Jodie, with their shared histories, could perceive the unspoken words, the silent cries for help, and the quiet hopes for a better tomorrow.

Their narratives also had the power to challenge stigmas, a topic often under-discussed yet crucial in addiction. Living proof that addiction was not a character flaw but often a result of intersecting traumas, genetic predispositions, and social circumstances (Kreek et al., 2005), Joey and Jodie became advocates, challenging societal perceptions.

In conclusion, lived experiences, as showcased by Joey and Jodie's journeys, strengthen therapeutic bonds exponentially. Their stories, filled with scars and stars, exemplified the transformative power of empathy and understanding. As they walked hand in hand, navigating the terrains of addiction treatment, they illuminated the path for countless others.

As we transition into the subsequent chapters, we dig deeper into the inherent biases and stigmas associated with addiction. Chapter 12: Overcoming Stigmas: A Call to the Medical and Academic Communities promises to shed light on existing stigmas in medical and academic communities, urging for change, understanding, and empathy.

CHAPTER 12

Overcoming Stigmas: A Call to the Medical and Academic Communities

Existing Stigmas in Medical and Academic Communities

Amidst the familiar scent of freshly brewed coffee and aging books, a hush falls over Whispers and Words. The usually lively nook, where knowledge meets passion, now holds a tension palpable in the air. Positioned center stage, a weathered medical book, its pages dog-eared and annotated, rests atop an old wooden table. Next to it lies an academic journal, its pristine pages promising modern insights yet echoing age-old biases.

Drawing the attention of onlookers, Joey gently taps the textbook, stating, "These pages might carry the weight of knowledge, but they also bear the burden of misconceptions." Jodie, flipping through the academic journal, nods in agreement. "These stigmas," she pauses, searching for words, "are shadows cast by ignorance, but they're not immune to the light of understanding."

In this pivotal chapter, join Joey and Jodie as they traverse the aisles of the bookstore and the nuances of the coffee shop conversations. Their mission is to challenge and change the narratives rooted in the medical and academic corridors. Dive deep into a world where empathy meets education and recognize the urgent need for reformation. Journey with them as they illustrate that by dispelling the myths, we can cultivate a community more compassionate and informed about the challenges and triumphs of recovery.

A cool breeze drifted through the aisles of the bookstore. With a steady hand, Joey leafed through the pages of an old medical textbook, its spine groaning as it gave way to countless stories and anecdotes. For him, some of those pages represented the glaring biases that still colored the perspective of healthcare professionals today. Beside him, Jodie skimmed through an academic journal, her face reflecting a similar turmoil.

"Why is it," Joey pondered aloud, "that even in this age of cutting-edge medicine and research, our past, fraught with addiction, is viewed as a moral failing?" He quoted a line from Van der Kolk's *The Body Keeps the Score*, relying on the intricacies of trauma and how it can shape an individual's path (Van der Kolk, 2014). "We were victims of trauma, Jodie. We self-medicated, as many do, in search of relief from that ever-persistent pain."

Khantzian (1997) proposed that substances were often used to self-medicate, a coping mechanism for distress and mental health issues.

Jodie responded, her voice tinged with frustration and hope, "And even as we stand tall today, having overcome our past, our credentials are overshadowed by society's view of addiction. Despite all our efforts, those in the medical and academic realms often unknowingly perpetuate harmful stereotypes, making it harder for individuals like us to find our footing." She referred to Simpson & Miller's review, which discusses the correlation between childhood abuse and subsequent substance use, emphasizing that understanding such relationships is paramount to informed treatment (Simpson & Miller, 2002).

Thinking back to the early days at the COE, Joey reminisced about a particularly challenging incident when a peer questioned the efficacy of addiction treatment. "He cited some outdated research, disregarding Maté's *In the Realm of Hungry Ghosts* and its in-depth exploration of addiction (Maté, 2008). The lack of comprehensive understanding is jarring."

Jodie nodded, adding, "In academic circles, many are content to view addiction through a narrow lens, sidelining the lived experiences of individuals. Our past, Joey, might have been marred by addiction, but it was also filled with resilience, learning, and growth."

She remembered their time at the OUD program. Joey's approaches often echoed Najavits's *Seeking Safety*—prioritizing trauma-informed care in the conversations with clients (Najavits, 2002). "Our methodologies in the COE were a testament to how lived experiences could inform and enrich medical and therapeutic approaches."

The couple's story was not unique. Many survivors of addiction grapple with these stigmas daily, affecting their self-worth and ability to seek and sustain recovery. The weight of stigmatization can become an unbearable burden. Harris & Fallot's work outlines the necessity of a trauma-informed approach in service systems, emphasizing understanding, empathy, and comprehensive support as critical to healing (Harris & Fallot, 2001).

In light of their struggles, Joey and Jodie found solace in their shared experiences, understanding the silver linings that arose from their pasts. Their connection, mutual support, and resilience became the foundation upon which they built their recovery journey. As Mead, Hilton, and Curtis (2001) noted, peer support offers a unique perspective, drawing from lived experiences to provide understanding, hope, and guidance.

Joey looked at Jodie, determination evident in his eyes. "Our journey, filled with scars, has also brought us the wisdom to see the stars. We are living testimonies of the need for change, Jodie."

As they moved forward, Joey and Jodie bore a shared dream: to challenge the existing stigmas in medical and academic communities. With every discussion, workshop, and intervention, they aimed to rewrite the narrative, advocating for a world where the experiences of individuals like them were not just acknowledged but celebrated.

While in the coffee shop, clutching the academic journal, Jodie said, "We are more than our past, more than our addiction. It is time for these pages to reflect our truth."

The weight of their message was evident, urging readers to recognize the multifaceted nature of addiction and recovery. Joey and Jodie's stories are stark reminders that while the medical and academic corridors may be riddled with biases, they are also pathways to change.

In the next section, dig deeper into the devastating impacts of these stigmatizations on treatment and recovery, emphasizing the dire need for a paradigm shift in understanding and approach. The time for reformation is now.

Impacts of Stigmatization on Treatment and Recovery

Jodie's fingers trembled as she gingerly held the tiny plastic cup containing her methadone medication. The anxiety was noticeable, her mind racing, fearing being judged and labeled as "another addict" (Maté, 2008). While Joey, her husband, went through some of the same stigmas on MAT in his journey to recovery.

Over the years, the stigmatization around addiction has weaved a daunting picture of negativity, placing unfair burdens on individuals seeking help (Livingston et al., 2012). The toxic nature of such stigmatization has been proven to create additional barriers in the recovery process, inducing feelings of shame, self-doubt, and internal conflict (Van der Kolk, 2014). When one's internal world is already reeling from trauma, the external animosity can amplify the internal chaos.

Joey and Jodie knew this all too well. Their journeys with addiction were fraught with painful episodes, worsened by society's disdainful views. When Jodie once bravely opened up about her addiction in a group therapy session, a family member later questioned why she would "air her dirty laundry." This stigmatization, steeped in ignorance and lack of empathy, makes the already difficult journey to recovery even more challenging (Harris & Fallot, 2001).

For Joey, working in the OUD program, stigmatization was constant. "You are just enabling them!" was a phrase he had heard one too many times. However, Joey had the wisdom of both lived experience and academic understanding. Drawing from the insights of White (2009) and Miller & Rollnick (2012), he understood the nuances of addiction and the paramount importance of trauma-informed care.

Joey often remembered his days with Jodie at the COE and how they had transformed their personal battles with addiction into a mission to support and uplift others. However, even in such supportive settings, shadows of stigma lingered. Both, coming from good families with their own sets of dysfunctions, often faced quiet judgment–as if addiction was a "choice," a moral failing rather than a complex interplay of genetic, environmental, and traumatic factors (Kreek et al., 2005; Dube et al., 2003).

The silver lining of their shared ordeal, though, was resilience and determination. Jodie often recalled an incident when a fellow client, overwhelmed with self-blame, broke down during a peer support session. Drawing from her own journey and Maté's (2008) insights, Jodie gently reminded the client that addiction is not a character flaw but rather an attempt, although maladaptive, to cope with profound pain. Their shared vulnerabilities became a source of strength, turning tears into tales of hope.

What is crucial for society, especially the medical and academic communities, to realize is that stigmatization does not just hinder the recovery of the individual and stymies our collective understanding of addiction (Najavits, 2002; Lieberman & Van Horn, 2009). By perpetuating stereotypes, we shut down avenues of conversation, research, and understanding. This lack of dialogue and continued perpetuation of harmful beliefs can lead to inadequate policies, treatment methods, and societal responses that further alienate those struggling with addiction (Harris & Fallot, 2001).

Recovery from addiction is not just about abstinence: it is about rebuilding a life, repairing relationships, and reclaiming one's sense of self-worth (Van der Kolk, 2014). Joey and Jodie's lives are testaments to this transformative journey. Through their past struggles, they have illuminated pathways for others. They highlight the importance of understanding trauma, creating safe spaces, and fostering peer support as cornerstones for effective recovery (Mead et al., 2001; Tracy & Wallace, 2016).

Moreover, as Joey once put it, drawing from his own life's tapestry of scars and stars, "The night is darkest before the dawn. Nevertheless, stars—our experiences, learnings, and connections—shine the brightest in that very darkness."

Yet, it is one thing to talk about the challenges and another to see its tangible impacts. One must look deeper into real-life narratives to truly comprehend the depth and breadth of the consequences that stem from stigmatization. This will provide a clear picture of how the weight of societal judgment impacts real lives. As we move forward, let us delve into some poignant case studies, shedding light on the adverse outcomes of stigma.

Case Studies Highlighting Adverse Outcomes of Stigma

The experience of stigmatization is powerfully detrimental. It reopens wounds, hinders recovery, and reinforces traumatic narratives. In the context of addiction recovery, where vulnerability is already heightened, stigmas can be deadly. This chapter researches two poignant case studies centering on Joey and Jodie, exemplifying the ramifications of such stigmas, and the resilience and hope they found in the silver linings of their lived experiences.

Joey's Ordeal

Joey's initiation into the world of opioids was not from some dark alley but from an individual trying to black out the years of bullying and stigmatization. Within weeks, the grip of an addiction was evident. As his dependence grew, the whispers began. Colleagues, friends, and even family members began viewing him through the myopic lens of his addiction. He was no longer Joey, the loving son or diligent worker; he was just another "junkie."

The term "junkie" is not benign. Van der Kolk elucidates how traumatic experiences can embed themselves within the body, causing emotional and physical distress (2014). Each derogatory label, every sidelong glance, and every whispered comment further deepened Joey's trauma. His brain, already grappling with addiction, was now additionally combatting a world that seemed to be against him.

However, amidst the despair, there were moments of grace. Joey's past, filled with its share of misdemeanors, also had moments where he reached out to fellow addicts, sharing his story, offering a listening ear, and becoming the embodiment of White's advocacy for peer-based addiction recovery support (2009).

Jodie's Struggle

Jodie's journey with addiction began at eighteen. The feeling of being "alone" made her vulnerable to the seductive allure of opioids. Jodie was battling the ghosts of her past and now the pernicious demon of addiction.

Topitzes, Mersky, & Reynolds have noted how early traumatic experiences can influence a person's predisposition to violent behaviors and substance abuse (2012). Jodie's usage was a misguided attempt at self-medication, a hypothesis well-articulated by Khantzian (1997).

Yet, society failed to see Jodie's pain. Instead of empathy, she was faced with prejudice. In her role at the COE, Jodie frequently felt the weight of this stigma. Instead of being seen as a professional, she was often relegated to the status of her addiction, an unfair label that did not represent her totality.

Nevertheless, Jodie's past was not devoid of silver linings. Like Joey, her lived experiences made her exceptionally empathetic. She was a beacon of hope for many at the COE, a testament to the transformative power of love, understanding, and professional help.

The Interplay of Stigma and Trauma

For both Joey and Jodie, addiction was not a solitary battle. It was intertwined with trauma, pain, and societal prejudice. The stigma exacerbated their trauma, creating a cycle that Maté refers to as being in the realm of hungry ghosts, where one is perpetually chasing relief in the wrong places (2008).

And while they found strength in each other, the medical and academic communities' roles must be noticed. Joey's position at COE and Jodie's role as a BCM are testaments to the importance of trauma-informed care.

Harris & Fallot stress the necessity of designing service systems around trauma theory (2001). Such systems understand and actively combat the adverse impacts of trauma and stigma. Recovery becomes tangible when individuals like Joey and Jodie find support in structures that recognize and work with their traumas.

Yet, one does not lie solely on the medical community. Society at large needs a paradigm shift in perception. Stigmatization is not just about labels; it is about refusing individuals their narratives and their complex tapestry of experiences.

Livingston et al. highlight the necessity of interventions to reduce stigma, primarily related to substance use disorders (2012). Such interventions can pave the way for individuals like Joey and Jodie to lead fulfilling lives free from the shadows of prejudice.

Joey and Jodie's stories are emblematic of the intertwined struggles of trauma, addiction, and societal prejudice. They underscore the urgency of a paradigm shift toward understanding, empathy, and trauma-informed care. These narratives also provide a seamless transition into our next focal point: the imperative for collaborative efforts to combat prejudice. The interplay of multiple stakeholders, from the medical community to society at large, can revolutionize the journey from scars to stars.

Collaborative Efforts to Combat Prejudice

The journey to recovery is never simple. The memories that still echoed in Joey and Jodie's minds—the euphoria of a high and the dread of withdrawal—intertwined with the shadows of prejudice and misunderstanding. Although they emerged as survivors of addiction, the stigmas often ran deeper than the scars of their past.

Working at the COE, Joey observed countless individuals challenged by OUD. At the COE, Joey bore witness to the multidimensionality of addiction beyond the stereotypes and preconceived notions. Goleman (1995) referred to emotional intelligence as the ability to manage and interpret emotions in oneself and others.

Through his lived experiences and professional background, Joey cultivated an emotional intelligence that reshaped the recovery process for many. For Joey, substance abuse was not about a lack of moral strength or self-control but was deeply connected to trauma, stress, and even genetic predispositions (Kreek et al., 2005).

On the other side, Jodie's move to another agency as a BCM illuminated the pervasive stigmas that transcend different settings. Prejudices persist even within medical and academic communities, which should be bastions of understanding and empathy (Livingston et al., 2012). Drawing from Maté (2008), Jodie often cited how addicts were like "hungry ghosts," forever craving, seeking, but never truly satisfied. The "ghosts" were not just substances but the trauma, childhood neglect, and dysfunctional family dynamics (Dube et al., 2003).

Both Joey and Jodie hailed from good families. But good does not always mean uncomplicated. Their family lives were peppered with dysfunction, mirroring the reality that many who struggle with addiction come from environments where external smiles mask internal struggles. Van der Kolk (2014) highlighted how trauma can persist within the body. For Joey and Jodie, their past addictions were not just fleeting impulses but embodied responses to past traumas.

Yet, even in darkness, silver linings emerge. In their days working together at the COE, Joey, and Jodie often reminisced about the clients who defied the odds. One particular story always resonated. Initially shunned by her family and community, a young female client rebuilt her life piece by piece, thanks to her peer support (Mead et al., 2001; Tracy & Wallace, 2016). This narrative was not unique; Joey and Jodie's stories were testaments to the transformative power of compassionate, trauma-informed care (Harris & Fallot, 2001).

A paradigm shift was desperately needed. Instead of isolating and stigmatizing, there was a clarion call to integrate and understand. But how could such a shift be catalyzed?

With Joey's executive, Cheryle Emala, lighting the way for people with life experiences, the COE leaned into the principles of MI (Miller & Rollnick, 2012), aiming to support individuals in evoking their intrinsic motivation for change. This method, blended with harm reduction strategies (Marlatt & Witkiewitz, 2002), offered a compassionate approach, acknowledging that recovery is a journey with its ebbs and flows.

Today, in her role, Jodie often collaborates with medical professionals, emphasizing the importance of understanding the biological underpinnings of addiction and PTSD (Kar, 2011; Krystal et al., 2004). By linking the cognitive, emotional, and physiological dimensions, she advocated for an interdisciplinary approach to combating addiction.

However, more was needed for interventions to be evidence-based; they needed to be human-based. The narratives of Joey and Jodie served as reminders of the importance of lived experiences in shaping interventions. Whether it was peer support, which has been lauded for its effectiveness (Davidson et al., 2012), or creating trauma-informed service systems (Harris & Fallot, 2001), the personal became universal.

Combating prejudice in addiction requires a symphony of voices, from those like Joey and Jodie, who bear the marks of their past, to academics, medical professionals, and policymakers. The scars of addiction are not just reminders of a painful past but emblematic of resilience, transformation, and hope.

As we transcend the boundaries of prejudice and envision a more inclusive approach, we must recognize the multifaceted nature of addiction. The subsequent discussions will highlight the future directions for inclusive thinking, emphasizing the imperative for medical and academic communities to be at the forefront of this revolution.

Understanding the past is essential but looking toward the horizon is equally crucial. As we explore the future directions for inclusive thinking, we must reiterate the shared responsibility of both medical and academic communities in shaping a more compassionate and understanding world.

Future Directions for Inclusive Thinking

The imprints of past trauma and addiction are etched in the psyche and the neural pathways of those affected. Van der Kolk (2014) posits that trauma resonates within the body, affecting the mind and overall well-being, and its echoes can be deafening for survivors like Jodie and Joey. Despite coming from loving, albeit dysfunctional families, both have weathered storms many could hardly imagine.

Every time Joey shared their pasts at the COE, a hush would fall over the room. His emotional recounting of their journey from addiction's vice-like grip to finding solace and purpose is miraculous. The raw vulnerability, the potent emotion, is palpable every time. And therein lies the strength of their tales—the lived experiences. Their past encounters with opiates bring forth the essence of Maté's (2008) narrative about close encounters with addiction; it is a haunting dance with the "hungry ghosts" that lurk within, awaiting an escape.

For far too long, the stigmas around addiction and trauma has been a suffocating blanket over the medical and academic communities. While science has made strides in understanding the biological underpinnings (Kreek et al., 2005), the emotional and societal aspects often remain uncharted. The dichotomy between the clinical coldness of medical diagnosis and the raw, heart-wrenching emotion of lived experiences needs bridging.

Take Jodie's transition to a new agency, for instance. While her professional role changed, her mission remained rooted in her past. Leveraging her past experience with addiction, she uses her story as a beacon for those lost in the tempestuous sea of substance use disorders. For Jodie and Joey, their scars have become their north star, guiding them and countless others toward a horizon of hope and recovery.

Their experiences also underscore the importance of trauma-informed care. The Substance Abuse and Mental Health Services Administration emphasizes a trauma-informed approach to care (Abuse, 2014). Recognizing trauma and integrating knowledge into policies, procedures, and practices, Joey has seen firsthand the transformative power of such an approach. It is not just about administering medication or holding therapy sessions but about holding space, understanding, and connecting.

Harris and Fallot (2001) advocate for the design of service systems through the lens of trauma theory. Considering the intimate tales of individuals like Joey and Jodie, this does not seem like a lofty academic ideal but an urgent, tangible need. Design systems that are not merely about healing but understanding and empathy. Systems that are not just about recovery but also about respect.

But how can the more comprehensive community foster this inclusive thinking, particularly the medical and academic ones? One way is through the potent medium of peer support. White (2009) emphasizes peer-based recovery's history, theory, and practice. Peer-support groups can offer a unique therapeutic milieu by leveraging lived experiences like those of Jodie and Joey. They provide a sense of belonging, a shared understanding, and, most importantly, hope. Tracy & Wallace (2016) reiterate the manifold benefits of such groups in treating addiction.

But with the promise of hope also comes the responsibility of the community to shed preconceived biases. Livingston et al. (2012) propose the need for interventions that reduce the stigma tied to substance use disorders. For every time Joey and Jodie share their tales, it is an opportunity for listeners to unlearn stereotypes, challenge stigmas, and embrace a more informed, empathetic perspective.

The stories of Joey and Jodie underscore a powerful truth. Trauma and addiction are not mere clinical terms; they are raw, unfiltered human experiences. They are about tears, despair, hope, and resilience. As Van der Kolk aptly puts it, the body might keep the score, but the spirit writes the narrative.

Thus, as we turn the pages to the next chapter, we investigate into tangible stories from the field that showcase the magic that unfolds when medical knowledge meets the raw power of human experience. These stories of integrated care enlighten and inspire, serving as testaments to the incredible resilience of the human spirit.

With a renewed understanding of the power of inclusive thinking, let us dive into the next chapter, showcasing real-life applications where the combination of medical acumen and lived experiences have crafted tales of redemption and recovery—Chapter 13: Case Studies: Real-life Applications of Combined Approaches.

CHAPTER 13

Case Studies: Real-life Applications of Combined Approaches

Success Stories of Integrated Care

Within the cozy embrace of Whispers and Words, amid the rhythmic dance of turning pages and the intoxicating scent of fresh coffee, lies a dedicated space known to locals as The Realms Corner. This particular niche, adorned with vintage bookshelves and ornate lamps, serves as a sanctuary for authentic stories that blur the lines between clinical expertise and the undiluted narratives of life.

As Joey and Jodie sit nestled in this corner, the atmosphere brims with a sense of reverence. Their shared table is a canvas, illustrating the confluence of clinical interventions with heartfelt personal journeys. The leather-bound notebook Joey holds is no ordinary diary; it's a testament to the triumphs and trials of souls battling addiction. Each handwritten account is tangible proof of strategies employed, interventions initiated, and lives reclaimed.

Beside the notebook, Jodie's photographs create a visual symphony, capturing raw moments of despair, hope, and eventual resurgence. Every image, every gaze locked within it, is a testimony to the power of merging clinical strategies with the profound resonance of personal tales.

Jodie, her fingers tracing the edges of a photograph, murmurs, "These snapshots are moments frozen in time, symbolizing the intersection of professional methods with personal battles and breakthroughs."

Engage deeply with this chapter as it beckons you to explore the labyrinth of real-life applications, where clinical techniques and personal narratives intertwine, painting a vivid picture of recovery, renewal, and resurgence. Dive deep into these case studies and witness the alchemy that arises when therapeutic approaches meld seamlessly with the factual realities of human existence.

Tucked away in The Realms Corner of Whispers and Words, Joey and Jodie's mutual reflection spanned more than just the pages of a leather-bound notebook and the evocative photographs Jodie captured. It was a silent tribute to the harmony that clinical interventions and personal narratives can create. The hum of conversations from other corners of the café dissolved into a muted background as they delved into their own stories.

Joey's fingers glided over a page he had penned after one particularly trying peer-support session at the COE. He had written, *"Jodie and I come from families where love was abundant, but so was dysfunction. We often danced on the thin line between guidance and chaos, unaware that this dance would one day be our very salvation."*

As Maté (2008) describes, backgrounds of familial affection often intertwine with scars that are hard to discern, making addiction's pull even more magnetic and confounding.

Jodie leaned closer, her eyes shimmering as they met an old photograph of them from their early days in recovery at Club Serenity. The image was a visceral memory of them, worn but hopeful, standing outside the club. "Remember this, Joey?" she whispered, tracing the photo's edges. "This was after an outreach event where you quoted Van der Kolk (2014), saying, 'the body keeps the score.' You emphasized how our traumas might have scarred us but also made us resilient." The scars, they believed, were indeed the stories of the stars they were becoming.

This resilience was further strengthened by the integrated approach they experienced at their jobs at the COE. Joey, harnessing methods like MI (Miller & Rollnick, 2012), channeled his own past struggles to form connections with clients, making therapeutic dialogues feel more genuine. Meanwhile, Jodie seamlessly incorporated trauma-informed care principles such as safety and empowerment she learned from her mentor, Cheryld, as detailed by Harris & Fallot (2001), into her case management, ensuring the clients felt seen, heard, and understood.

Drawing from their lived experiences, their combined efforts were more than professional strategies. They were lifelines. Drawing parallels from Najavits (2002), the COE's peer-support framework intertwined PTSD treatment with substance abuse strategies. As Joey narrated cases from his notebook, the emphasis was evident on the "Seeking Safety" model, where personal narratives formed the backbone of the therapeutic process.

However, it was not just therapeutic models that carved their journey. As Jodie reminisced about the peer-support groups she once attended, she was reminded of Tracy & Wallace's (2016) assertion of their efficacy. Joey, too, benefited from peer-based recovery support, as delineated by White (2009), finding solace in shared experiences, mutual understanding, and unspoken bonds.

And yet, as they journeyed together, they were also mindful of the silver linings from their past addiction experiences. The seemingly dark episodes of their pasts were, in fact, steppingstones that imparted vital lessons. For Joey, it was about self-awareness. Goleman's (1995) "emotional intelligence" resonated deeply with him. He had learned to read between the lines, discern emotions in clients that even they weren't aware of, and navigate treatment accordingly.

For Jodie, her silver lining lay in her fierce advocacy for reducing the stigma associated with substance use disorders, drawing inspiration from Livingston et al. (2012). Her photographs, often showcasing addiction survivors' raw, unfiltered journeys, became powerful tools for community awareness and sensitivity.

Like many others, their stories were testaments to the intricate tapestry that integrated care could weave. They had witnessed firsthand the profound impact of merging clinical techniques with personal tales, navigating the treacherous waters of addiction, trauma, and recovery with grace and determination.

As the café's ambiance shifted with the setting sun, Joey and Jodie's recollections also drew to a pause. Closing the notebook, Joey mused, "Jodie, we've come so far, yet the road ahead remains filled with challenges." She nodded, adding, "But these challenges have always molded us, shaped our response, and taught us to innovate."

Their shared stories and insights were not just about success, echoing from The Realms Corner. They were about continual evolution, learning, and growth. We'll explore more into their challenges, innovative solutions, and the undying spirit of hope that fuels every step of their journey.

Challenges Faced and Solutions Implemented

Two recovery champions, Jodie and Joey, were tucked away in the COE's bustling corridors. Their individual journeys through addiction and the subsequent path to redemption weren't merely tales of survival: they were symbolic of resilience, grit, and the transformative power of lived experiences.

With her gentle disposition, Jodie vividly remembers the harrowing nights marred by substance abuse. Despite having a loving family, the underlying dysfunction created an environment ripe for addiction (Dube et al., 2003). She found solace in the very substance that threatened her existence. Joey, on the other hand, mirrored a similar trajectory. The cocoon of familial love was always overshadowed by latent dysfunctions, driving him toward the treacherous maze of opiates.

The journey of addiction is not just about the chemical shackles; it's a dance between trauma and substance (Van der Kolk, 2014). Joey's despair was more than the numbing effect of the drugs; it was an escape from the traumas that plagued his psyche. This sentiment resonates with Gabor Maté's assertion: "Not why the addiction, but why the pain?" (Maté, 2008). Delving into the emotional realm, they both echoed a common theme: a desperate quest to self-medicate their emotional wounds (Khantzian, 1997).

Yet, amidst the seemingly endless nights and the relentless grip of addiction, silver linings began to manifest. Joey, during his most vulnerable phase, found solace in art. Those canvas strokes became a testament to his pain and a precursor to his healing. On her end, Jodie channeled her anguish through writing, penning down verses of poetry that bore witness to her struggles.

Their paths converged at the COE. They used their lived experiences to foster an environment rooted in empathy and trauma-informed care. Harris & Fallot (2001) echoed this approach's efficacy, advocating for trauma theory as a foundation for service systems.

The COE faced an influx of individuals grappling with OUD. The underlying trauma in many of these cases necessitated a treatment model that was comprehensive and holistic. As Van der Kolk (2014) articulated, trauma impacts the mind, brain, and body. Integrating this understanding, Joey and Jodie played pivotal roles in implementing Najavits's (2002) "Seeking Safety," a trauma-informed approach tailored for PTSD and substance abuse. As their clinical knowledge grew, it complemented their lived experiences.

However, challenges were abundant. Despite their best intentions, resistance from clients was common. Here, Joey tapped into Miller & Rollnick's (2012) MI techniques. By cultivating an environment of collaborative conversation, clients were gradually ushered into recognizing their own reasons for change.

Yet, as Jodie astutely observed, treating addiction couldn't merely be clinical; it had to resonate at a human level. Drawing from her past, she championed peer-based addiction recovery support (White, 2009), emphasizing the transformative power of shared experiences. Peer support wasn't just a therapeutic intervention but a beacon of hope, a testament that recovery was possible (Davidson et al., 2012).

Yet, the most profound transformations often stemmed from the smallest gestures. Recalling his pain, Joey became the guiding light to continue serving the vulnerable populations.

They also recognized the pressing need to address the stigma surrounding addiction. As Livingston et al. (2012) elucidate, stigma reduction is paramount for effective interventions. They made real strides in humanizing addiction and foregrounding recovery by weaving their narratives into the COE's fabric and galvanizing others to share theirs.

Jodie and Joey would attest that the road to recovery isn't linear. Relapses occurred, and with them came a wave of guilt and self-recrimination. However, drawing insights from Marlatt & Witkiewitz (2002), they emphasized harm reduction, underscoring the journey's importance over the destination.

In retrospect, their stories exemplified the convergence of trauma-informed care and lived experiences. Their scars were testaments to their pasts, but the stars in their narrative were their indomitable spirit, their unwavering commitment to healing, and their ability to transform pain into purpose.

As we segue into understanding the insights gleaned from diverse treatment settings, we must remember the profound impact of humanized, trauma-informed approaches. Jodie and Joey's journeys illuminate the possibilities when clinical interventions meld seamlessly with the transformative power of shared human experiences.

Insights From Diverse Treatment Settings

The recovery journey from addiction is as diverse as the human experience, interwoven with moments of despair, insight, resilience, and transformation. Delving into the poignant narrative of Joey and Jodie offers a unique perspective, highlighting the potency of combined treatment modalities in diverse settings.

In their early days working at the COE program, Joey and Jodie were exposed to numerous cases that pulled at the fabric of their own traumatic pasts. The COE was not just a workplace for them but a living testament to their personal battles with addiction. Their shared pasts, laden with emotional turmoil amidst familial dysfunction, provided them with an unparalleled depth of understanding. As Van der Kolk expounds, trauma impacts the mind and body, making the healing process intricate and multi-dimensional (Van der Kolk, 2014).

Despite their harrowing experiences, there were silver linings in Joey and Jodie's pasts that made their approach to the COE human-centric and palpably genuine. Jodie recalled the warmth of family dinners, a tradition that was an oasis amidst the chaos. Joey often reminisced about his father's love for music—a shared bond that provided fleeting moments of connection and solace. Their pasts became tapestries of pain and beauty, intricately woven, informing their therapeutic interactions.

Today, Joey often implements MI, which focuses on evoking change by harnessing intrinsic motivation (Miller & Rollnick, 2012). Based on his lived experience, Joey could relate to many clients' ambivalence.

As a BCM, Jodie brought a wealth of insights from a harm reduction approach. This method, which Marlatt & Witkiewitz (2002) highlight, focuses not on abstention but on minimizing the adverse effects of substance use.

Joey and Jodie were proponents of peer-based recovery support, recognizing the transformative power of shared experiences (White, 2009). Jodie frequently cited the importance of community and interpersonal relationships, echoing Tracy & Wallace's assertion of the benefits of peer-support groups in addiction recovery (2016).

With both serving many roles but in the field of social work, they became a sanctuary for many. As a couple, they modeled a partnership grounded in empathy, mutual respect, and resilience, epitomizing Harris & Fallot's vision of a trauma-informed service system (2001).

A particular time at the COE with a lady named Dani remains indelible. Dani's narrative was hauntingly reminiscent of the Adverse Childhood Experiences study, which delineates the connection between childhood trauma and subsequent risk of substance use (Dube et al., 2003). As she recounted tales of neglect and abuse, Joey and Jodie tapped into their shared reservoir of pain and healing, validating her emotions. Leveraging Goleman's Emotional Intelligence principles helped her navigate her whirlpool of emotions (Goleman, 1995).

Through such peer-support sessions, they unveiled an underlying theme. Many battling addictions tried to self-medicate, attempting to numb unbearable pain, reflecting Khantzian's hypothesis (1997). Their combined approaches encompassed understanding addiction neurobiology and recognizing social contexts' role, as Heilig et al. (2022) elaborated.

Yet, amidst these narratives of pain, Joey and Jodie's sessions were not devoid of hope. They recognized the importance of giving voice to the unspeakable (Lieberman & Van Horn, 2009) and combating the pervasive stigma associated with addiction (Livingston et al., 2012). Their approach was holistic, aware of the interplay of genetics, impulsivity, and environmental triggers, as expounded by Kreek et al. (2005).

However, it wasn't all seamless. Working in such intense settings brought back haunting memories. Joey recalled nights where the weight of his clients' stories melded with his, leading to restless nights and vivid nightmares, underscoring the biological basis of PTSD (Krystal, Neumeister, & Charney, 2004). Jodie, too, grappled with moments of self-regulation failure, an intricate dance between her neural circuits and external triggers (Heatherton & Wagner, 2011).

Yet, their shared journeys were their anchors. Their personal experiences and professional expertise made them embodiments of hope, resilience, and transformation. This duality of their lived experience and professional knowledge set the stage for exploring the transformative power of combined expertise, demonstrating that sometimes, our scars can indeed pave the way to the stars.

While the insights from diverse treatment settings are paramount, the amalgamation of lived experience and professional insight truly revolutionizes recovery. In the next section, we examine "the transformative power of combined expertise," spotlighting the symbiotic synergy of personal narratives with therapeutic modalities.

The Transformative Power of Combined Expertise

It was a brisk morning when Joey and Jodie sat down at their favorite breakfast spot, *Whispers and Words* discussing their previous week's encounters with clients. Over the hum of the coffee machine and the distant chatter of other patrons, they reflected on their intertwined past, full of chaos, hurt, and then rebirth.

Joey's eyes, though showing lines of age and experience, shone with empathy, an embodiment of the saying by Maté (2008), "The question is not 'Why the addiction?' but 'Why the pain?' As they recalled their memories, their past experiences with addiction loomed like omni-present specters but with silver linings. Joey often spoke of his darkest moments in addiction, using them as tools to connect with his clients. "The isolation I felt back then," he replied, "gave me a perspective I now use to build bridges."

Jodie, with her intuitive understanding, often remembered her nights of despair. But through it all, the fond memories of her family kept her going. Even though they were riddled with dysfunction, their innate goodness acted as a beacon. "Understanding my trauma," she said, touching upon Van der Kolk's work, "helped me see the patterns of my behavior and chart a path to recovery."

Their professional journeys had seen them working hand in hand with shared clients in human services. Jodie and Joey exemplified the marriage of trauma-informed care and lived experience. Joey's role was enriched by White's (2009) assertion that peer support plays a crucial role in recovery, while Jodie's role allowed her to use MI, as extolled by Miller & Rollnick (2012), to effect transformative change in her clients.

There's an inherent power in combining professional expertise with personal experience. This synergy allows professionals like Joey and Jodie to tap into a deeper understanding beyond academic knowledge. Such a union exemplifies Najavits's (2002) emphasis on treating PTSD and substance abuse concurrently, recognizing the interplay of trauma and addiction.

One of the cases that stood out was that of a young woman named Kendra. She came to the COE grappling with OUD after traumatic events during her past relationships. For Jodie, Kendra's story eerily echoed her own, punctuated by family dysfunction and deep-rooted pain. Drawing from her personal experience and the trauma-informed care model by Harris & Fallot (2001), Jodie seamlessly bridged her understanding of trauma with its role in Kendra's addiction.

Gorski's (1990) relapse prevention model became the cornerstone of Joey's approach with many clients. "Relapse is not a failure," Joey would often tell them, echoing the sentiments of harm reduction strategies described by Marlatt & Witkiewitz (2002). Joey and Jodie's personal narratives of addiction, struggle, and recovery gave them a unique lens, enabling them to help their clients see relapse as a bump in the road rather than the end of it.

A poignant moment in their shared journeys was when they initiated a peer-support group inspired by Tracy & Wallace's (2016) findings on its benefits. They believed in the power of community, especially when that community had shared lived experiences. Joey often shared tales of resilience from his past, while Jodie shed light on the importance of self-awareness, drawing from Goleman's (1995) work on emotional intelligence.

But the emphasis on the "human" element stood out starkly in all their interactions, be it with clients or each other. Whether they discussed neuroscience's role in addiction, as Heilig et al. (2022) did, or the importance of understanding trauma's effects from infancy, as highlighted by Lieberman & Van Horn (2009), they never lost sight of the person behind the disorder.

As their breakfast meeting neared its end, an actual emotion lingered in the air—a mix of gratitude, empathy, and hope. Their lived experiences, combined with their academic expertise, were more than just tools; they were testimonies of resilience.

With their cups empty but their spirits full, Jodie and Joey readied to part ways, ever dedicated to their mission. Their shared stories, laden with pain but also redemption, stands as testaments to the transformative power of combined expertise.

In the shadows of their pasts and the brilliance of their combined expertise lie a compelling story that paves the way for future applications, the very lessons we delve into next.

Lessons for Future Application

The iridescent sheen that addiction casts is misleading, almost surreal. When we plunge into the heart of Jodie and Joey's journeys, it is not a walk in a park but a trek through a wild, unpredictable terrain. The challenges they faced, the lessons they learned, and the triumphant moments they celebrated can illuminate paths for others treading similar courses.

Hailing from families that were, by most standards, "good," the couple was not exempted from familial dysfunction, a thread seen in many addiction tales (Dube et al., 2003). In their roles at the COE, the couple found themselves drawing from their professional knowledge and their lived experiences.

In the past, Joey encountered numerous instances where his personal story became the cornerstone of hope for many. In contrast, Jodie continued to resonate with her message of resilience, drawing from the deep wells of her own past.

While both fought with the devils of addiction, it is essential to understand that their battles were deeply rooted in pain—mostly stemming from unresolved traumas (Van der Kolk, 2014). The theory that trauma becomes a precursor to addiction has been well-discussed in literature, notably by Najavits (2002) and Harris & Fallot (2001). This connection between trauma and addiction was visible in Joey and Jodie's stories, which blended intricately with their work. Their trauma-informed approach to healing played a pivotal role in the success of their interventions, highlighting the significance of acknowledging the trauma-addiction nexus (Abuse, 2014).

Yet, what made their recovery journeys uniquely powerful? The silver linings. Joey often recalled the early days of his addiction, describing them as "pain cloaked in fleeting euphoria." But in those dark moments, he found friendships, solidified his values, and learned the art of self-compassion (Goleman, 1995). These unintended lessons became the building blocks of his recovery journey.

Similarly, Jodie's addiction path was riddled with instances where she explored the depths of her emotional strength. A vivid memory she often shared was the evening she spent feeling alone, lost in her thoughts. That night, the soothing way of walking outside and the company of a stray cat became her anchors, teaching her the value of finding beauty in the bleakest situations (Maté, 2008).

Their experiences were also enriched by the peer-based recovery support system (White, 2009). The camaraderie they shared with others with similar lived experiences testified to Mead et al.'s (2001) assertion that peer support offers a perspective rooted in empathy and genuine under-standing. These interactions often served as a protective factor, ensuring relapse prevention (Gorski, 1990). Joey and Jodie's tales emphasized the instrumental role of such supports in bolstering recovery.

Their shared recovery journeys and professional paths highlighted the importance of an integrated approach to addiction management. This approach melded evidence-based strategies, like MI (Miller & Rollnick, 2012) and harm reduction techniques (Marlatt & Witkiewitz, 2002) with insights from their personal stories.

In essence, the powerful lessons Joey and Jodie imparted were multi-fold. Their stories underscored the need for personalized, trauma-informed interventions in addiction treatment. It showcased the invaluable role of lived experiences in designing recovery strategies and emphasized the importance of holistic support systems.

Drawing insights from their journeys, future applications in addiction care need to:

1. Recognize and validate the trauma that often lies at the heart of addiction.

2. Integrate personal lived experiences into professional roles for a more empathetic approach.

3. Prioritize peer-based recovery support systems as foundational to addiction management.

To say that Joey and Jodie's journeys were inspirations is an understatement. Their stories, teeming with raw emotion, despair, hope, and triumph, showcased the full spectrum of human experience. They taught us that even in the depths of addiction, one could find moments of clarity, learn profound life lessons, and draw strength from the most unexpected sources.

However, their narratives also point to something crucial—despite the strides made in understanding and treating addiction, several challenges remain. As we transition into the next chapter, we will dig into the nitty-gritty of these challenges, exploring the barriers in treatment and finding ways to overcome them.

CHAPTER 14

Challenges and Resilience: Overcoming Barriers in Treatment

Identifying Common Challenges in Treatment

Amidst the rhythmic chatter of patrons and the soft hum of turning pages, Whispers and Words becomes a haven for introspection, especially on rain-kissed days. As droplets dance on the windowpanes, they paint a canvas of reflection and anticipation, much like the one in Joey and Jodie's contemplative expressions.

As Jodie adjusts her scarf, taking comfort from its warmth, she muses, "Therapeutic journeys are akin to reading a riveting novel. There are chapters of suspense, pages where the protagonist feels lost, and times when turning back seems tempting. Yet, navigating these challenges makes the story's essence truly shine."

Joey nods in agreement, tracing a droplet's path on the window. "Indeed. Much like every book chapter, every therapy or peer support session brings its share of uncertainties. But it's in confronting these barriers that the narrative of resilience unfolds."

Their gazes shift to a young woman immersed in her journal, a silent testament to the myriad stories that unfold within the hallowed walls of the cafe-cum-bookstore. Jodie reflects, "Each ink stroke, every whispered conversation here, echoes the universality of struggle and triumph."

Joey sets down his cup, its warmth lingering "In this chapter, we'll journey through these intricate mazes, understanding that challenges in therapy aren't mere obstacles. They are, in fact, opportunities–doors that lead to deeper insights and transformative growth."

As you examine this segment with Joey and Jodie, you'll discover the profound interplay between challenge and resilience, revealing the potential of barriers not as dead-ends but as catalysts driving therapeutic evolution and personal empowerment.

Stepping back into the intimate realities of their pasts, Joey and Jodie vividly recall their battles with addiction. As they often expressed, their memories were like well-read books: every page held a story, lesson, and testament to the human spirit's resilience.

Having spent considerable time at the COE, Joey and Jodie witnessed countless individuals with stories as harrowing, if not more, than their own. The journey of recovery, they knew, was far from a straight path. Instead, it was an intricate maze with challenges that often seemed insurmountable.

One such challenge that both Joey and Jodie resonated deeply with was the omnipresent shadow of trauma. In his seminal work, *The Body Keeps the Score*, Van der Kolk delineated how trauma gets engraved in both the mind and body, making its healing a complex, multilayered process (Van der Kolk, 2014). For many individuals with addiction, past traumatic experiences often become intertwined with their substance use, forming a protective yet destructive armor against raw, painful memories (Khantzian, 1997; Simpson & Miller, 2002).

Jodie once mentioned an encounter with a young woman at the COE. This woman, whose history was punctuated with episodes of childhood maltreatment, found solace in opiates. They provided her with a fleeting escape from the nightmares of her past, although, in the long run, they only added to her trauma (Dube et al., 2003; Topitzes, Mersky, & Reynolds, 2012). Such intertwined traumas made the treatment more intricate, demanding an understanding of the multifaceted relationship between trauma and addiction.

However, this dual challenge of addiction and trauma is not the only barrier. The societal stigma associated with addiction further compounds the recovery process. Despite emerging scientific evidence, many still view addiction as a mere "lack of willpower" rather than understanding its deep-rooted biological, psychological, and social dimensions (Livingston et al., 2012; Kreek et al., 2005). While reflecting on his past, Jocy often lamented the hurtful stereotypes and prejudice he faced. These external judgments often internalize, creating a daunting internal barrier of shame, self-loathing, and hopelessness.

Amidst these challenges, the silver lining for Joey and Jodie lay in their bond and shared experiences. When Joey would recount the time they worked together at COE, there was always a sparkle in his eyes. Their collective strength became a beacon of hope for many at the center. They demonstrated the immense power of peer support beyond clinical interventions, offering solace through shared pain, mutual understanding, and relentless hope (Mead, Hilton, & Curtis, 2001; Davidson et al., 2012).

But why is peer support so powerful? Why did Jodie still find solace in Joey's presence, despite shifting to a different agency? As Harris and Fallot (2001) describe in their trauma theory, individuals with lived experiences can offer a unique form of empathy. They understand the clinical dimensions of addiction and deeply resonate with the emotions, vulnerabilities, and aspirations of those walking the recovery path (Harris & Fallot, 2001).

With her ever-present insight, Jodie often emphasized the importance of individualized care. Drawing from Najavits's "Seeking Safety," she advocated for a trauma-informed approach, which focuses not on "What's wrong with you?" but "What happened to you?" (Najavits, 2002). This shift in perspective, Jodie believed, held the power to revolutionize addiction care by acknowledging and validating every individual's unique journey and challenges.

Joey had a broader view from his vantage point as a clinical supervisor. He saw systemic challenges, from inadequate resources to a need for updated professional training. Yet, he remained undeterred. Drawing strength from his and Jodie's journey, he continuously advocated for a more inclusive, evidence-based, and empathetic approach, emphasizing MI, harm reduction, and resilience building (Miller & Rollnick, 2012; Marlatt & Witkiewitz, 2002).

As we transition through this chapter, we acknowledge that treatment barriers, whether internal or external, personal or systemic, are undeniable realities. Yet, as Joey and Jodie's stories illuminate, these barriers are not insurmountable. With every challenge faced, there's an inherent opportunity, a chance to learn, adapt, and grow stronger.

But how does one cultivate this strength? What role does resilience play in shaping one's recovery journey? Let's explore this further as we dig into the subsequent segment: role of resilience in overcoming barriers.

Role of Resilience in Overcoming Barriers

The role of resilience in overcoming barriers is akin to a candle burning bright amidst darkness. For Joey and Jodie, the arduous journey from addiction's abyss to their present roles in addiction care is a testament to the power of this internal flame. Their narrative uniquely portrays the human spirit's capacity to rebound and remake through their past addictions, the subsequent despair, and the redeeming power of resilience.

When delving into addiction, one must recognize its multilayered nature. Van der Kolk (2014) elucidates how trauma leaves an indelible mark on both the brain and body, making it evident that recovery isn't merely about abstaining: it's a journey toward reconfiguring one's emotional, psychological, and physiological responses.

Within the walls of the COE, where Joey and Jodie once collaborated, they bore witness to the profound impact of resilience. As they progress, Joey and Jodie wield their personal histories as tools. They were drawing from experiences such as Joey's vulnerable moments seeking safety from PTSD, while entangled in substance abuse, and Jodie's encounters with the "hungry ghosts" Maté (2008) discusses—those insatiable cravings and haunting pasts.

Good families don't equate to flawless upbringings. The dysfunction in Joey and Jodie's early environments amplified their vulnerabilities. The Adverse Childhood Experiences study (Dube et al., 2003) accentuates the profound relationship between childhood trauma and subsequent risk for substance use disorders. This invisible emotional inheritance perhaps ushered them toward addiction, a desperate attempt, as Khantzian (1997) suggests, at self-medication.

Yet, there were silver linings. Amid the turmoil, their shared experiences in the COE, those authentic moments of empathy and connection illuminated recovery paths for themselves and countless others. In White's (2009) exploration of peer-based addiction recovery, there's an acknowledgment that lived experiences can sometimes offer a depth of understanding that traditional therapies might overlook. Joey and Jodie's synergistic partnership, rooted in shared battles against addiction, became a beacon for many.

Emotionally, the challenge is visceral. Resilience isn't merely about bouncing back; it's a metamorphosis. Maté (2008) recognizes that behind every case of addiction lies pain, an agony often echoing unaddressed traumas. Joey's resilience meant confronting these past shadows, employing strategies like CBT, and fostering emotional intelligence, as underscored by Goleman (1995).

For Jodie, resilience manifested in forging connections, both personal and professional. Leveraging peer support, as highlighted by Mead et al. (2001) and Tracy & Wallace (2016), she built bridges to recovery for herself and others.

Despite the challenges, both harnessed the trauma-informed approach. Harris and Fallot (2001) stress the importance of viewing addiction treatment through the lens of trauma. Every setback, be it a relapse or a challenging day at the COE, was not seen as a failure but as an integral component of their healing journeys. Joey and Jodie internalized the ethos that every individual brought into the COE was not defined by their addiction but by their human potential.

Yet, like the most intricate of mosaics, this journey wasn't solely about the struggles. There were memories of laughter, love, and profound moments of shared understanding. Remembering the time Joey played his guitar, giving a fleeting escape from the clutches of their current plight. Or when Jodie told a story, helping clients feel safe where both tales of despair and hope reverberated, echoing the sentiments of Lieberman and Van Horn (2009) about the reparative nature of vocalizing trauma.

Understanding the challenges of addiction and the monumental role of resilience in navigating these hurdles is not about glorifying struggle. Instead, it's an acknowledgment of the strength innate in every individual. As Joey and Jodie have shown, resilience isn't about the absence of adversity but the capacity to use it as a steppingstone, a testament to the boundless power of the human spirit.

As we transition to the next segment, let us assess the heart of our discussion, exploring how harnessing these lived experiences can be channeled as powerful tools for building resilience.

Harnessing Lived Experiences for Resilience Building

In the vast expanse of trauma recovery, lived experiences offer a unique potency. Joey and Jodie are not just names but embodiments of lived resilience and hope. Their stories, woven with trauma and recovery, isn't just a testament to their strength but a beacon for countless others treading the murky waters of addiction.

Growing up in seemingly good families, Joey and Jodie had the camouflage of normalcy. However, beneath the surface lurked dysfunction and hidden traumas. Van der Kolk insightfully pens *The Body Keeps the Score*, highlighting that trauma embeds itself deeply, often manifesting in ways one least expects, like addiction (Van der Kolk, 2014). For Joey and Jodie, the internal struggles met the inviting arms of opioids, offering a brief respite from the chaos.

Working hand in hand at the COE, they observed how addiction was not just an isolated problem. Still, they intertwined with past trauma and wounds that never truly healed. Najavits (2002) echoes this sentiment in *Seeking Safety*, emphasizing the close relationship between PTSD and substance abuse (Najavits, 2002). Their shared understanding and lived experiences became instrumental in fostering a trauma-informed care approach at the COE.

There's a moment Joey often recalls from their time together at COE. It was a chilly winter evening, and a young woman, clearly in the throes of addiction, walked into their COE waiting room. Her eyes, though weary, looked familiar. It was the same look Joey and Jodie once carried–a mélange of despair, hope, and desperate yearning for change. As they conversed, Joey and Jodie shared snippets of their journeys with her, the dark alleys of addiction, the overwhelming urge to escape, and the ray of hope that eventually led them out. It was an evening where past traumas met healing, all facilitated through the power of shared experiences.

But why are these experiences so potent? Mead, Hilton, and Curtis (2001) suggest that peer support isn't just about shared experiences but also about the shared understanding and empathetic resonance it fosters (Mead, Hilton, & Curtis, 2001). When Joey spoke of the warmth opioids provided against the cold trauma of his childhood, or when Jodie narrated her constant struggle against relapse, triggered by early memories of feeling isolated, they weren't just sharing stories. They were laying down a roadmap of resilience built on the traumas that once imprisoned them.

Even as they navigated different professional paths, with Joey ascending to the role of a clinical supervisor and Jodie transitioning to a BCM, their shared narrative never ceased to inspire. They became living examples of how one can repurpose pain into a driving force for change.

However, understanding addiction's intricate relationship with trauma requires a deeper dive. Dube et al. (2003), in their study on childhood abuse and neglect, found a stark link between early adverse experiences and the propensity for illicit drug use (Dube et al., 2003). This confluence of trauma and addiction underscores the importance of a trauma-informed treatment approach, as Harris and Fallot stressed (2001). Instead of simply treating the addiction, there's a paramount need to address the root—the underlying trauma (Harris & Fallot, 2001).

In essence, Joey and Jodie's journeys weren't just about overcoming addiction; they were about confronting and healing the wounds of the past. Their shared experiences became tangible evidence of the transformative power of resilience and hope.

Yet, for every Joey and Jodie, countless others are yet to find their path to recovery. This necessitates a shift in treatment approaches, placing lived experiences at the forefront. As White (2009) expounds, peer-based addiction recovery support anchors itself in history, theory, and practice, and this amalgamation makes it so effective (White, 2009). Joey and Jodie's narratives offer glimpses into this efficacy, illustrating the undeniable power of empathy, understanding, and shared resilience in fostering recovery.

As this chapter unfolds, it beckons a deeper exploration into harnessing these lived experiences. If Joey and Jodie's stories tell us anything, it's that within every scar, there's a star waiting to shine. Their pasts, marred by addiction and trauma, sowed the seeds for a future of hope, resilience, and unwavering support for others.

Transitioning forward, we look at the strategies providers can employ to enhance client resilience, ensuring that stories like Joey and Jodie's aren't mere anomalies but become the norm in addiction treatment.

Strategies for Providers to Enhance Client Resilience

Joey and Jodie's intertwined histories are testaments to the endurance of the human spirit in the face of unimaginable challenges. Both emerged from the crushing jaws of addiction, with tales of resilience that offer hope to every service provider in the addiction treatment domain. Their past experiences provide invaluable lessons to inform strategies for enhancing client resilience.

Understanding Trauma and Its Implications

Trauma has been noted to be an underlying thread in the fabric of addiction (Van der Kolk, 2014). Even when suppressed, the memories can insinuate themselves into every facet of an individual's life. While reflecting on his years of misuse, Joey shared how trauma-induced feelings of shame and worthlessness exacerbated his addiction. On the other hand, Jodie recognized patterns from her traumatic past that led to her self-destructive choices. The body and mind constantly seek ways to process traumatic experiences, and sometimes, substances become the maladaptive solution (Maté, 2008). Providers must recognize these traumatic triggers and design interventions sensitive to clients' trauma histories (Harris & Fallot, 2001).

Individualizing the Recovery Path

Every journey through addiction and recovery is unique, and providers must tailor their approaches. As clinicians like Joey in human services observed, the key is to balance evidence-based interventions and the individual's unique narrative (Najavits, 2002). Leveraging personal strengths, such as Joey's managerial abilities and Jodie's aptitude for empathy, can play a vital role in enhancing resilience.

Peer Support as a Pillar of Resilience

White (2009) emphasized the value of peer-based recovery support. Joey and Jodie's relationship is emblematic of this principle. Their shared histories, mutual understandings, and combined strengths formed a supportive foundation for their recovery. Peer interactions foster an environment where individuals feel understood, accepted, and empowered. Service providers should actively facilitate peer- support groups, acknowledging the mutual benefits of shared experiences in addiction recovery (Tracy & Wallace, 2016).

Encouraging Emotional Self-Regulation

Emotional self-regulation is central to resilience (Goleman, 1995). Overcoming addiction often involves understanding and mastering one's emotional responses. The ability to regulate emotions can determine how effectively one deals with stressors that might trigger a relapse (Heatherton & Wagner, 2011). Thus, by instilling skills for emotional self-regulation, providers can offer clients tools to navigate the tumultuous seas of recovery.

Understanding the Biological Dimensions

The interface between genetics and addiction must be considered. The disposition for addiction in some individuals may be amplified due to genetic factors (Kreek et al., 2005). Understanding this interplay can allow for more targeted and effective interventions. As a social worker, Joey understands the importance of this biological understanding, urging his colleagues to stay updated on the latest research and findings.

Reducing Stigma: The First Step towards Healing

Livingston et al. (2012) underscored the adverse impacts of stigma related to substance use disorders. Joey and Jodie, despite their pasts, faced societal prejudices. Combating stigma is paramount for the affected individuals and the larger community to be involved in recovery.

Empowering Through Knowledge

Equipping clients with knowledge about addiction, its triggers, and strategies for coping can be empowering. Informed clients are better equipped to make choices that bolster their resilience (Miller & Rollnick, 2012). Joey and Jodie felt that being educated about their conditions allowed them to take ownership of their recovery journeys.

As providers embark on this path to enhance client resilience, they must remember that every strategy and intervention must be imbued with compassion, understanding, and patience. The stories of Joey and Jodie shine a light on the importance of hope, determination, and mutual support. They demonstrate that the right approach can overcome even the most daunting barriers in treatment.

To further illustrate the power of resilience in the recovery journey, the next section will examine real-life case studies showcasing resilience in action.

Case Studies Showcasing Resilience in Action

In addiction, resilience is often likened to a phoenix rising from its ashes. Joey and Jodie's stories encapsulate this transformative journey from profound darkness to gleaming light.

Jodie and Joey first met in recovery while in twelve-step meetings. Their paths crossed as two individuals seeking solace from the relentless grip of addiction and as two souls intertwining in a shared purpose. Over the years, they would face immense challenges, yet they remained unyielding, each becoming the other's rock.

Van der Kolk writes about the profound effects of trauma and how the body often holds onto these memories long after the mind believes it has moved on (Van der Kolk, 2014). Jodie's experience bore testimony to this idea. Growing up in a seemingly "good" family, she was subjected to layers of dysfunction, which fueled her need to find solace in substances. The drugs offered her an escape–a space where she didn't have to confront her past and felt temporarily freed from the chains of her traumatic memories.

Maté (2008), in *In the Realm of Hungry Ghosts*, discusses how many people who struggle with addiction are battling traumas and emotional pains. Similarly, Joey's addiction originated from a place of deep emotional turmoil. He grappled with the suffocating weight of family expectations and societal pressures while trying to mask the internal chaos and emotional abyss he felt.

Despite the shadows of their pasts, there were silver linings in Joey and Jodie's experiences. While addiction had trapped them, it was also where they found each other. This connection became the cornerstone of their recovery. Together, they navigated the complexities of their treatment. MI (Miller & Rollnick, 2012) played a critical role in their journeys, allowing them to confront and challenge their internal narratives.

Jodie's transition to a BCM role was challenging. The change took her away from the familiar COE environment where she and Joey had begun their healing journeys. However, it also provided her a platform to leverage her lived experience to help others with mental health disorders. She employed trauma-informed care, a holistic approach that acknowledges the pervasive impact of trauma and integrates this understanding into her work (Harris & Fallot, 2001).

Joey's growth within COE to a clinical supervisor role showcased his resilience and determination. His work drew heavily from the principles of *Seeking Safety*, a treatment manual that underscores the importance of addressing both PTSD and substance abuse concurrently (Najavits, 2002). Joey's deep understanding of trauma, compounded by his lived experiences, allowed him to empathize deeply with his clients.

Joey and Jodie's stories demonstrate the intricate and profound connections between trauma, resilience, and recovery. While painful, their shared pasts and battles with addiction also offered rich tapestries of experiences. These experiences, woven with threads of silver linings, became vital tools in their arsenal as they worked to support others navigating similar challenges.

In retrospect, their journey illustrates the essential truth that physical and emotional scars can indeed transform into stars, guiding lights for others in the vast expanse of addiction recovery.

As we explore deeper into the intricacies of substance use treatment, it becomes increasingly evident that our understanding is evolving. While we celebrate stories of resilience like Joey and Jodie's, we must also look forward to the potential future landscape of substance use treatment.

CHAPTER 15

A Vision for the Future of Substance Use Treatment

The Future Landscape of Substance Use Treatment

A corner stands transformed in the cozy enclave of Whispers and Words, where the aroma of coffee intertwines with the musk of old books. Today, it resembles a collaborative space. On a table, carefully laid out, are blueprints depicting future therapy modalities and books placed in volumes that hint at revolutionary approaches in substance use treatment.

As Joey flips open a book detailing technology integration in therapy, he replies, "The potential advancements in treatment could reshape our entire understanding of recovery." Peering at a blueprint illustrating community-based recovery hubs, Jodie adds, "It's a future where treatment isn't just a standardized protocol but a tailor-made journey."

She sips her coffee, its warmth contrasting with the cool touch of her metallic bookmark, engraved with the words "A Personalized Future." "Our approach," she ponders aloud, "must be as dynamic and evolving as the individuals we aim to help."

Dig into this chapter with Joey and Jodie as they traverse the pages of possibility. Witness the innovative confluence of technology, human touch, and the promising horizons of substance use treatment. Allow yourself to be engrossed in a narrative that paints a future where care and innovation walk hand in hand.

Joey and Jodie sat across from each other, a reflective atmosphere enveloping them. Jodie's fingers danced over the pages of Van der Kolk's *The Body Keeps the Score*, remembering her own body's score of addiction. Joey glanced over at his wife, reminded of the days when they walked through the dark abyss of addiction. The mere fact they sat here today, looking at the future of substance use treatment, was nothing short of a miracle.

"Remember when we believed there was no way out?" Joey began, his voice edged with emotion, recalling their traumatic pasts marred by substance abuse. They both belonged to loving families, but family dysfunction often exacerbated the complex layers of their addictions (Dube et al., 2003). Their shared histories gave them unique insights into the multifaceted nature of addiction and recovery.

Jodie nodded, brushing a tear from her cheek. "We've come so far. We were fortunate to find each other and recover together. But many don't have that privilege. That's why creating a future where every individual's journey is recognized and addressed is crucial."

She turned a page to a quote that resonated deeply with her: "Trauma results in a fundamental reorganization of the way the mind and brain manage perceptions" (Van der Kolk, 2014). Reflecting on her trauma and subsequent substance use, Jodie remembered how she'd once tried to numb her overwhelming emotions. «Addiction,» she whispered, recalling Maté's words, "is a complex flight from distress, from a reality that seems too painful to endure" (Maté, 2008).

Joey leaned in, placing his hand on the blueprint of community-based recovery hubs. "There's a growing consensus that personalized care, especially with the trauma-informed approach, is key to successful treatment," he commented, referencing Harris & Fallot's work on using trauma theory in designing service systems (2001). "It's not just about treating the addiction; it's about understanding the underlying causes, the deep-seated traumas, and crafting a path to healing."

Jodie looked up, her eyes sparkling with a blend of hope and determination. "We're living proof that trauma and addiction can be confronted and conquered.

Our experiences, our scars, are testament to that."

Their intertwined pasts served as rich tapestries of lessons for the future. Joey often spoke about their early days at the COE, the challenges they faced, and the individuals they helped. Their encounters with countless others, each with unique scars, shaped their understanding of substance use disorders. While they may have moved on to different roles, their commitment to revolutionizing substance use treatment remained strong.

Turning her attention to White's "Peer-based Addiction Recovery Support," Jodie mused, "Peer support plays a pivotal role. We've both benefited from it, and we've seen its transformative power in others" (White, 2009). Joey nodded in agreement, remembering their days at COE, where peer support was paramount.

But Jodie had concerns, too. "While peer support is essential, we must also address the stigmas associated with substance use disorders," she said, referencing Livingston et al.'s study on the effectiveness of interventions for reducing stigma (2012).

"The trauma many experiences lead them to substances as a coping mechanism," Joey added, "Yet society often looks down on them, further entrenching their pain. As treatment evolves, we must prioritize compassion and understanding, combining the power of emotional intelligence (Goleman, 1995) with evidence-based treatments."

They both envisioned a future landscape where treatment wasn't just a clinical process. Instead, it was an intertwining of personal experiences, trauma-informed care, technological advancements, and community support, leading to holistic healing—a future where the very fabric of substance use treatment resonated with empathy, personalization, and innovation.

Jodie looked up, her face a picture of hope and determination. "We've come so far, but the journey ahead is long. Every story, every scar, every star is a testament to human resilience. The future of substance use treatment isn't just in the pages of these books: it's in the lived experiences, the collective wisdom, and the shared journeys."

Joey nodded, "Indeed, as we look ahead, we see a horizon where trauma-informed care isn't just an option but a necessity." This thought acted as the bridge, leading to the next vital juncture in their exploration.

As they investigated deeper into the future chapters, Joey and Jodie knew that trauma-informed care would be central to effective substance use treatment. But what evolutions awaited this paradigm, and how could it be made even more robust? The journey continues as they explore the "potential evolutions in trauma-informed care" in the recovery world.

Potential Evolutions in Trauma-Informed Care

When we hear the term trauma, our minds often paint a visceral image of life's more harrowing events. Trauma can be a spectrum, and its shadow doesn't only cast on those who have experienced catastrophic events. For Joey and Jodie, life was full of moments that ranged from good memories to those steeped in dysfunction and turmoil. Their experiences testify to the broader idea that trauma-informed care must be multidimensional, compassionate, and ever-evolving.

Dr. Van der Kolk once wrote that the body keeps the score, suggesting that emotional and physical traumas aren't just forgotten; they resonate within our physiology (Van der Kolk, 2014). For Joey and Jodie, their own bodies' scores reverberated deeply. Their experiences with addiction and work at the COE shaped their perspective on substance use treatment. Jodie's move to another agency as a BCM and Joey's role as a clinical supervisor at the COE was no mere transition but a reflection of their commitment to growth and change.

Substance abuse can be traced back to various underlying factors—sometimes trauma being one of them. Maté (2008) illustrated how addiction can be viewed as an attempt to fill an insatiable void, a symptom of an underlying trauma or mental anguish. Jodie and Joey understood this. The scars from their shared pasts of addiction, once painful and debilitating, gradually became their stars. These scars became lessons, stories of resilience, and foundations for their future.

As we anticipate the future of substance use treatment, trauma-informed care is destined to play a monumental role. Incorporating this form of care into addiction recovery plans has shown increased effectiveness in treatment (Najavits, 2002; Harris & Fallot, 2001). Why? Because it addresses the underlying reasons for substance use, weaving together the fragmented parts of an individual's psyche.

The couple's history is a poignant reminder of how trauma and substance use intertwine. They emerged from good families, yet layers of dysfunction beneath the surface pointed to a complex interplay of factors influencing their paths to addiction (Dube et al., 2003). Not every person with a history of trauma will develop a substance use disorder, but it's undeniable that such histories can increase vulnerabilities (Topitzes et al., 2012).

The current trajectory of trauma-informed care in addiction treatment pivots toward a more integrated, personalized approach. Marlatt & Witkiewitz (2002) elucidate the potential of harm reduction approaches, suggesting that helping individuals make safer, healthier choices can be transformative.

Let's humanize this with Jodie and Joey's narrative. Remember those early days at the COE, where they worked side by side? Their empathetic approach stemmed from their personal narratives. They knew firsthand the power of being seen, heard, and understood. Their shared experiences created a bridge to those they served. They were living proof that understanding trauma wasn't just about clinical knowledge but about shared humanity. Through their trauma-informed care, they could address the self-regulation failures often associated with addiction (Heatherton & Wagner, 2011).

There are silver linings in their shared journeys. Moments where their past experiences allowed them to create genuine connections with their patients. Moments when Joey's intuitive grasp of emotional intelligence (Goleman, 1995) or Jodie's understanding of the complexities of self-medication (Khantzian, 1997) became invaluable.

One cannot overemphasize the role of peers in substance use recovery. White (2009) chronicled the history, theory, and practice of peer-based addiction recovery support. Jodie and Joey's narratives highlight the tangible benefits of this support. Their stories provided beacons of hope for many in their own battles with addiction.

But what of the future?

The next leap in trauma-informed care must be a synthesis of therapeutic interventions grounded in robust neuroscience research, while also allowing for the lived experiences of individuals. This dual approach will create a holistic environment where trauma can be addressed clinically and emotionally.

Joey once shared a touching moment from his past. Amidst the chaos of addiction, he remembered his mother's unwavering faith in his recovery. This belief wasn't rooted in naivety but in love. Love, that despite the bleakness, saw the potential for growth, healing, and evolution.

The future of trauma-informed care in substance use treatment beckons us to bring love, compassion, and hope to the forefront. As the field advances, the essence of recovery will always be deeply human, rooted in science and heart.

With this evolving vision for trauma-informed care emerges another significant element in the trajectory of substance use treatment. The invaluable presence and growing role of those with lived experiences...

The Growing Role of Those With Lived Experiences

The tangible pulse of healing begins when stories are shared. Joey and Jodie's lives were testaments to this truth. Their pasts were marred with addiction, threatening their very existence. Yet, their intertwined journeys showed the transformative power of trauma-informed care and the integral role of those with lived experiences in revolutionizing substance use treatment.

In the dim-lit room of the COE, Joey once recounted his initial days of addiction. The trauma rooted in his childhood, a medley of love and dysfunction, became an internal wound that drove him to substances. Khantzian (1997) presented the self-medication hypothesis, which posits that individuals use drugs to relieve emotional distress. Joey's life mirrored this hypothesis: a bid to silence the chaos within (Khantzian, 1997). Jodie's story echoed similar chords—searching for solace in substances amidst the overwhelming feelings from the past.

According to Van der Kolk (2014), trauma is not just the story of something awful that happened but also the residue that lingers in the minds and bodies of survivors.

The weight of their struggles became their strength. After braving the tumultuous waves of addiction, they discovered that their redemption lay in leveraging their lived experiences to illuminate the path for others. Joey and Jodie's roles were not a coincidence. It was their personal mission.

Their firsthand experience allowed them to craft an environment of authentic empathy at COE. Maté (2008) articulates that compassionate curiosity toward an individual's life story is instrumental in understanding addiction. Joey and Jodie exemplified this sentiment, listening deeply, recognizing triggers, and offering tailored interventions.

One of the pillars of their approach was emphasizing the significance of trauma-informed care, which recognizes the prevalence and impact of trauma in individuals' lives (Harris & Fallot, 2001). Their mission was aligned with SAMHSA's concept, which outlined that recognizing signs and symptoms of trauma is paramount (Abuse, 2014). They knew trauma was not an isolated incident but a series of cascading events ripple through every aspect of one's life.

The duo's sessions always incorporated discussions about traumatic experiences. Najavits' (2002) *Seeking Safety* was often a reference point—a beacon of hope emphasizing coping skills and cognitive-behavioral strategies. Through these, they unearthed memories and triggers, often rooted in adverse childhood experiences (Dube et al., 2003).

Yet, it wasn't just about recalling the past. Joey and Jodie's methodology harmoniously blended the past with the present. They integrated Miller and Rollnick's (2012) MI techniques, helping clients harness their intrinsic motivation to foster change. In tandem, harm reduction approaches proposed by Marlatt & Witkiewitz (2002) focused on reducing adverse consequences of drug use.

However, the most potent weapon in their arsenal was peer support. Mead, Hilton, & Curtis (2001) elucidated that peer support, grounded in shared experiences, offers unique therapeutic benefits. White (2009) further highlighted its historical and scientific significance in addiction recovery. For Joey and Jodie, their stories weren't just tales of despair;

they were silver linings illuminating the dark corners of many lives, making recovery palpable.

Tracy & Wallace (2016) accentuated the advantages of peer support groups in addiction treatment. Through their stories, Joey and Jodie humanized the recovery process and created a compassionate community. Their pasts were testimonies that stars of hope can still shine amidst the harshest storms.

To look at Joey and Jodie was to witness resilience incarnate. They embodied Goleman's (1995) assertion of emotional intelligence, using self-awareness, empathy, and interpersonal skills to foster genuine connections. Their journey showcased that recovery wasn't merely about abstaining from substances—it was about reclaiming one's life, stitching past wounds, and kindling hope.

As we reflect on the indomitable spirit of Joey, Jodie, and countless others who use their lived experiences to light the way, we must recognize their invaluable contribution to substance use treatment. Intertwined with evidence-based approaches, their stories sow seeds of hope, illuminating a path paved with empathy, understanding, and resilience.

As we transition to the subsequent discussions on innovative approaches on the horizon, let Joey and Jodie's journeys serve as testaments to the transformative power of lived experiences, showing us that our scars, when embraced, can indeed become stars.

Innovative Approaches on the Horizon

Life and recovery have always been a dance between the past's scars and the future's hope-filled stars. No individuals reflect this journey better than Joey and Jodie. Survivors of addiction's brutal grip, this couple now stands at the forefront of addiction treatment, transforming their pain into beacons of hope for countless others. Their stories show that innovative approaches are on the horizon in a world where the vicious cycle of trauma and substance use spirals into devastating outcomes.

At the COE, Joey and Jodie continually emphasized the power of lived experiences in shaping treatment pathways. Through this lens, we explore the evolving vistas of substance use treatment fueled by trauma-informed care and the passion of personal narratives.

One such innovation emerging is the emphasis on trauma's insidious influence on substance misuse. As Van der Kolk posits, the body does indeed keep the score; trauma manifests physically and mentally, leaving individuals more susceptible to addiction as they seek relief (Van der Kolk, 2014). Understanding this, the COE's approach has shifted toward an integrated model that bridges the gap between trauma care and addiction treatment. This paradigm shift mirrors Harris & Fallot's envisioning of a trauma-informed service system, emphasizing the recognition and responsiveness to trauma's pervasive presence in afflicted individuals (Harris & Fallot, 2001).

Jodie often recounted her experiences working with clients and the undercurrent of childhood traumas. Reflecting Dube et al.'s findings, adverse childhood experiences dramatically increase the risk of substance misuse later in life (Dube et al., 2003). The tales of Joey and Jodie exemplify the urgency of this nexus between trauma and addiction. Born into families replete with love yet marred by dysfunction, their descent into addiction became an unconscious attempt at self-medication, echoing Khantzian's hypothesis (Khantzian, 1997).

Yet, as the scars become more evident, so do the stars. MI, a client-centered counseling approach that mobilizes an individual's desire to change, stands as a beacon (Miller & Rollnick, 2012). With his compassionate demeanor, Joey often employed this technique, tapping into a person's intrinsic motivation and awakening their dormant aspirations for recovery.

Moreover, the future lies in embracing peer-based addiction recovery support, as proposed by White (2009). There's a transformative power when survivors guide survivors. Joey and Jodie's stories are potent testaments to the power of shared lived experiences. Mead et al. emphasize that peer support offers a unique, empathetic perspective, creating an environment where healing thrives (Mead, Hilton, & Curtis, 2001).

Leveraging harm reduction approaches, another promising avenue focuses on minimizing the negative consequences of substance use rather than on strict abstinence (Marlatt & Witkiewitz, 2002). It's a philosophy Jodie and Joey stood by; they recognized that the journey to recovery isn't a straight path. Often, it's filled with setbacks, but every step, no matter how small, moves toward a healthier life.

Lastly, technology's role in rehabilitation cannot be underestimated. From leveraging data analytics to predict relapse tendencies based on Gorski's CENAPS model (Gorski, 1990) to utilizing virtual reality for exposure therapy in PTSD-induced substance abuse patients (Kar, 2011), the digital age promises a revolution in addiction treatment.

As we examine these innovative approaches, it's vital to remember that the emotional core remains paramount. Substance misuse and trauma intertwine deeply with emotions. Goleman's notion of emotional intelligence underscores the importance of understanding and managing our emotions, especially when navigating the tumultuous waters of recovery (Goleman, 1995). Joey and Jodie's journeys reflect this emotional dance–from the depths of despair to the pinnacles of hope and back again.

Yet, the silver linings from their past addiction experiences illuminate the way forward. Whether it was Joey's resilience in facing relapse or Jodie's unwavering commitment to helping others, even as she battled her demons, their narratives emphasize that the stars always shine amidst the scars.

As we stand at the crossroads, reflecting upon the innovations on the horizon, it becomes clear that collaboration and unity are the true power in revolutionizing recovery. The following section delves deeper into this sentiment, cementing the belief that we can construct a future where recovery isn't just a possibility but a promise.

Collaboration and unity as the way forward beckons us toward this new dawn in substance use treatment.

Collaboration and Unity as the Way Forward

Amidst the COE corridors, two souls who had once grappled with addiction had now become its beacon. Joey and Jodie not only united in matrimony but also in their commitment to change. Their combined scars from past addiction became the stars guiding others toward recovery.

With her soft-spoken manner, Jodie often recounted her early days. She would fondly remember the rhythm of her and Joey's steps echoing in the hallway, symbolizing their harmonious effort. As the couple grew in their lives, the unison of their mission remained strong.

From Van der Kolk's pioneering work, it becomes evident that trauma is embodied–it lingers, it remains (Van der Kolk, 2014). The haunting grip of trauma had once tethered Joey and Jodie to a vortex of substance use. However, they transcended. Joey would often muse, "Our past is not our destiny." They embraced Maté's perspective, viewing their past battles not as signs of inherent dysfunction but as encounters with "hungry ghosts"–manifestations of unmet needs and unresolved trauma (Maté, 2008).

The silver lining of their past experiences was the rich tapestry of lessons learned, which informed their collaborative approach to treatment. Where Joey became an expert in applying the trauma-informed principles detailed by Harris & Fallot (2001), ensuring the care environment was secure and empowering, Jodie shone in implementing peer support, helping her own PTSD (Najavits, 2002).

Drawing from their roots, they understood the nuances of addiction. Good families, like theirs, were not immune. But, beneath the façade of good families, they also knew the undercurrents of dysfunction that often flowed. Referencing Dube et al.'s seminal work, they stressed the undeniable link between childhood trauma and susceptibility to addiction (Dube et al., 2003).

Their vision was clear: a collaborative and unified approach to substance use treatment. Integration was their keyword. They championed the peer-based recovery system, taking a leaf from White's book emphasizing the unparalleled power of shared lived experiences (White, 2009). Miller & Rollnick imbibed the ethos of MI, ensuring that the individual's motivation was the guiding star of their recovery journey (Miller & Rollnick, 2012).

But their genius lay in recognizing the blend. Inspired by Marlatt & Witkiewitz, Joey often suggests, "It's not about total abstinence for everyone. Harm reduction is just as valid" (Marlatt & Witkiewitz, 2002). Together, they envisioned an adaptable fabric of care, recognizing individual trajectories of healing.

A significant learning, they brought to the table was the power of emotion. As Goleman elucidated, emotional intelligence is the rudder steering us through life's tumultuous waters (Goleman, 1995). Joey and Jodie utilized it as the cornerstone of their programs, helping clients navigate their emotional landscapes and making them understand the self-medication hypothesis Khantzian put forth (Khantzian, 1997). It was about understanding one's pain and not just numbing it.

But the duo emphasized unity beyond the theories, methods, and techniques. Whether it was the unity of systems, treatment models, or people, convergence was the key. As Mead et al. wrote about the power of peer support, the lived experiences of Joey and Jodie became the bedrock on which others could build their recovery stories (Mead, Hilton, & Curtis, 2001).

Reflecting on their journeys, the underpinning emotion was hope. Joey would often say, "In unity, there's strength. In collaboration, there's change." Every scar they bore was a testament to their resilience and their commitment to ensuring others saw the stars amidst their battles.

As we draw this chapter close, Joey and Jodie's message resounds more clearly: the way forward in substance use treatment is one of unity and collaboration. With their vision as the guiding star, the horizon looks promising. And as we step into the next chapter, it's crucial to acknowledge that healing is not confined to a center, a city, or a country. It's a global calling, urging us to shift from localized treatment to a universal embrace–a movement transcending borders.

CHAPTER 16

Creating a Global Movement: The Road Ahead

From Localized Treatment to Global Change

Nestled between a rustic bookstore and a coffee shop on a bustling street, Joey and Jodie found a quiet space to brainstorm their next big move. The aromas of freshly ground coffee beans intermingled with the scent of old books, providing a fitting ambiance for such a significant discussion.

Clutching a well-worn novel she'd just bought, Jodie said, "You know, Joey, this story speaks of uniting people under a common cause. It reminds me of our goal: creating a global movement."

Sipping his americano, Joey replied, "Every great movement starts with a single step, a story. We have the power to pen ours."

As the couple discussed their roadmap, they realized that crafting a worldwide initiative would require weaving together countless stories, each representative of diverse backgrounds and perspectives. This chapter prepares the reader for the intricacies of sparking a movement that breaks barriers. With Joey and Jodie at the helm, the journey promises to be an inspiring tale of determination, collaboration, and hope.

The arduous journey from addiction's dark abyss to recovery's luminous embrace is marred with tales of despair and hope, trauma and redemption. Joey and Jodie stood at the center of such tales, not as mere survivors but as architects of a future they envisioned—one devoid of judgment and teeming with understanding and support.

Jodie often reminisced about the tumultuous times they endured together at the COE. While battling the clutches of opiates, they also battled societal stigma, ignorance, and a lack of trauma-informed care. As Van der Kolk (2014) wisely puts it in *The Body Keeps the Score*, trauma isn't just an event that occurred sometime in the past: it's an imprint left by that experience on the mind, brain, and body. This resonated deeply with Jodie and Joey. Their personal struggles weren't isolated events but a continuous battle against the scars left behind, intensified by an environment that often failed to understand or acknowledge their pain.

There were, however, silver linings. Jodie's memories were peppered with moments when they would laugh together about some absurdity in the middle of a peer-support session or when Joey would share stories from his past, providing a stark yet vital reminder of the human side of addiction. These instances were underpinned by the emotion and passion they felt for their cause. Joey's role at the COE and Jodie's being a BCM bore testament to their resilience and commitment.

But the more significant challenge lay ahead. How could they channel their unique lived experiences and knowledge into a force for global change? Drawing inspiration from Maté (2008), who explored the intricate world of addiction in *In the Realm of Hungry Ghosts*, they realized that the answer lay not just in the mind but in the soul, heart, and human connection.

There's a vital need for the world to move beyond isolated treatments and understand addiction from a holistic perspective. Such a perspective recognizes the critical role of trauma and socio-cultural factors (Harris & Fallot, 2001) while emphasizing the role of peer-based recovery (White, 2009). Joey, recounting a time when he felt utterly alone, spoke of the power of shared experiences, highlighting the importance of peer support in substance abuse recovery (Tracy & Wallace, 2016).

Their blueprint for change necessitated the integration of diverse stories, backgrounds, and perspectives. In their discussions, they constantly referenced *SAMHSA's concept of trauma and guidance for a trauma-informed approach* (Abuse, 2014). Jodie passionately spoke of creating global networks where individuals from different cultures could share their stories, allowing for a richer, more holistic understanding of addiction and recovery. Their vision also emphasized emotional intelligence (Goleman, 1995) and understanding the neurobiology of addiction (Heilig et al., 2022) to tailor interventions effectively.

What was distinct about their approach was the emotional depth. Joey and Jodie's past experiences weren't mere anecdotes but palpable lessons. They vividly remembered their days of despair, where trauma often played a dual role–both as a trigger and a consequence of their addiction. The link between childhood maltreatment, later violent offenses (Topitzes et al., 2012), and substance use (Dube et al., 2003) made their endeavor even more crucial. The world needed to understand that trauma and addiction were profoundly interconnected, demanding an empathetic and comprehensive approach to treatment.

Yet, as they planned, they were also mindful of the challenges. Taking their local experiences to a global stage requires understanding diverse cultural nuances and systemic intricacies. They needed allies who understood the biological (Krystal et al., 2004), psychological (Kar, 2011), and social dimensions (Livingston et al., 2012) of addiction.

However, a spirit of hope enveloped them as their discussion deepened in that quaint coffee shop. Joey recalled a statement from Najavits (2002): "Safety first." They knew the road ahead wouldn't be easy. They would face skepticism, resistance, and perhaps even ridicule. But they were grounded in the belief that they could forge a path toward a more understanding world with a trauma-informed approach.

Clasping Jodie's hand, Joey said, "Our story, our scars are our strength. From here, we take the first step. We've survived, now it's time for us to ensure others thrive."

With that affirmation, they embarked on their quest, fully aware of the *challenges and opportunities on the global stage* that awaited them.

Challenges and Opportunities on the Global Stage

The vast, interconnected world thrums with voices echoing their truths, longings, and traumas. Beneath the cacophony lies the universally experienced scourge of addiction, a shadowy villain that often lurks undetected until its consequences ripple out, touching everyone in its path. As Joey and Jodie can attest, the face of addiction isn't always what you'd expect. Born into good families—though marred by dysfunction—the couple's journeys into the world of addiction and their triumphant emergence sheds light on the profound challenges and opportunities facing addiction recovery on a global scale.

A Scar Deepens: The Emotional Undertow of Addiction

Jodie's transition to another agency didn't just signify a career shift but created a reminder of her past struggles with addiction. At the COE, where she once worked side by side with Joey, their combined lived experiences were their most potent weapon against the perils of addiction. Their scars, once painful reminders, became badges of honor and resilience.

Yet, in the broader context, understanding addiction isn't merely about recognizing its physical manifestations. It digs deeper, often rooted in trauma, as Van der Kolk aptly put in *The Body Keeps the Score*: our brains, minds, and bodies become intricately tied to our traumas (Van der Kolk, 2014). This trauma-informed perspective underscores the importance of treating the addiction and the underlying emotional and psychological wounds that often give birth to it (Harris & Fallot, 2001).

Starlight Amidst Darkness: The Silver Linings

One cannot ponder on the vast challenges without recognizing the gleams of hope. Joey, having overcome his struggles, flourished in his role at COE. As he often shared, the darkest moments of their addiction, where despair loomed large, became the very foundation upon which they built their recovery.

Remembering one instance, Jodie recalled a client, a young woman, mired in the depths of heroin addiction. The woman's hopelessness was real. However, drawing from her lived experience, Jodie shared her story—punctuated with the raw emotions of despair, hope, and eventual recovery. By the end of their session, the young woman, tears in her eyes, whispered, "If you could do it, maybe I can too."

Such moments epitomize the power of peer-based addiction recovery support, where lived experiences form the cornerstone of healing (White, 2009).

The Global Stage: Recognizing The Challenges

While Joey and Jodie's stories are powerful, they are but two stars in a galaxy of lived experiences. Addiction, a global epidemic, is a multifaceted adversary. With its deep roots in both biology and environment (Kreek et al., 2005), solutions must be equally comprehensive.

The pervasive stigma associated with addiction forms a significant barrier, often discouraging individuals from seeking the help they desperately need (Livingston et al., 2012). Moreover, childhood traumas, ranging from neglect to abuse, significantly elevate the risk of substance abuse later in life (Dube et al., 2003). This interplay between trauma and addiction creates a vicious cycle that is challenging to break.

Transforming Scars into Constellations: Opportunities Await

The road ahead, while fraught with challenges, also teems with possibilities. Harnessing the power of shared stories, like Joey and Jodie's, offers a glimmer of hope in dark times. Peer support, rooted in empathy and lived experience, provides an invaluable tool in addiction recovery, forging connections that transcend cultural and geographical barriers (Mead, Hilton, & Curtis, 2001).

Moreover, understanding the intrinsic link between trauma and addiction opens doors to holistic treatment approaches, targeting both the root causes and their manifest symptoms (Najavits, 2002).

The scars of addiction and trauma are real, raw, and often painful. Yet, as Joey and Jodie's journeys show, these very scars, when viewed through the lens of hope and resilience, can transform into guiding stars, illuminating the path for countless others.

As we transition into the world stage, seeking global collaboration and synergy becomes not just an aspiration but a necessity. The next segment researches strategies for fostering this global unity, envisioning a world where scars become symbols of hope, guiding everyone toward a brighter tomorrow.

Strategies for Global Collaboration and Synergy

There's a profound stillness in a room where two souls share their most vulnerable truths. For Joey and Jodie, it was more than just the raw intimacy of a relationship–it was the stark convergence of two tormented pasts, from the mires of addiction, aiming toward a future founded on mutual recovery and strength.

Jodie's memories of her time at the COE with Joey were vivid. As they worked side by side, aiding others in the grip of opiate addiction, she felt an undercurrent of energy. There was an undeniable synergy between them, fueled by the scars of their own lived experiences with addiction and their dedication to turning those scars into stars, beacons of hope for others (Harris & Fallot, 2001).

Van der Kolk (2014) once eloquently stated that the body remembers trauma. This sentiment was no stranger to Joey and Jodie. Their bodies bore the testament of their pasts, but it was in each other's company that they learned that the heart remembers hope. Hope was the bridge between the shared dysfunction of their upbringing and the life they envisaged ahead (Van der Kolk, 2014).

Maté (2008) explored the haunting realm of addiction, suggesting that these struggles often emerge from places of profound pain and unaddressed trauma. Joey and Jodie's pain might have been individual, but their healing was collaborative. They learned the power of transformation through trauma-informed care, which emphasizes understanding, respecting, and appropriately responding to the effects of all types of trauma (Abuse, 2014).

The collaboration and synergy in their personal lives need to be elevated on an international platform to create a global movement. The emotions of those involved in trauma-informed care should be acknowledged, respected, and understood as integral parts of the recovery process (Najavits, 2002). This would require vast networks of peer-based addiction recovery support, whereby survivors like Joey and Jodie use their lived experiences to inform and guide others on similar journeys (White, 2009).

The strategy rests on several pillars:

1. **Understanding the Trauma-Addiction Nexus**: It's crucial to recognize the intricate relationship between trauma and substance misuse (Simpson & Miller, 2002). By acknowledging that many addiction stories stem from unhealed wounds, caregivers and professionals can tailor their approaches, ensuring they're holistic and trauma-sensitive.

2. **Building Peer Networks**: Joey and Jodie's narrative proves peers' profound impact on recovery processes. Having walked a similar path, a peer can offer unique perspectives, shared empathy, and an understanding others might lack (Mead et al., 2001). Their stories become instrumental in guiding, comforting, and inspiring those at different stages of recovery (Tracy & Wallace, 2016).

3. **Embracing Emotional Intelligence**: Goleman (1995) emphasized the importance of emotional intelligence in understanding oneself and others. By building capacities to recognize, process, and manage emotions, those in recovery can navigate challenges more effectively and develop healthier relationships.

4. **Harm Reduction**: Not everyone is ready for complete abstinence. Harm reduction strategies provide an interim solution, ensuring that while individuals might not be completely drug-free, they reduce the potential harm associated with their substance use (Marlatt & Witkiewitz, 2002).

5. **Educating Communities and Reducing Stigma**: Society's perception can either accelerate or hinder recovery. There's an urgent need to combat the stigma associated with addiction, ensuring that survivors like Joey and Jodie can reintegrate into society without judgment (Livingston et al., 2012).

6. **Leveraging Technology and Virtual Platforms**: As the world grows increasingly interconnected, leveraging technology can be pivotal. Virtual support groups, online counseling, and digital resources can bridge geographic divides, ensuring everyone can access quality care regardless of location.

Joey often reminisced about their early days at COE in the golden rays of the setting sun, recalling how he and Jodie transformed their lives from despair to purpose. It was a purpose beyond personal redemption and about lighting the way for countless others.

Creating a global movement is no small task, and it's one fraught with challenges, complexities, and emotional whirlwinds. But as Jodie often said, "Our scars are our stars. They light the way." The road ahead is long, but with collective effort, dedication, and an unwavering commitment to trauma-informed care, it's a journey that promises hope, healing, and transformation.

As we forge ahead, it becomes clear that collaboration extends beyond individual stories and shared experiences. It's also about uniting policymakers, professionals, and peers in a cohesive, integrated approach. Together, they will play a pivotal role in shaping the contours of this global movement. As we transition into the next segment, we dig deeper into the significance of their roles in "The Role of Policymakers, Professionals, and Peers."

The Role of Policymakers, Professionals, and Peers

The road to recovery is not just a series of steps one takes personally but a collaborative journey shaped by the shared efforts of policymakers, professionals, and peers. When Joey and Jodie began their recovery journeys, it wasn't just the strength of their bond that helped them heal. It was the trauma-informed care they received and the compassionate souls they encountered along the way.

As Van der Kolk highlights, "Trauma is not just an event that took place sometimes in the past; it is also the imprint left by that experience on mind, brain, and body" (Van der Kolk, 2014). This spirit guided the approach in the halls of the COE, where Joey and Jodie once worked side by side. It was understood that addiction wasn't just a symptom of poor choices but rather the aftermath of pain, often deep-seated and stemming from early adverse experiences (Dube et al., 2003).

Jodie often shared stories from her past, reflections of a childhood marred by neglect, and instances that made her question her self-worth. Joey would nod, understanding more than anyone the torment of past traumas and how they often push individuals toward substance abuse as a means of self-medication (Khantzian, 1997). Both had witnessed in their families the dichotomy of love and dysfunction. And both knew the weight of carrying that dichotomy into adulthood.

Policymakers play an instrumental role in providing the landscape for healing. With the right policies, facilities like the COE can receive the necessary funding and resources to implement trauma-informed care (Harris & Fallot, 2001). By acknowledging the connection between childhood maltreatment and subsequent substance abuse (Topitzes, J., Mersky, J. P., & Reynolds, A. J., 2012), they have the power to reshape the framework of addiction recovery.

Professionals are the torchbearers, guiding individuals through the dark tunnels of their pasts. They empower individuals to confront and move beyond their trauma through techniques like MI (Miller & Rollnick, 2012). Joey, with his innate understanding of addiction, embodied such a beacon. At the COE, he took pride in understanding that everyone's path to recovery was different, emphasizing harm reduction over abstinence-only models (Marlatt & Witkiewitz, 2002).

And then there are the peers. Jodie and Joey's stories of resilience are testaments to the power of peer support. As White (2009) elucidates, the history of addiction recovery is embedded with peer support, stemming from the realization that those who've been through the storm often provide the best shelter. Their shared experiences, as different as they were, became the cornerstone of their recovery. With her role as a BCM, Jodie often harnessed the power of shared experiences to foster connections, drawing from Mead's perspective on the therapeutic value of peer support (Mead, S., Hilton, D., & Curtis, L., 2001).

Despite their professional roles, Joey and Jodie never hid the silver linings from their pasts. Jodie often spoke of her turning point—the moment she realized that her past traumas didn't define her, referencing Najavits's principles of safety and grounding (Najavits, 2002). Joey reminisced about his epiphany after reading Maté's *In the Realm of Hungry Ghosts*, realizing the importance of understanding the emotions behind addiction, not just its neurochemical aspect (Maté, 2008).

The recovery world isn't just about abstaining from substances; it's about healing, understanding, and, most importantly, connection (Tracy & Wallace, 2016). By leaning on each other and embracing the support of peers, professionals, and the larger framework of policies, one can emerge from the shadow of addiction as a survivor and as a torchbearer for others.

As we delve deeper into this global movement, the tales of Joey and Jodie remind us of the importance of collective effort and the role every individual plays in shaping the road ahead. Their past may be scarred, but their present and future are paved with stars. Stars that illuminate the path for many others. As we stand at this juncture, let's take a moment to reflect and recognize the power of unity, shared experiences, and the immense potential that lies ahead.

With that, we transition to the heart of our message, setting the stage for a worldwide transformation–a resounding call to action for every soul touched by the specter of addiction and trauma. Let the revolution begin.

A Call to Action for Worldwide Transformation

There's a prevailing notion, which has been rooted deeply in our societal narrative, that the painful circumstances of our lives, those marked by trauma and hardship, are weaknesses. They are seen as cracks in our armor, vulnerabilities that leave us forever wounded. Yet, this couldn't be further from the truth for Joey and Jodie. Their scars, products of the gut-wrenching struggle with addiction, became their most potent strength, their north star that guided their mission.

Joey and Jodie's journeys began in the grim corridors of the COE, where they battled the weight of opiate use disorders. The experience was not gentle, as Van der Kolk (2014) so poignantly describes, "The body keeps the score," highlighting that trauma finds its dwelling in every muscle and nerve: for Joey and Jodie, the memory of needles, midnight cravings, and the agony of withdrawal became engraved in their strengths. Yet, in this maze of despair, they found one another. Their union, both in matrimony and mission, would go on to inspire countless souls.

Jodie's departure to become a BCM and Joey's elevation to the role of a clinical supervisor in COE signifies a professional progression and a personal transformation. Harris & Fallot (2001) emphasize the importance of designing service systems that recognize trauma, and in Joey and Jodie's work, the impact of such understanding was profound.

In Maté's (2008) *In the Realm of Hungry Ghosts*, addiction is likened to haunting specters continually chasing their victims. This powerful imagery captures the relentless grip of addiction, a force that once ensnared both Joey and Jodie. Their past, while marred with the sufferings of addiction, wasn't entirely bereft of silver linings. Joey recalls when, in the throes of withdrawal, an elderly woman in the COE offered to share her food while barely eating herself–a small act of kindness that he credits as the starting point of his belief in humanity. For Jodie, it was a therapist's gentle hand on her shoulder, a gesture that spoke louder than words, reminding her that there was still hope.

Theirs are stories not just of personal resilience but are symbolic of the collective spirit that's needed for worldwide transformation. In the exhaustive battle against addiction, White (2009) argues the indispensability of peer-based recovery support. And who better exemplifies this than Joey and Jodie? Their lived experiences became their credentials, their shared pasts a bridge to those who felt misunderstood and isolated.

So, where does this take us on the road ahead? Transformative movements don't sprout in isolation; they are the products of collective effort, of a global community coming together. Jodie and Joey's advocacy is merely a chapter in this larger narrative. Miller & Rollnick (2012) emphasize the power of MI, an approach rooted in empathy and understanding. Joey and Jodie's endeavors align with this principle as they endeavor to impart skills, knowledge, and, most crucially, hope to the afflicted.

The emotional gravitas of their pasts become a powerful motivator for change, not just for them but for everyone they touch. Marlatt & Witkiewitz (2002) underline the importance of harm reduction approaches, which Joey and Jodie have passionately endorsed, integrating them into their professional lives.

However, to achieve a truly global movement, the world needs more than just understanding and empathy; it requires actionable strategies and widespread adoption of trauma-informed care. This calls for robust support systems, destigmatization efforts, and broadening our perspective on addiction–to view it not as a moral failing but as a complex interplay of genetics, environment, and personal experiences (Kreek et al., 2005).

Following a family dysfunction backdrop, Joey and Jodie shattered several addiction myths. Their stories remind us that trauma and adversity can strike anyone, regardless of background. However, their recovery journeys serve as beacons of hope, symbolizing that healing, transformation, and redemption are within reach for all.

As we reflect on this journey, it becomes evident that the worldwide transformation sought is not just about combating addiction. It's a movement toward compassion, understanding, and unity. As witnessed in the tales of Joey and Jodie, it's a journey from scars to stars.

Looking back at our exploration, the power of unity becomes the indisputable force propelling the change we hope to achieve...

CLOSING

The Power of Unity: A Call to Action

Reflections on the Journey Through the Book

The air was dense with anticipation as Joey and Jodie sat in a cozy nook of the beloved coffee shop and bookstore that had witnessed their many profound discussions. Jodie, her fingers tracing the embossed cover of a book titled *Unison Echoes*, looked at Joey thoughtfully.

"It's incredible, isn't it?" she began. "How words, when united with purpose, can ignite change."

Joey nodded, setting down his cup. "Indeed. Just like us. Movement is born when people come together, pooling their strengths and passions. Our journey has been a testament to that."

Surrounded by walls adorned with the wisdom of centuries, the duo felt an overwhelming sense of responsibility. As they penned down their final thoughts, their message was clear: Unity is power. And now, it was up to the readers, every individual, to harness that power, to come together, share their stories, and make a lasting impact.

This closing beckons you, dear reader, to reflect on your role in this tapestry of change. With Joey and Jodie's narrative as a guiding beacon, the world awaits your contribution to this united call to action.

The realm of addiction is desolate, intricately linked with memories of trauma and shadows of self-destruction. For Joey and Jodie, the landscape of addiction was not unfamiliar. Born in families with their share of dysfunction, their journeys were not just about redemption but also about unity and synergy, forging a bond stronger than the chains of their pasts. And their stories echo hope, illuminating the dark alleys of countless lives entangled in the throes of addiction.

Van der Kolk (2014) illuminated the profound connection between trauma and the body, suggesting that traumatic experiences leave indelible imprints on the soul. This understanding resonates deeply when we reflect upon the lives of Joey and Jodie. Their descent into addiction, as Maté (2008) aptly captures, wasn't a mere indulgence but an escapade from the "hungry ghosts" of their pasts.

As the narratives of trauma (Dube et al., 2003) merged with the dysfunctional family dynamics, the couple found solace, although momentarily, in the brief high of opiates.

Yet, every scar they bore held a story, and every story sparkled with a silver lining. Joey and Jodie's partnership transformed their lived experiences into catalysts for change at the COE. It was here that they first realized the power of unity. Where the standardized interventions from MI (Miller & Rollnick, 2012) to harm reduction strategies (Marlatt & Witkiewitz, 2002) played their roles, it was the peer-based addiction recovery support that truly revolutionized their healing process (White, 2009). It was not merely about textbook therapies but about sharing stories, empathizing with the pain, and reigniting the spark of hope.

For Joey, one poignant memory stands out. During peer support, a young woman, almost skeletal from drug use, shared her story of childhood maltreatment, echoing the findings of Topitzes et al. (2012) linking being bullied with violent offending. As her tears flowed, Joey recalled his own experiences, and instead of offering clinical advice, he shared a fragment of his journey. That moment was transformative. Finding solace in Joey's words, the woman embraced recovery, a living testament to the therapeutic power of shared experiences.

Similarly, as a BCM, Jodie constantly leverages her past to light the way for those still trapped in addiction's grip. She fondly remembers a session where she introduced her clients to Najavits's (2002) *Seeking Safety* protocol. Incorporating her personal journey, she emphasized the need to build a trauma-informed care system, echoing the sentiments of Harris & Fallot (2001). Her words, laden with emotion and sincerity, resonated deeply, leading to many of her clients' breakthroughs.

These instances weren't singular; they were symbolic of a broader truth. The lived experience of Joey and Jodie, combined with trauma-informed care, was therapeutic for themselves and countless others. They demonstrated that while the roots of addiction might be grounded in genetics (Kreek et al., 2005) or impulsivity (Heatherton & Wagner, 2011), the journey to recovery is deeply human, requiring compassion, understanding, and unity.

Their stories also shattered the misconceptions surrounding addiction. Despite coming from good families, their descent into this world underscores that addiction isn't a mere choice but often a confluence of genetics, environment, and trauma (Khantzian, 1997; Simpson & Miller, 2002). Their resilience, however, serves as a beacon of hope, showcasing that while addiction might have a multifaceted genesis, the road to recovery, too, can be multi-pronged.

So, as we reflect upon the collection of stories and insights shared throughout this book, Joey and Jodie's narratives become the lustrous thread that binds them all. Their scars, symbolic of their tumultuous past, and their stars, symbolizing their hopes and dreams, remind us that unity holds immense power in all its forms.

The air might have been dense with anticipation that day in the bookstore, but now, it's heavy with reflection and realization. Unity, indeed, is power. As Joey once replied, "Movement is born when people come together," this closing beckons every reader to reflect upon their role, journey, and potential to influence change.

As we transition to the next phase of this reflection, let's look deeper into the synergistic power of combined approaches, exploring how various methods, when united, can lead to monumental shifts in addiction recovery.

The Synergistic Power of Combined Approaches

Joey and Jodie's tales stand out as testimonies to the astounding resilience of the human spirit and the indomitable power of unity within the vast expanse of humanity. They symbolize what is possible when trauma-informed care intersects with lived experience—a synergy that holds transformative potential.

Like many others, their early lives were filled with profound joy and heartrending pain. The dysfunction within their apparently good families became the theater for the drama of addiction that would ensue. Jodie and Joey's narratives are poignant reminders of the oft-quoted assertion by Dr. Bessel van der Kolk that "the body keeps the score" (Van der Kolk, 2014). Indeed, their bodies bore the scars of trauma, and their souls carried its weight.

As Joey fondly recounts, there were silver linings amidst the darkness. The time they danced in the rain to wash away the pain of withdrawal. Or Jodie's infectious laughter in the face of despair, a momentary yet profound act of defiance against the grip of addiction. These gleaming moments were not just footnotes in their chronicles but pivotal landmarks on their journey to healing.

In their battle against addiction, the COE emerged as a beacon of hope. Working side by side in this opiate use disorder program, they confronted their demons together, drawing strength from each other and the COE's innovative approaches. Joey's role and Jodie's compassionate work as a BCM showcased how two individuals, deeply mired in addiction, could transcend their past and become agents of change.

At the heart of their journeys was the realization that addiction wasn't merely about substance abuse. As Dr. Gabor Maté suggests in *In the Realm of Hungry Ghosts*, addiction is more about the void one attempts to fill, or the pain one seeks to numb (Maté, 2008). Their shared experiences attested to the profound truth that the roots of addiction often lay buried in the traumas of the past (Najavits, 2002; Harris & Fallot, 2001).

As survivors, they became apostles of a new paradigm emphasizing a trauma-informed approach combined with lived experience. They believed peer-based addiction recovery could be pivotal in healing (White, 2009). This was about professional intervention, human connection, mutual understanding, and shared journeys.

Their advocacy was grounded in rigorous evidence. Research has consistently shown that combining trauma-informed care with personal experience can revolutionize recovery processes (SAMHSA, 2014; Topitzes et al., 2012). Through this lens, addiction wasn't a personal failing but a symptom of deeper wounds (Gorski, 1990; Dube et al., 2003).

But it wasn't just about their personal tales but the stories of countless others they interacted with. Reports of childhood neglect, domestic abuse, shattered dreams, and stifled hopes. Every individual narrative was a stark reminder of the risk factors leading to addiction (Simpson & Miller, 2002) and the power of understanding and empathy in facilitating recovery (Miller & Rollnick, 2012; Marlatt & Witkiewitz, 2002).

Joey and Jodie's love for each other was unwavering despite their challenges. Their commitment to recover and help others was real in every interaction, workshop, and counseling session. Their story is a testament to the profound words of Dr. Maxie Maultsby: "Happiness and self-worth come from the quality of your thoughts, choices, and actions" (Harris & Fallot, 2001).

Lastly, while uniquely their own, Joey and Jodie's journeys offer lessons for us all. It underscores the transformative power of combined approaches in addiction recovery. Their narrative serves as a clarion call, urging us to harness collective strengths in our quest for revolutionizing care—a topic we will explore deeper into in the succeeding section.

Harnessing Collective Strengths for Revolutionizing Care

Amidst the glaring fluorescent lights and haunting echoes of fading conversations, Joey and Jodie took their seats at the COE. Now, Joey and Jodie were testaments to the arduous journey from addiction's abyss to a renewed purpose.

Van der Kolk (2014) aptly wrote, *The Body Keeps the Score*, Joey and Jodie's bodies were indeed memoirs of their pain. But they weren't just tales of suffering: they were chronicles of resilience, the power of unity, and what it means to find purpose amidst the wreckage.

Every scar on their bodies, every hesitation in their voices, spoke of a tumultuous past packed with memories that most would shudder to recall. Yet, every time they shared their narratives, there was a glint in their eyes, reflecting the stars they had turned their scars into.

With her gentle manner, Jodie often narrated the chilling accounts of her childhood heightened her vulnerability to substance abuse (Dube et al., 2003). The household dysfunctions from their seemingly "good families" had left lasting imprints. She cited Najavits (2002) when discussing the complex interplay between PTSD and substance abuse, emphasizing the need for trauma-informed care.

Meanwhile, with a firm tone that belied his traumatic past, Joey would mention the *Realm of Hungry Ghosts* (Maté, 2008), drawing parallels with their personal battles with addiction. Their stories were not just their own; they were reflective of millions who grapple with addiction, trauma, and a relentless search for healing.

But it wasn't just about reminiscing the past but shaping the future. The couple firmly believed in harnessing collective strength to revolutionize care. They were avid proponents of peer-based addiction recovery support, realizing that lived experiences could pave the path to recovery for others (White, 2009). Their advocacy focused on understanding addiction as a clinical ailment and a multifaceted issue intertwined with personal trauma, societal stigmas, and systemic inadequacies (Harris & Fallot, 2001).

To truly revolutionize care, they believed in giving voice to the unsayable (Lieberman & Van Horn, 2009). The therapeutic power of empathy, validation, and shared stories became their guiding principle. They championed the cause of peer-support groups, emphasizing their instrumental benefits in addiction treatment (Tracy & Wallace, 2016).

But they were also firm believers in the power of research and evidence-based approaches. Joey, as a clinical supervisor, professor, therapist, and researcher, integrated techniques from MI (Miller & Rollnick, 2012) with harm reduction approaches (Marlatt & Witkiewitz, 2002) to offer a holistic treatment module. Their approach to trauma-informed care was shaped significantly by SAMHSA's concept of trauma (Abuse, 2014), emphasizing physical, psychological, and emotional safety.

Their lived experiences became a beacon of hope for many. Recounting silver linings from their addiction journey, Jodie would share moments of unexpected kindness, the solace she found in art, or Joey's unyielding support. On the other hand, Joey would speak of the transformative power of introspection and how, in his darkest moments, the idea of change became a glimmer of hope. As Goleman (1995) elucidated, their emotional intelligence became their compass, guiding them through the storm.

The culmination of their efforts was a call to action—a plea for understanding addiction beyond its medical definition, acknowledging the role of social context (Heilig et al., 2022) and embracing the power of unity for revolutionary care. They embodied the spirit of their message, living examples of the change they hoped to see.

Joey and Jodie's journeys are testaments to the transformative power of unity, empathy, and resilience. Their scars tell tales of pain, but their stars radiate hope. As we transition to our next theme, "Opportunities for readers to make a difference," let Joey and Jodie's stories remind us that revolutionizing care isn't just a professional obligation; it's a collective moral responsibility.

Opportunities for Readers to Make a Difference

The complexity of addiction and its stranglehold on victims often seems impossible, daunting, and overwhelming. Yet, Joey and Jodie's poignant journeys through addiction, recovery, and resilience are testaments to the possibility of triumph over adversity.

When Joey and Jodie first walked through the COE doors, their pasts weighed heavily on them. As Maté (2008) illuminates in *In the Realm of Hungry Ghosts*, addiction often stems from deeply rooted traumas and emotional pain. It's a desperate attempt to self-soothe and find solace. And this truth echoed in the life stories of our resilient couple. Despite coming from good families, a jumble of dysfunction created an environment ripe for addiction.

This truth is supported by Dube et al. (2003), who directly link childhood adversities and the increased risk of substance abuse later in life.

However, it wasn't all darkness for Joey and Jodie. The silver linings from their shared pasts became the touchstones of hope for countless others. At the COE, while they both were sculpting paths.

Their shared experiences made them acutely aware of the importance of trauma-informed care. The power of this approach, as Van der Kolk (2014) beautifully articulates in *The Body Keeps the Score*, lies in the understanding that trauma leaves indelible marks on the mind and body, and true healing demands addressing both.

Joey and Jodie became living embodiments of what White (2009) termed "Peer-based Addiction Recovery Support." Their experiences, far from mere tales of despair, became tools of empathy and connection. Joey often recounts a memorable moment when a newcomer opened up about his struggles amidst a twelve-step support meeting. Remembering his days of desperation, Joey shared a story from his past. That story, tinged with vulnerability and hope, became a bridge. It resonated with the newcomer and served as a beacon of hope that recovery, while challenging, was indeed possible.

Jodie's approach to healing was influenced by Najavits's (2002) *Seeking Safety*. She often emphasized that recovery is not merely about abstaining from substances but seeking safety in relationships, emotions, and behaviors. This approach resonated deeply with many in her care, particularly women, who found in Jodie's story a reflection of their own pain and the promise of healing.

Their lived experiences were testimonies of personal resilience and a powerful impetus for system-wide change. Harris & Fallot (2001), in "Using trauma theory to design service systems," stress the need for a paradigm shift in how service systems view and address trauma. Joey and Jodie, with their firsthand knowledge, became champions of this change. The personal became political, and their stories became catalysts for restructuring how addiction care is approached and delivered.

However, for readers, Joey and Jodie's journeys are not just inspirational stories to admire from a distance. It is a call to action—a plea to look beyond the stigmatized narratives of addiction and see the human stories of pain, resilience, and hope. Livingston et al. (2012) suggest that battling the stigma surrounding substance use disorders is paramount in the fight against addiction. Every reader has the power to be an agent of change through policy advocacy, community engagement, or simply by altering perceptions.

Jodie often recalls a silver lining from her darkest days. In the throes of her addiction, she met a therapist in an inpatient facility, who, instead of judging, said, "You have a purpose. Your pain will lead to healing for many." Today, Jodie realizes the profundity of those words. Every scar, every painful memory, can be transformed into a beacon of hope, a star guiding others out of the abyss of addiction.

While deeply personal, Joey and Jodie's stories have universal implications. Their journey underscores the power of unity and collaborative efforts in overcoming even the most insurmountable challenges. As we transition to our next section, "A plea for continued collaboration and innovation," let's carry forward this spirit of unity and hope, for collective endeavors lie the seeds of revolutionary change.

A Plea for Continued Collaboration and Innovation

Amidst the turmoil of battling addiction, some stories stand out, reminding us that resilience and human connection are integral in the journey to recovery. Among the most captivating tales are those of Joey and Jodie, whose intertwining narratives have fostered profound change in their lives and the larger world.

Good families, we are often told, provide safe havens. Yet, family can also be a site of dysfunction where overt and insidious traumas originate (Dube et al., 2003; Harris & Fallot, 2001). Joey and Jodie emerged with deep scars from their respective families, both marked by love and struggle. But the luminosity of stars—their unyielding hope—guided them through the darkest nights of addiction.

There were moments when their paths to self-destruction seemed irreversible. However, as Van der Kolk (2014) aptly explains, the body and mind are intrinsically connected in their pursuit of healing. Through mutual understanding, Joey and Jodie cultivated an indomitable spirit of collaboration, using their lived experiences to recover and revolutionize the approach to trauma-informed care.

During their time at the COE, they witnessed the dawning of this transformative collaboration. Joey's role saw him integrating techniques from Motivational Interviewing (Miller & Rollnick, 2012) and principles from the Harm Reduction approach (Marlatt & Witkiewitz, 2002) to help clients identify their own motivations for change. In a parallel narrative, Jodie, with her unique insights as a BCM, observed that trauma often acts as a catalyst for substance abuse, echoing the findings of Topitzes et al. (2012).

It was not merely their professional roles that made them trailblazers. Their shared experiences—of slipping into the shadows of addiction and re-emerging into the light—offered a silver lining to many. Recalling a particular encounter, Jodie once spoke of a patient who'd described addiction as being trapped in a room of mirrors, each reflection amplifying self-loathing (Maté, 2008). With her characteristic empathy, Jodie would often share stories from her past of times when she felt trapped in a similar maze. But she'd always end on a hopeful note, emphasizing the potential of human connection to shatter those mirrors.

Joey, too, had his stories of silver linings. He'd often recount when, during his own battle with opiates, a stranger at a park bench who once was a therapist before turning to addiction had shared an insight from Seeking Safety (Najavits, 2002), explaining how trauma and addiction were interlinked. That conversation was a turning point for him. Joey's vulnerability became his strength, encouraging others to share their stories and demonstrating the powerful healing that occurs in mutual understanding and peer-based recovery (White, 2009).

Their work emphasizes the symbiotic relationship between clinical expertise and lived experiences.

As crucial as it is, theoretical knowledge needs the human touch of empathy and understanding (Mead, Hilton, & Curtis, 2001). As Joey often replied, "Clinical textbooks can teach you the 'how,' but lived experiences teach you the 'why.'"

The dual narratives of Joey and Jodie's lives underscore the importance of unity in combating addiction. They embody the essence of Goleman's (1995) Emotional Intelligence, using their traumas to attune to the emotional needs of others, empowering them with tools for self-regulation (Heatherton & Wagner, 2011) and resilience. Their commitment to trauma-informed care demonstrates how addressing underlying traumas can lead to sustainable recovery (Harris & Fallot, 2001; Kar, 2011).

This journey with Joey and Jodie—though fraught with scars—highlights the brilliant constellations that can be formed when individuals come together for a shared purpose. The beauty of their collaborative spirit is a clarion call to all of us, emphasizing the need for continuous innovation, compassion, and unity in addressing the multifaceted challenge of addiction.

We end this closing with a vision of hope—a world where collaboration and innovation reign supreme and every individual, regardless of their past, is empowered to redefine their narrative. As we transition to the epilogue, we invite you to step into the intimate world of Joey and Jodie once more, to revisit the cafe where it all began, and to feel the warmth and inspiration that emanates from "The Traveling Social Workers," a beacon that still glows brightly, touching lives and changing destinies.

EPILOGUE

As sunlight streamed through the cafe windows, casting a golden hue on the scattered books and coffee mugs, Joey and Jodie settled into their favorite coffee shop corner. Both were no strangers here; it was where they dreamt up their initiative, "The Traveling Social Workers."

Skimming an old classic, Jodie mused, "Every ending in literature signals the dawn of a fresh narrative."

Joey's eyes filled with nostalgia and hope, added, "Our chronicle might be documented here, but the countless lives touched and changed through 'The Traveling Social Workers' still ripple outward."

This coffee shop, once just a haven for bibliophiles and coffee enthusiasts, had silently observed their brainstorms and their dedication to societal betterment. The murmur of conversations, the scent of ancient books mingling with fresh prints, and the rhythmic brewing of coffee—everything hinted at new beginnings.

Their venture, born from personal experiences and mutual aspirations, was more than just an organization. It was a testament to the belief that positive change was always within reach.

As you, dear reader, turn this final page, understand that the story doesn't truly end here. Let the adventures of Joey and Jodie serve merely as an introduction. Now, inspired by their journeys, write your own chapter of change and influence in the world.

ABOUT THE AUTHORS

Joey Pagano, MSW, LSW, CRS, is not only a luminary in the realm of trauma-informed care but also a past #1 best-selling author, recognized for his trailblazing work, *No Addict Left Behind: It's a Recovery Medicine State of Mind*. His acclaim extends to a nomination for the Pulitzer Prize, further solidifying his reputation as a thought leader in the addiction recovery space.

Jodie Pagano, BSW, CRS, brings to the table her academic background and her deeply personal journey of resilience and recovery. Together, they surmounted the trials of addiction and turned their pain into a purpose, forging a life dedicated to educating, enlightening, and empowering others. United in love and purpose, they are affectionately known as "The Traveling Social Workers."

Their joint ventures have taken them across the globe, where they have left indelible marks through their impactful presentations, training sessions, and heartfelt book signings. *From Scars to Stars: Revolutionizing Recovery Through Trauma-Informed Care & Lived Experience* is a testament to their shared mission and unwavering commitment. Through their experiences and expertise, Joey and Jodie light the way for countless others, transforming despair into hope and scars into stars.

REFERENCES

Abuse, S. (2014). SAMHSA's concept of trauma and guidance for a trauma-informed approach. HHS Publication No. (SMA) 14-4884. Rockville, MD: Substance Abuse and Mental Health Services Administration.

Davidson, L., Bellamy, C., Guy, K., & Miller, R. (2012). Peer support among persons with severe mental illnesses: a review of evidence and experience. *World Psychiatry*, 11(2), 123-128.

Dube, S. R., Felitti, V. J., Dong, M., Chapman, D. P., Giles, W. H., & Anda, R. F. (2003). Childhood abuse, neglect, and household dysfunction and the risk of illicit drug use: The adverse childhood experiences study. Pediatrics, 111(3), 564-572.

Goleman, D. (1995). Emotional intelligence. New York: Bantam.

Gorski, T. T. (1990). The CENAPS model of relapse prevention. Independence, MO: Herald House/Independence Press.

Harris, M., & Fallot, R. D. (2001). Envisioning a trauma-informed service system: A vital paradigm shift. New Directions for Mental Health Services, 2001(89), 3-22.

Harris, M., & Fallot, R. D. (2001). Using trauma theory to design service systems. Jossey-Bass.

Heatherton, T. F., & Wagner, D. D. (2011). Cognitive neuroscience of self-regulation failure. Trends in cognitive sciences, 15(3), 132-139.

Heilig, M., Epstein, D. H., Nader, M. A., & Shaham, Y. (2022). Time to connect: bringing social context into addiction neuroscience. Evaluating the Brain Disease Model of Addiction, 35-49.

Kar, N. (2011). Cognitive behavioral therapy for the treatment of post-traumatic stress disorder: a review. Neuropsychiatric disease and treatment, 167-181.

Khantzian, E. J. (1997). The self-medication hypothesis of substance use disorders: A reconsideration and recent applications. *Harvard review of psychiatry*, 4(5), 231-244.

Knight, K. R., Lopez, A. M., Comfort, M., Shumway, M., Cohen, J., & Riley, E. D. (2014). Single room occupancy (SRO) hotels as mental health risk environments among impoverished women: the intersection of policy, drug use, trauma, and urban space. *International Journal of Drug Policy*, 25(3), 556-561.

Kreek, M. J., Nielsen, D. A., Butelman, E. R., & LaForge, K. S. (2005). Genetic influences on impulsivity, risk-taking, stress responsivity and vulnerability to drug abuse and addiction. Nature neuroscience, 8(11), 1450-1457.

Krystal, J. H., Neumeister, A., & Charney, D. S. (2004). The Biological Basis of PTSD. *Psychiatric Quarterly*, 75(4), 341-362.

Lieberman, A. F., & Van Horn, P. (2009). Giving voice to the unsayable: Repairing the effects of trauma in infancy and early childhood. Child and Adolescent Psychiatric Clinics, 18(3), 707-720.

Livingston, J. D., Milne, T., Fang, M. L., & Amari, E. (2012). The effectiveness of interventions for reducing stigma related to substance use disorders: a systematic review. Addiction, 107(1), 39-50.

Marlatt, G. A., & Witkiewitz, K. (2002). Harm reduction approaches to alcohol use: Health promotion, prevention, and treatment. Addictive behaviors, 27(6), 867-886.

Maté, G. (2008). *In the Realm of Hungry Ghosts: Close Encounters with Addiction.* Vintage Canada.

Mead, S., Hilton, D., & Curtis, L. (2001). Peer support: A theoretical perspective. *Psychiatric Rehabilitation Journal,* 25(2), 134.

Miller, W. R., & Rollnick, S. (2012). Motivational interviewing: Helping people change. Guilford press.

Moos, R. H. (2007). Theory-based active ingredients of effective treatments for substance use disorders. Drug and Alcohol Dependence, 88(2-3), 109-121.

Najavits, L. M. (2002). Seeking Safety: A Treatment Manual for PTSD and Substance Abuse. Guilford Press.

Simpson, T. L., & Miller, W. R. (2002). Concomitance between childhood sexual and physical abuse and substance use problems: A review. Clinical psychology review, 22(1), 27-77.

Tracy, K., & Wallace, S. P. (2016). Benefits of peer support groups in the treatment of addiction. Substance abuse and rehabilitation, 7, 143.

Topitzes, J., Mersky, J. P., & Reynolds, A. J. (2012). From child maltreatment to violent offending: An examination of mixed-gender and gender-specific models. *Journal of Interpersonal Violence,* 27(12), 2328-2357.

Van der Kolk, B. A. (2014). *The Body Keeps the Score: Brain, Mind, and Body in the Healing of Trauma*. Viking.

White, W. (2009). Peer-based Addiction Recovery Support: History, Theory, Practice, and Scientific Evaluation. Great Lakes Addiction Technology Transfer Center and Philadelphia Department of Behavioral Health and Mental Retardation Services.

9 798218 347857